FREEDOM GAMEPLAN

Build Wealth. **Live** Free. **Reclaim** Time.

Amir Rodnia

Dedication

To my **parents**
for their unwavering sacrifices, endless encouragement,
and the strength that shaped the person I am today.

To my partner, **Renee**
for making life unbelievably beautiful, believing in me
through every season, and always spurring me on.

To my dear sister, **Sara**, and my brother-in-law, **Daniel**
for opening the first door that allowed me to begin this journey.

To **Paul** and **Sarah**
for welcoming me into the family with open arms
and supporting Renee and me along the way.

And to our dear **friends**
whose encouragement, laughter, and belief
made the journey lighter and the destination sweeter.
I am forever indebted to you all.

Amir

First published in 2026 by RWP Media Pty Ltd

A catalogue entry for this book is available from the National Library of Australia.

ISBN: 978-1-923630-36-9

Printed in Australia by Pegasus
Book production and text design by Publish Central
Cover design by Julia Kuris

The paper this book is printed on is certified as environmentally friendly.

Disclaimer: General advice only

The information contained in this book is of a general nature and has been prepared without taking into account your individual objectives, financial situation, or needs. Before acting on any information in this book, you should consider its appropriateness with regard to your personal circumstances and consult a qualified financial adviser.

While care has been taken to ensure the accuracy of the information provided, no warranty is given as to the reliability or completeness of the information. The author and publisher disclaim all liability for any loss or damage arising from reliance on the content in this book.

Any case studies or examples are for illustrative purposes only and do not constitute a recommendation or personal advice.

The author, Amir Rodnia, is a licensed financial planner. However, this book is not intended to constitute financial product advice or personal advice as defined by the *Corporations Act 2001*. This book does not replicate the personalised process used in professional financial advice. The outcomes of the Real People Real Success Stories sections are not typical and are shown for illustration only. Different choices and market conditions can lead to very different results.

CONTENTS

INTRODUCTION
SINK OR SWIM

Picture this.

It's early evening, already dark outside. The rain's been bucketing down for hours, and the streets look like swimming pools separated by thin strips of dry land.

You're standing by your window, watching the floodwaters creep higher, when you notice something strange: a man walks up to the edge of the water. He pauses for just a second, as if deciding whether to turn back. But then, to your disbelief, he steps forward into the floodwaters.

Soon the water climbs from his knees up to his waist. Before long, he's swimming – awkward, clumsy strokes, splashing everywhere while branches, rubbish, and bits of fence float past him. You can't help thinking: *what on earth would make someone swim through floodwaters?* Maybe there's a child trapped somewhere. Maybe he's saving his dog. Maybe he's just cuckoo crazy.

But I bet you'd never guess what actually happened.

You see, this guy's true story had an unusual twist. And I should know because it's my story.

I was working at a restaurant in 2013, when Brisbane had a major flood. That day, I'd gone home for a break, but by the time I headed back, the streets were underwater. The roads to the restaurant were blocked in all directions.

The restaurant, though, was only a couple of hundred metres away, across a flooded park and a roundabout I could no longer see. Through the rain and flickering streetlights, I could make out faint figures on the other side.

So I thought: *I need the cash from that shift. What's the harm in getting a bit wet? Let's just go through the water to the other side.*

And, in a moment of financial desperation, I did what anyone in their right mind would never even consider.

I walked straight into the flood.

At first it was ankle-deep. Then knee-deep. Then waist-deep. I figured, *that's as bad as it'll get.*

It wasn't.

Soon I was dog-paddling in the dark, fighting the current, dodging debris and trying not to think too hard about what else was in that murky brown water. And just a pro tip, I don't recommend drinking floodwater. Doesn't taste the best.

By halfway across, I thought about turning back. But I could see people on the other side and my brain did the maths:

If I make it, I get paid.

If I don't ... well, that wouldn't make much difference anyway, would it? Better to go forward.

When I finally crawled onto solid ground, drenched, muddy and exhausted, Mal and Bec, the couple who owned the restaurant, were standing there. They'd come in earlier that day to sandbag the place and try to save their stock.

They stared at me in total bewilderment.

'We saw some crazy guy swimming through the flood,' Mal said, while giving me a massive pat on the back. 'Didn't realise it was you! Mate, you're the most dedicated employee I've ever had!'

Everyone had a good laugh and kept talking about how crazy I was. I smiled, took the compliments as gracefully as anyone dripping head to toe could, and headed straight into the kitchen like it was business as usual.

Back then I was a casual kitchenhand. No shift meant no pay. Missing that hundred-dollar shift didn't just cost me money; it meant running on empty for days, with no fuel to get to work, and a week of scraping by. I wasn't motivated by pride or passion. I was motivated by survival.

If I'd been thinking clearly, I never would've risked my life for a hundred bucks. But when survival is at stake, logic gets washed away by the emotional current that money creates.

By the next day, Mal had told everyone the story. They paid me for the shift even though we barely did any work that night. To them, it was a tale about commitment.

But it wasn't.

I didn't swim that night because I loved my job.

I swam because I couldn't afford *not* to.

It wasn't dedication that got me through that flood.

It was desperation.

And that right there is what this book is about. It will show you how to replace dependence on a pay cheque with a system that gives you time, choice, and peace of mind.

> “ Freedom Gameplan is not about getting rich. It's about getting free.

THE NUMBER THAT CHANGES EVERYTHING

This book revolves around one simple idea I call your *Freedom Score*™. It's an easy way to measure how much freedom your money gives you, and how much of your life still depends on a pay cheque.

Most people work 40 years and never work out this number.

Every strategy, tactic, and tool in this book exists for one reason only: to improve that score.

Because when money dictates your every decision, when you're working shifts you hate, missing family moments you love, and swimming through floods just to survive, you're not living free. You're trapped in an invisible cage.

When life keeps forcing you into sink-or-swim choices because of money, your options shrink. And sometimes, those choices pull you into places you were never meant to go.

Back then, my Freedom Score was zero, which meant I had no real choices.

And once you see your life through that lens, you can't unsee it.

Financial freedom isn't about making millions or never working again.

It's about choice.

That's why *Freedom Gameplan* is about building a life where you never have to risk your sanity, your relationships, or your health for money. It's about dignity, peace of mind, and the power to choose how you spend your time, live life on your terms, and do work you love.

That night in the flood taught me something I'll never forget: I wasn't in control of my life. Money was.

And over the years, I've realised I'm far from the only one. You might not have swum through a flood for a hundred-dollar shift, but if money has ever made you say yes when every bone in your body wanted to say no, you know that feeling. And that's why your Freedom Score matters: because until it rises, your choices are never fully your own.

WHY YOU FEEL STUCK

Let's see if this sounds familiar:

The alarm goes off.

Not a soft chime, more like an air raid siren at 6 am.

You roll over, smack the phone, and stare at the ceiling.

You already know how the day will go.

Get up. Show up. Do what's expected. Earn just enough to keep the wheels turning.

Now let me ask you: when was the last time you woke up and felt truly free?

Not on holiday. Not on a weekend. I mean *free*.

Free to wake up and spend your day exactly how you want, not because you have to, but because you choose to.

For most people, the answer is … never.

Steel-caps or suits, shifts or boardrooms – it's the same loop.

Monday to Friday, grind it out, living for the weekend.

By Sunday night, dreading Monday's alarm.

Most people are trapped in a modern cage of rent, mortgages, bills, and routines that quietly steer their lives while an invisible clock ticks away their time.

I call this the 'wage cage', and 'clocking off the cage' is what happens when you no longer *need* a wage to survive. Just like you clock off at the end of a shift, financial freedom is clocking off the need for that next paycheque.

Freedom Gameplan is my rebellion against that wage cage.

Think about it. What if financial freedom isn't about earning more or chasing the next investment fad, but about reclaiming your time and your choices? What if it's about learning to think clearly, adapt quickly, and act with confidence?

Inside these pages, you'll find the framework I've used to help real people (in their 20s, 30s, 40s, 50s, even 70s) to move towards building lives of freedom on their own terms.

Today, modern life gives us comforts our ancestors couldn't have imagined: instant access to food, medicine, technology, clean water, warm homes. Most of us live better than kings and queens once did.

But comfort isn't the same as freedom. Our lives are cushioned by conveniences, yet squeezed by invisible pressures of rent, mortgages, bills, and subscriptions. The quiet pull of money still shapes our choices more than we like to admit. It's as if we made a deal without signing anything:

> “Here, have all the comforts you want. The price? Your peace of mind. Your freedom of choice.

If you've ever seen the movie *In Time* with Justin Timberlake, it's a striking metaphor for our reality. In that world, time is money. People pay for coffee, rent, even bus rides with minutes of their lives. They have a glowing clock on their arm that counts down their remaining time, and when it hits zero, they die.

We don't have glowing clocks on our arms, but the countdown is real. It's called your life.

The real price of everything is time.

For some, that $20 burger might cost 20 minutes of work. For others, it's an hour. You're not just eating lunch, you're chewing on a chunk of your Tuesday.

As long as you're trading time for money, every swipe of the card is really an exchange. Hours of your life spent on things.

Most of us sacrifice 80% of our waking hours just to enjoy the other 20%. It's like booking a seven-day cruise and spending five of them scrubbing dishes below deck.

UNLOCKING TRUE FREEDOM

Freedom does not come free.

The price of freedom has shifted with history.

In the Agricultural Age, it was noble birth.

In the Industrial Age, wealth.

Today, in the Information Age, the price is still wealth, but the rules have changed – drastically. Just showing up is no longer enough. Technology is rewriting the playbook at lightning speed. AI is already replacing jobs once thought untouchable, and the pace is only accelerating.

That's why we've never had a greater need to have a modern gameplan. Otherwise, we'll end up playing today's game with yesterday's rules.

But here's the good news: there's still time.

Start planning now and you can build genuine financial independence. In a world of uncertainty, financial freedom is your best defence.

> " True freedom isn't the absence of work.
> It's the presence of choice.

So, if trading time for money is being stuck in a cage, how do you escape?

Two powerful words: **passive income**.

That's what this book will show you: how to reclaim your time and build the one thing that changes everything – income that works while you don't.

A simple but powerful engine

At the heart of this gameplan lies a simple but powerful engine I call the *RICH Trifecta*™, designed to systematically improve your Freedom Score. This is built around:

- Four decision filters (R: Risk, I: Income, C: Capital, H: Hassle).
- Three core asset types (Trifecta).
- One integrated wealth-building machine.

In the chapters ahead, I'll show you exactly how it works. I'll also show you how to use it to build wealth in property, shares, and business as you create your own Freedom Gameplan.

But let me tell you, before I built this gameplan, I had to find a way to clock off my own cage.

MY PERSONAL JOURNEY: FROM JERRY CANS TO FREEDOM PLANS

Today, I live a comfortable life doing work I love. I'd happily do it for free because it's a life built by choice, not by necessity.

But, as the flood story hinted, my journey wasn't a straight line. It was filled with failure, humility, and a fair bit of chaos before my own Freedom Gameplan began to take shape.

I was always determined to be my own man. At 19, I was studying engineering and working at my dad's workshop when I decided to start my own business manufacturing CNC machines (devices that etch VIN numbers on car parts). And so Rodnia CNC Co. was born, complete with an office, a workshop, and even a secretary.

Imagine the smugness of a 19-year-old with a secretary!

Amazingly, I managed to land a contract with a major auto parts manufacturer. They gave me a generous deposit and a tight deadline. I still wonder what those guys were thinking, trusting a first-year uni student with a large deal.

My prototype was full of bugs, but I was sure it would all come together … somehow. So for the first few months, I celebrated my newfound 'wealth' by partying with mates, taking life easy, and 'working on it' here and there.

But when the delivery day came, barely half the machines worked. So I had to swallow my pride and call my dad to help me face the client. And that ended in one of the most humbling moments of my life. I was kicked out of the meeting and had to sit in the car while dad negotiated to save me from bankruptcy.

It then took me a year of hard slog to pay back what I had spent of the deposit.

But that wasn't the end of my lessons. I started other businesses that each humbled me in their own way. A few years later, in my mid-20s, my partner Renee and I found ourselves so broke that we scavenged coins from between our car seats just to afford fuel.

Have you ever been too broke to pull up at a petrol station?

I used to carry a little jerry can to the servo around the corner, buy two litres of fuel, pour it into my car, and pray it was enough to get to work, where I washed dishes for 80 hours a week.

Meanwhile, Renee had just lost her business when her car, vital for her work as a personal trainer, was written off. Our bank account was constantly in the negative. Every time a bill landed, the bank hit us again with another overdraft fee. And when you're broke, the fees seem to multiply faster than rabbits!

But despite all that, Renee and I always look back on those years fondly. Because they toughened us, grounded us, and gave us the grit this book is built on.

Every failure taught me something no textbook ever could:

- to plan better
- to under-promise and overdeliver
- to master money instead of being mastered by it.

Those lessons became the foundation of the wealth-building system I now teach. The one that took me 15 years to figure out the hard way, so you can get a head start on your freedom quest without repeating my mistakes.

> “It took me 15 years to figure it out. It only took a few more to live it.

If I can clock off the cage, so can you.

YOUR FREEDOM GAMEPLAN

With time, I've learned that helping others reach their goals brings even more joy than achieving my own. I'll never forget helping a friend buy his first home when everyone said it wasn't possible. His excitement was so contagious that I felt like I'd bought the house myself. And I've been lucky enough to feel that same rush again and again with different people over the years.

I decided to share my journey and my plan for freedom in this book because I know that freedom isn't found by luck, it's built with strategy. The guidance in this book is what I share with my own family and friends and are the very principles I've followed in my own journey.

As a financial planner, I've had the privilege of a front-row seat to people's lives, their hopes, fears, and dreams about money. I sit with young professionals, families, business owners, and retirees, everyday Aussies doing their best to build a better future. People just like you and me.

Over the years, I've noticed something powerful: while everyone's story is different, their questions are almost always the same:

'Where should I start?'

'Am I doing the right thing?'

'How do I actually get ahead?'

'How can I retire early?'

'How can I stress less about money?'

'How do I financially set my family up?'

This book is my answer to those questions.

I've kept the content simple, clear, and practical, because I know from hundreds of real-world conversations that people don't want jargon. They just want guidance they can understand and apply.

It's written for Australians. Unlike the flood of US and UK money books that often miss the mark here in Australia, everything inside *Freedom Gameplan* is built for us and for our system, so you can learn it all with clarity and confidence.

This book IS for you if ...

- You earn reasonable money but still feel trapped.
- You want a long-term plan, not shortcuts or hype.
- You're Australian and want advice that actually fits our system.
- You want clarity, structure, and confidence around money.
- You're willing to think differently and act consistently.

This book is NOT for you if ...

- You want fast money or speculative wins.
- You're looking for day trading, investment hype, or shortcuts.
- You're not prepared to take responsibility for your decisions.

Along the way, you'll see *real people with real success stories.* These are genuine profiles of people who applied the ideas in this book and transformed their lives. Some turned things around despite being told it wasn't possible. Others built wealth from scratch. They're a reminder that you don't need to be perfect, lucky, or wealthy to start. You just need the right knowledge, a clear path, and the courage to take action.

BUT WAIT, ISN'T MONEY THE ROOT OF ALL EVIL?

We've all heard the saying, but it's usually the absence of it that causes the most pain.[1] Poverty breeds desperation, not virtue. Where wealth grows, so do health, opportunity, and dignity.

Money doesn't corrupt; it empowers. It's not the enemy; it's the tool. Financial freedom isn't selfish; it's the foundation that lets you contribute, create, and live with purpose.

HOW TO USE THIS BOOK

Let's be real, it's tempting to jump straight to the tactics. That's normal. I get it. Who doesn't want the juicy stuff first?

---

1 The phrase 'money is the root of all evil' is actually a common misquotation. The biblical verse it comes from – 'For the love of money is a root of all kinds of evil' (1 Timothy 6:10) – criticises the obsession with money rather than money itself.

But this isn't just another 'do this, buy that' money manual. This book is your detailed roadmap, designed to reshape how you think, plan, and build lasting wealth with actionable steps.

It's structured around what I call the *Freedom Framework*™. It's a simple but powerful four-step system for building momentum and repeatable success, not just once but over a lifetime.

We start broad, with the right mindset and strategic lens. Then we zoom in on what to do, what tools to use, and how to stay on track.

The Freedom Framework

Here's how it flows:

1. **THINK – Sharpen your money mindset:** Rewire your financial operating system, your beliefs, psychology, and blind spots. This is the stuff most books skip, but it's the difference between temporary wins and lasting success.
2. **PLAN – Build your *RICH Trifecta*™:** Map out your long-term wealth strategy across real estate, shares, and private business.

You will learn to use the RICH filters: Risk, Income, Capital, and Hassle. This is your master plan.

3. **DO – Tactics that work:** This is the action zone: actionable property, shares, and business tactics that meet you where you are and grow with you.
4. **GEAR UP – Your wealth-building toolkit:** The nuts and bolts, bank accounts, loans, insurance, apps, and platforms that you need to put your gameplan into action.

The THINK, PLAN, DO, and GEAR UP Framework is part of a machine. And the output of that machine is your *Freedom Score.*

THREE WAYS TO READ THIS BOOK

There's no single 'right' way to read *Freedom Gameplan*. You can choose the path that best fits where you are right now from the following options:

1. **The Full Gameplan (recommended):** Read THINK and PLAN in full → focus on the Must Read DO tactics and the ones most relevant to you → read GEAR UP fully → complete the 30-Day Kickstart.
2. **The Fast-Track Builder:** Skim THINK → read PLAN fully → focus on the Must Read DO tactics and selected tactics that fit your situation → use the matching GEAR UP tools as needed → start the 30-Day Kickstart.
3. **The Tactical Sampler:** If you're already confident in your mindset and are aware of mental financial pitfalls: skip THINK → read PLAN fully → read only the Must Read DO tactics → start the 30-Day Kickstart.

For those of you who choose paths 2 or 3, I'll briefly reintroduce key concepts throughout the book to ensure you don't miss any important details.

Whichever track you choose, make sure to do the one-step action at the end of each part, read the short intro into Property, Shares, and Business in each chapter of the DO section and finally, don't skip the final WRAP UP section.

You can switch tracks at any time.

You don't need to read this book quickly.

You don't need to agree with everything you read.

And you don't need to understand it all in one pass.

Some ideas will make immediate sense. Others will sit quietly in the background and connect later. It's how this book is designed to work. Take it at your own pace.

Choose the path that best fits where you are right now

Full Gameplan
THINK: read in full
PLAN: read in full
DO: read 'Must Reads'
+ relevant tactics
GEAR UP: read in full
Complete 30-Day **Kickstart**

Tactical Sampler
PLAN: read in full
DO: read 'Must Reads' only
GEAR UP: read in full
Complete 30-Day **Kickstart**

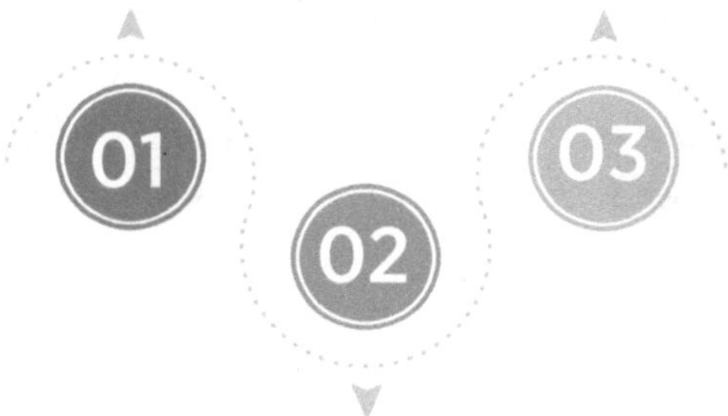

Fast-Track Builder
THINK: skim
PLAN: read in full
DO: read 'Must Reads'
+ selected tactics
GEAR UP: matching tools
Complete 30-Day **Kickstart**

QUICK WINS ALONG THE WAY

While this book is written with long-term wealth-building in mind, you'll also come across some ideas you can apply immediately and start seeing results. You don't need to wait years to experience progress.

Each part ends with one clear action you can take right now towards your freedom. Don't try to do everything at once. Do the one thing at the end of each part before moving on. That's your first play in *Freedom Gameplan.*

HOW TO USE THE TACTICS IN DO PART

Part III of the book is dedicated to actionable tactics you can choose from, based on where you are in your gameplan. Not all tactics are created equal. Some are for beginners, others for more advanced builders. Pick the tactics that best suit your situation right now. Skipping tactics you don't need yet isn't procrastination. It's strategy.

To keep it clear, I've labelled each tactic like this:

- **Foundation level:** Perfect if you're just getting started.
- **Intermediate:** For those with some wins under their belt, ready to level up.
- **Advanced:** High-leverage tactics for when you're ready to go big.
- There's also a '**Best For**' label attached to each tactic so you can quickly scan if it's for you.

Oh, and keep your eyes peeled later in the book. There's a single-page visual Freedom Map in PART II that could reshape your entire trajectory.

Everything is explained as you go. But if something slips your mind, there's a handy glossary at the back of the book. Think of it as your cheat sheet – quick, simple, and always there when you need it.

At the end of the book, you will find a *30-day Freedom Kickstart* plan to help you put the ideas from this book into action.

This book is here to change your options.

CONNECT, LEARN, GROW, TOGETHER

You don't have to go through this journey alone. That's why I created the *Freedom Gameplan Community* (FG Community), a space where readers from all walks of life share wins, swap tactics, and keep each other accountable. Throughout this book, I'll point you to free tools, templates, and this community of readers. They're here so you can actually apply what you learn.

Whether you're just starting out or already building momentum, you'll find others on the same path, and often a few steps ahead to light the way.

DO YOU HAVE WHAT IT TAKES TO BECOME FINANCIALLY FREE?

Most people never clock off the wage cage.

Most people stay stuck, worrying, and repeating the same mistakes.

Most people stay broke. Or at least struggling.

Will you be the exception?

The strategies in this book have the power to bring meaningful change, but only if you *act*.

You've been misled your whole life.

Knowledge isn't power.

It's only *potential*.

And only action activates it.

You could walk into the grandest library, surrounded by centuries of wisdom, and still leave unchanged if you don't act.

So, here's a challenge:

Let finishing this book be the one big thing you do for yourself this year.

Read it. Take notes. Reread sections if you need to.

If you do, I promise, you'll come out the other side with more clarity, more confidence, and a practical gameplan to build a financially free life.

> "You're either money's master or its slave. The choice is yours.

INTRODUCTION RECAP

Some will read these pages, feel inspired, and then do nothing. Others will take what's here, apply it with discipline, and build a life of financial freedom. Which one will you be?

Freeing yourself starts with first recognising the cage.

As long as money runs your life, you're stuck.

In every decision lies a piece of your freedom.

Read it. Live it. Share it. And if you laugh once or twice along the way, well, I won't be mad!

PART I
THINK
Sharpen Your Money Mindset

WHAT TO BELIEVE AND WHY IT MATTERS

THINK is the first step of the Freedom Framework, and it's all about building the right mindset. Because if your mindset isn't right, nothing else matters. Not your budget, not your investments, and definitely not that shiny new app you downloaded last month and have never opened again!

THINK is here to save you time, not slow you down. Most people rush to tactics and spend years undoing mistakes. You can have the best strategy, the smartest tactics, and all the right tools, but without the right *thinking*, you'll sabotage yourself before you even begin.

Why?

Because your thinking drives your actions, and your actions shape your circumstances. Poor thinking results in poor circumstances, and empowered thinking leads to desirable outcomes.

You don't need to agree with everything in this section.

You don't need to remember it all.

Think of this part like installing the operating system before the apps. Once it's in place, everything else works smoothly.

Most people want to skip ahead to the question: 'What should I invest in?' But that's like trying to run the latest high-powered app on an old, glitchy operating system. It just can't handle it.

Without the right mindset, you could stumble into the best opportunity in the world and still blow it. But with the right mindset, small sparks can ignite big wealth.

THE FARMER AND THE GOOSE

Let me paint the picture with a classic little story from 2600 years ago, one of Aesop's Fables.

A farmer wakes up one morning to find that one of his geese has laid a golden egg.

Solid gold.

At first, he thinks it's a fluke. But the next day comes another golden egg. And another. Day after day, the gold keeps coming. Soon, the farmer and his family are lifted out of poverty.

But as time goes by, the farmer grows restless. He thinks to himself: *one lousy egg a day? That's not enough. I want them all, right now!*

So, armed with impatience and a sharp knife, he does the unthinkable: he cuts open the goose, hoping to find a stash of golden eggs inside. But there's nothing inside. No stash of gold. No hidden treasure. All he's left with is one very dead goose and a lifetime of regret.

In one rash decision, he managed to turn a miracle of wealth creation into Sunday dinner.

> “A poor mindset can destroy the opportunity of a lifetime.

That's why we begin here, by reprogramming your thinking. So that when the golden opportunity lands in your lap, you're ready to make the most of it. You seize the moment, and keep making opportunities work, again and again.

KICK-OFF: WHAT YOU'RE ABOUT TO DISCOVER

Now, before we get any further with sharpening your money mindset, let me give you a glimpse of what's coming up in the PLAN, DO, and GEAR UP parts, because I know you're itching to take action.

In the following parts, you'll discover:

- How a couple in their 30s bought their first home *without* a single dollar of deposit (using a tactic most people have never heard of).
- Why I consider *one specific type of investment account* one of the most underused vehicles in Australia (and a way to significantly reduce or even eliminate tax on investment earnings and capital gains – and no, I'm not talking about super).
- The *one metric* I look at before purchasing any property. And why ignoring it could cost you a fortune.
- How to use one simple negotiation tactic that would allow you to outwit even the most seasoned real estate agents when buying property.

- The strategy I call the *RICH Trifecta*, a framework that lets you build wealth with the flexibility to adapt to any market cycle and make big gains when markets go down.

Oh, and at some point, you'll come across something unexpected: a one-page map to unlock your next move. I won't spoil it now … but once you see it, you won't unsee it. It's a powerful visual tool that can reshape how you see your financial journey.

All of that is coming. But here's the catch: none of it will matter if your mindset isn't right.

That's why we start here. With the foundation. The part most people skip, until life forces them to circle back.

You don't need to change anything yet. In fact, I don't even want you to. The real action comes later in the 30-Day Freedom Kickstart. For now, just notice how you think.

THE ONE NUMBER THAT QUIETLY CHANGES EVERYTHING

I want you to do one simple thing.

Because before you build wealth, you need to see where you actually stand.

Most people track their money using the wrong scoreboard.

They watch net worth, bank balances, or investment returns – and still feel stuck.

But none of those numbers tell you the truth that matters most:

How close you are to freedom.

So here's a quick exercise. Don't overthink it. Just estimate.

Right now, write down three numbers:

1. **Your annual living cost:** What it actually costs to live your life for a year.
2. **Your annual passive income:** Income that keeps coming in even if you stop working. If you don't have any, that's totally okay. That's what this book is for.
3. **The gap between the two:** That gap is the space this book is designed to close.

Later in the book, I'll show you how to turn this into a single, simple metric I call your *Freedom Score*™. These three numbers are the raw ingredients. Everything you'll read next – mindset, strategy, tactics, tools – serves one purpose: to shrink that gap without increasing stress.

The moment your Freedom Score starts rising, your life starts changing. Not all at once, but in subtle, powerful ways. You start saying no more often. You start choosing more carefully. You start feeling in control.

For now, you don't need the formula. Just notice the direction. Are you moving closer to freedom … or further away?

Keep these numbers in the back of your mind as you read. They'll quietly shape how everything else lands.

Now, let's build your foundation properly.

CHAPTER 1
LIGHT THE FUSE

A LEAP OF IMAGINATION

Throughout history, the world's greatest achievers – those who reshaped industries, societies, and even the course of human development – have all tapped into one powerful, often-overlooked truth. Once discovered, whether consciously or unconsciously, this became their superpower.

For me, few stories hint at this precious, little-known truth better than Thomas Edison's.

Everyone knows Edison for his invention of the light bulb. But what most people don't realise is that Edison wasn't alone in his quest to perfect the incandescent light bulb. In fact, many inventors were racing towards the same goal. If he hadn't cracked it, someone else would have.

No, the real marvel in Edison's story isn't the light bulb.

It's the moment he dreamed up something no one else had even dared to imagine. Something the world thought impossible.

I'm talking about the moment Edison captured the most invisible of all natural forces, and locked it inside a tin.

CAPTURING THE INVISIBLE

In the late 1870s, while tinkering with telegraphs and telephones, Edison had an incredible idea:

> What if sound could be captured? Not just transmitted through the telephone, but recorded and played back at will?

At the time, this idea was unthinkable. Not just because it was too complex, but because no one had even conceived it. The concept of preserving sound seemed so out of reach that it didn't even exist in anyone's mind. That is until Edison imagined it in his marvellous mind.

He sketched out a crude design: a vibrating needle, a diaphragm, and a cylinder wrapped in tin foil to etch vibrations into grooves. Then he built a prototype.

When the machine was ready, Edison gathered his workshop team and leaned into the mouthpiece. Slowly, deliberately, he recited a nursery rhyme: 'Mary had a little lamb … '

He reset the needle, cranked the cylinder back to its starting point, and began turning the handle.

And then, the unthinkable happened. From the tin-foil cylinder came a faint, scratchy voice, echoing his words back.

The room froze. The impossible had just happened.

Sound, once fleeting and untouchable, had been captured, preserved, and replayed.

The ephemeral had been made permanent.

Thomas Edison with his phonograph, Washington, D.C., April 1878

Edison would go on to hold over 1000 patents. When asked which invention was his favourite, it wasn't the light bulb. It was the phonograph, his sound recording marvel. The one no one saw coming. The one that wasn't born out of necessity, but from a vision no one else dared to dream.

The invention of the phonograph changed the world. It opened entirely new industries and transformed how we experience music, speech, and entertainment to this day.

And here's the twist that will blow your mind: Edison was nearly deaf!

Don't you think that's just amazing? A man who could barely hear gave the world the gift of recorded sound.

Edison spent most of his life with significant hearing loss. In fact, he used to bite down on a piano to feel the vibration through his jaw, just to 'hear' the music.

His breakthrough didn't come from tools; it came from vision.

From believing in possibilities that others couldn't see.

A COMMON THREAD BEHIND EXTRAORDINARY ACHIEVEMENT

So, what made Edison so unstoppable? The answer is that he understood the most potent ingredient for human achievement:

Self-belief fused with imagination.

When I first grasped the power of this principle, I was so awe-struck that I began diving into the biographies of other super-achievers to see if it held up. And sure enough, I found its undeniable fingerprint in all of them. Let's see if you can spot the common thread:

Arnold Schwarzenegger:
'The mind is the limit. As long as the mind can envision the fact that you can do something, you can do it, as long as you really believe 100 percent.'

Oprah Winfrey:
'You become what you believe, not what you think or what you want.'

Albert Einstein:
'Imagination is everything. It is the preview of life's coming attractions.'

Steve Jobs:
'The people who are crazy enough to think they can change the world are the ones who do.'

Henry Ford:
'Whether you think you can or you can't, you're right.'

These perspectives point to the same underlying pattern: that *self-belief*, paired with *imagination*, is the seed of meaningful achievement.

> " I strongly believe that if you took nothing else from this book but this one principle, you'd have a far greater foundation than most people ever build.

Today, we understand the science behind this principle. We now know that the human mind thinks in images, not logic. It responds not just to what is real, but to what it *believes* is real. The brain often struggles to distinguish between vividly imagined outcomes and physical reality. So, when you feed your mind with a powerful image, something clear and specific in your imagination, it starts to treat that imagined reality as a target. When your current circumstances don't match that mental picture, your brain creates tension.

And here's where it gets powerful: that tension activates your subconscious. You begin scanning your environment, looking for clues, solutions, and opportunities to close the gap. You take action when others hesitate. You persist where others give up.

Why?

Because your brain has already accepted your vision as reality. It's simply working to make your outer reality match the inner one you've already claimed.

To see just how powerful this mechanism is, take a look at the following image.

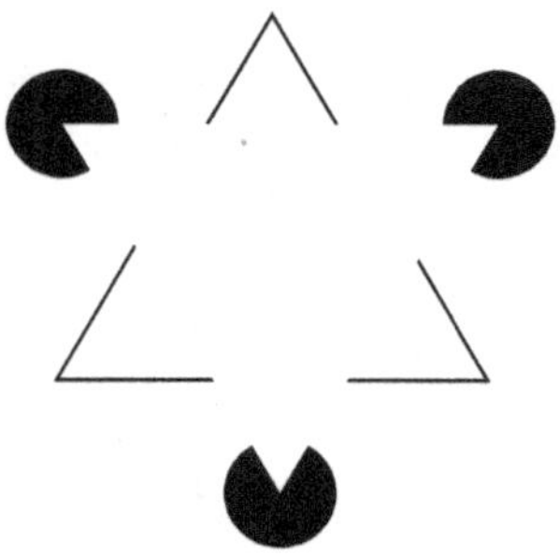

The Kanizsa Triangle

Look closely at the three 'Pac-Man' shapes to find the triangle hidden inside the image. Can you see the white triangle?

At first, it might be invisible. But once you spot it, it's obvious. And from that moment on, you can't unsee it. That's the Kanizsa Triangle, a stunning example of how your brain completes incomplete information to create a meaningful image. There *is* no white triangle. No lines. Just gaps and hints. But your brain fills it in anyway.

Now, think of this as a metaphor for your own mind.

Just as your visual system constructs the triangle from suggestion, your brain does the same with your goals, particularly through something called the Reticular Activating System (RAS). The RAS isn't what creates illusions, but it *does* filter your experience based on what you've trained your mind to look for.

If you've primed your brain with a clear, emotionally charged vision, your RAS begins highlighting information that aligns with that vision, the same way your eyes zero in on a triangle that isn't really there.

> “Once your mind sees something clearly, it starts working, consciously and unconsciously, to bring it into view.

I've closely studied many visionary achievers – Edison, Jobs, Da Vinci, Coco Chanel, Temple Grandin, Ford, Rockefeller, Carnegie, Churchill, and many more – across different centuries, cultures, and fields. And I noticed something remarkable. Despite their wildly different lives, they all shared this one quality with stunning consistency. This way of thinking is what took us to the moon, split the atom, and allowed humans to contact each other across vast oceans and freeze time in a photo.

And it's not just something I've observed in others. It shaped my own life, long before I ever realised it. In my personal life, *nothing* I've done would've been possible without it.

BUILD YOUR SELF-BELIEF MUSCLE, ONE TAP AT A TIME

A few years ago, I was reminiscing with my mum when she reminded me of a childhood story, one that perfectly captures why self-belief is such a powerful force.

I was about four or five, at my grandparents' house, where a kitchen tap was leaking. Even as a kid, I had a thing for fixing stuff. While other children played with toy cars, I preferred to play tradie with spanners and screwdrivers.

I still remember running up to Grandma and declaring, 'I'll fix it!' So I dashed off to grab a spanner from Grandpa's toolbox. But I was too small to reach the sink, and so Grandma had to lift me up. I twisted, tapped, did my thing, and then, miraculously, the dripping stopped.

I felt like a hero. Mum and Grandma cheered. In that moment, a powerful seed was planted in my mind: *I believed I was capable.*

But as Mum retold the story when I was in my mid-30s, she added a small detail I'd never heard before – that nearly floored me. It turns out that as Grandma held me up to 'repair' the tap that day, she quietly turned off the shut-off valve under the sink with her other hand, timed perfectly so it looked like *I* had fixed it.

Here I was, having gone through my whole life believing I'd fixed that tap, when actually, I hadn't. Yet the impact it had on me was real.

For years, that memory lived in me as proof of my ability. It shaped my confidence and gave me a lasting sense of empowerment. And that's the beauty of self-belief: whether it begins by accident or by design, it has the power to shape your life.

Self-belief works just like a muscle. Every small win, every 'tap fixed', is another rep. Over time, those moments build strength you can lean on when the stakes are higher. You don't need to start big. You just need to start.

And the best part is that you can design, recreate, and relive those moments of belief for yourself.

In finance, this is where the journey truly begins. The simple belief that you can grow your wealth, even from a modest start, is often the line between those who invest consistently and those who never begin. You'll put this to work in PLAN and DO parts of the book.

Now meet Danielle and see what happens when belief is put into motion.[2,3]

---

2 All stories are shared with the permission of the individuals involved.

3 I'd love to hear your story! If this book helps you on your journey to financial freedom, or provides you with the clarity you need to get a start, share your story with me at: www.rodnia.com.au. Maybe, just maybe, you will be the next profile for the Real People Real Success Story section!

REAL PEOPLE, REAL SUCCESS STORIES

DANIELLE

'If you want something done, ask a busy person'

Danielle is a living example that excuses don't build empires – belief and imagination do. Not long ago, Danielle decided that she wanted to start her own consulting practice. She already had a full plate: three young children and everything else that comes with a busy family and work life. Most people would have said, 'Now's not the time', and no one would have argued otherwise.

But Danielle isn't most people. Instead of waiting for the perfect moment, she trusted her instincts and made the leap. And in true form, she named her business Bold Fox Consulting, because bold is exactly what she is.

She's got that classic winner's mindset: no obstacle too big, no challenge too daunting. Nothing gets in the way of her vision.

Just one year after launching, her business was flourishing. In fact, she could barely keep up with demand. How did she do it?

She started with people who already knew her work, her skillset, and her reliability. By reconnecting with past colleagues, co-workers, and professional contacts, she offered services they genuinely needed, positioning her success as a win–win partnership. Her self-belief gave them confidence. That trust opened doors, and soon word of mouth spread.

Within a year, demand had grown so much that she could barely keep up.

Danielle's story proves a powerful truth: resources and timing matter far less than the belief you carry and the imagination you apply. She didn't wait for circumstances to change – she changed the circumstances by daring to see possibility and backing herself to pursue it.

What an incredible human!

CHAPTER 2
ROOT FIRST, FRUIT LATER

BUILDING FROM WITHIN

Some time ago, I found myself lost in thought, struck by a curious observation; we name a tree by its fruit: apple tree, olive tree, fig tree. But it's not the fruit that creates the tree. It's the tree that produces the fruit.

Why do we do that?

This simple observation reveals something profound about how we see the world – and ourselves.

In much the same way, we label people by their visible outcomes.

'She's a brilliant actress.'

'He's a successful entrepreneur.'

'They're a talented musician.'

We often attribute success to talent or luck. But in doing so, we're naming the fruit, not recognising the root. We forget that before the spotlight, the awards, the headlines, there was a person quietly cultivating habits, discipline, and vision. The actor, the musician, the entrepreneur – they were not born with those titles. They became the kind of person capable of producing those outcomes.

> Success is the by-product. Character is the source.

And that's good news. Because it means the fruit doesn't define the tree. You don't need to wear the label of success to be someone of worth. When you invest in your mindset, your character, and your effort, when you focus on growing the roots, the fruits will follow, in time, as a natural result.

The real work isn't in chasing recognition. It's in becoming the kind of person who produces consistent results.

And if you ever doubt what's possible, remember that even physical limitations can't block someone who is deeply rooted:

- **Ludwig van Beethoven:** profoundly deaf – composed symphonies that still echo through concert halls centuries later.
- **Stephen Hawking:** confined to a wheelchair by ALS – expanded our understanding of the universe with nothing but his mind and a single functioning cheek muscle.

These extraordinary individuals had deep roots. And because of that, their results were extraordinary.

This shift in mindset has been one of the most empowering realisations of my life. Now, whenever I'm at the beginning of something big, I don't feel overwhelmed by how long it might take or how far I have to go.

I feel calm. Certain.

Because I know how this works. I've done it before. Once I made this shift, obstacles stopped being frustrations. They became part of the process.

Now, instead of rushing for immediate and visible results, I focus on strengthening the roots – because I know everything I'm building depends on what's happening beneath the surface.

The journey isn't just the path to success. It *is* the success.

> “Focus on the roots, the habits, discipline, and vision. The fruit will follow.

CHAPTER 3
RELEASE THE UNSHAKABLE INNER WARRIOR

SAY HELLO TO MY LITTLE FRIEND

One of the greatest obstacles to success is doubt, whether it's self-doubt, the doubt of others, or the nagging question of whether you're on the right path.

Doubt is a barrier in your mind. And, if you want financial freedom, learning to manage doubt is not optional; it's essential.

Take the story of the legendary actor Al Pacino. During the filming of *The Godfather*, considered one of the greatest films ever made, almost everyone wanted him gone. Studio executives thought he was wrong for the role of Michael Corleone. They doubted his ability to carry the character and even considered firing him. But Pacino stayed the course. He ignored the noise and delivered a legendary performance.

Then came *Scarface*. Once again, the critics attacked. They called his performance excessive and the film a failure. And yet, *Scarface* became a cult classic. 'Say hello to my little friend,' is now etched into pop culture, and the film remains one of Pacino's most financially successful.

Now imagine if he had listened to the doubters. If he'd walked away. Those iconic roles, the ones that defined his legacy, would've never happened.

The lesson is simple: banish doubt. Don't let others decide your path. Trust in your ability. Stay the course. Even when the world questions you.

> “ Doubt is the real dream killer. Failure just teaches you how to do it better next time.

In the pursuit of wealth, crushing self-doubt is often what separates the average from the exceptional. Doubt is a luxury you cannot afford. Those who endure early setbacks and still stick to their vision are the ones who create lasting financial freedom.

A CASE FOR DECISIVENESS

Hesitation kills momentum. It's the enemy of opportunity. Too many people freeze when it's time to decide, paralysed by the fear of making the wrong move. Luck favours the bold. But more importantly, it favours the prepared.

Most successful people don't need countless chances. They seize one or two pivotal moments that change everything. The key is to decide quickly and change your mind slowly.

Nobel Prize–winning psychologist Daniel Kahneman, in his classic book *Thinking, Fast and Slow*, explains that our brains make choices using two systems:

- **System 1:** Fast, intuitive, emotional.
- **System 2:** Slow, deliberate, analytical.

Great decision-makers know how to blend these. They trust their gut in urgent moments, but that gut is grounded in careful, deliberate preparation. That's the secret: quick decisions based on slow learning.

But here's the truth: not deciding is often the biggest mistake of all. Time passes. Opportunities fade. Overthinking leads to analysis paralysis. Kahneman's research confirms that trying to account for every variable often prevents people from acting at all. But you'll never have 100% certainty. Success belongs to those who move *despite* uncertainty.

Over time, I learned that you can tell whether your decisions are moving you closer to freedom or quietly pulling you away. Later in the PLAN part of the book, I'll show you how I track that in a simple, practical way. For now, just remember this: every decision either moves you closer to freedom … or further away from it.

DECIDE QUICKLY, CHANGE SLOWLY

Once you've made a solid, informed decision, commit. Don't waste energy second-guessing. People who constantly doubt themselves go in circles. Those who stick to their course, even through turbulence, make real progress.

Most life-changing opportunities don't look obvious. They appear risky, uncomfortable, and uncertain. They test your courage. My best decisions made me nervous, and I acted anyway.

Take our first home purchase. The thought of owing the bank $400,000 kept me awake at night. I'd lie in bed replaying 'what if' scenarios in my head until my stomach started to ache from tension and stress. It felt terrifying. But deep down I knew I'd done my research and planning. So, I bit the bullet and signed the contract.

That single decision, as frightening as it was, became the catalyst for everything that followed.

System 1 thinking exists for a reason. It helps us move when time is short. But it only works well when it's built on a strong foundation of System 2 thinking: slow, thoughtful preparation. Prepare deliberately. Then, when the moment comes, you can act fast using your intuition.

No certainty needed, just the courage to take the next step.

DON'T LET THE CRABS KNOW YOU'RE ESCAPING

Even with a strong mindset, you're still vulnerable to the influence of others. Sometimes, the biggest threat isn't your own doubt, it's *other people* doubting you.

That's why it's often wise to keep your goals to yourself. Not out of secrecy, but self-protection. Many people simply won't understand your vision. And what people don't understand, they often criticise, dismiss, or worse, try to sabotage.

There's a powerful metaphor for this: crabs in a bucket.

Place a single crab in a bucket, and it'll climb out with ease. But put a group of crabs together, and as soon as one tries to escape, the others pull it back down. None escape, not because they can't but because they keep each other trapped.[4]

4 You can look up 'crabs in a bucket' on YouTube.

Humans behave in much the same way. When you try to grow, elevate, or step outside the norm, you'll often encounter resistance, not out of malice, but because your ambition threatens others' comfort zones. They may tell you it's too risky, too ambitious, too unrealistic. But really, it's *you* changing that makes *them* feel uncomfortable.

The philosopher Socrates was forced to drink poison. Giordano Bruno, the cosmologist, was burned at the stake in part for defending the idea that the Earth was not the centre of the universe. Galileo, the famous astronomer, was forced to deny what he knew to be true, that the Earth and planets revolve around the sun.

History is full of these examples because human nature often resists new ideas, especially when those ideas challenge the status quo. A hundred years ago, if you'd said we'd walk on the moon, they might have locked you up in a lunatic asylum.

And today?

Tell people you want financial freedom, to start a business, or retire young, and they'll likely call you 'ambitious' if they're being kind, or 'delusional' if they're not.

So, here's the lesson: protect your dreams. Let your actions and results do the talking. You don't owe anyone an explanation, especially those unwilling or unable to see what you see.

Financial freedom demands that you climb out of the bucket, even when others cling to you to pull you back. Protect your dream, then let results speak for themselves.

> “Keep climbing. Just don't let the crabs see you!

Next is a real story of preparation meeting decisiveness. Sergio and Katherine lived it.

REAL PEOPLE, REAL SUCCESS STORIES

SERGIO AND KATHERINE

'Experts said it couldn't be done. But they did it anyway.'

Meet Sergio and Katherine. They are an amazingly hardworking, down-to-earth couple with a big dream: buying their first home.

Like many first-time buyers, they didn't tick all the usual boxes. After being turned down by eight different banks, they were told, again and again, it just wasn't possible. Their deposit was short of the standard 20%, and other hurdles stood in the way too.

But here's what set them apart: they didn't freeze. They kept moving, asking questions, learning, and pushing forward.

Eventually, they came across a first-home buying tactic that changed everything. Then, with sheer persistence, they found a lender willing to back them. And with a little help from Sergio's brother, they scraped together the final bits they needed.

Katherine was overseas for work, so Sergio took the lead. He built rapport with a local real estate agent and uncovered a hidden gem – an off-market townhouse that was tidy, well-kept, and full of promise. It was the very first property they inspected.

Sergio saw beyond the surface. He saw what this home could become. The price guide?

'Mid-600s,' said the agent.

But Sergio had done his homework, using the same tools you'll discover in the *GEAR UP* part of this book. A similar home had just sold for $675,000. Armed with the negotiation tactic I'll share in the *DO* part, he managed to secure the property for $615,000 – well below market value.

Katherine, still overseas, was all in. Within 48 hours, the deal was done.

One year later, their home was valued at around $730,000. A strong outcome that reflected the purchase price and market conditions at the time.

CHAPTER 4
ASSEMBLE YOUR GAMEPLAN CREW

POWER IN PARTNERSHIP

One of the most overlooked principles in achieving financial freedom is this: *you're not meant to do it alone.*

I've experienced this firsthand at a leadership retreat I attend each year, organised by my good friend Michael Calam, author of *Brave Enough to Change*. Michael, an ex-cop turned business coach, has a gift for bringing the right people together. His work is a powerful reminder that real change begins on the inside, exactly the foundation you need before you build wealth with others.

At his retreat, ideas spark, perspectives shift, and connections flourish. Every time I leave, I'm buzzing with clarity, energy, and excitement. And it's not just me; everyone who attends says the same.

For me, it's living proof of what I call the *Gameplan Crew* principle: when likeminded, motivated people move towards a shared goal, something emerges that's bigger than any one of them.

Now you don't need a retreat to experience this.

> “ If you're serious about building wealth and freedom, one of the smartest things you can do is form your own crew.

Start with your life partner, a close friend, or a trusted peer, someone who shares your vision, values, and hunger for financial independence. Personally, my strongest crew member is my life partner, Renee.

When you align incentives and support each other's progress, you create a multiplier effect. You grow faster and stay accountable and motivated through setbacks.

Australian business is filled with examples that remind us success is rarely a solo mission:

- **Melanie Perkins** and **Cliff Obrecht** founded Canva in 2013 after years of rejection. A decade later, their vision scaled into a global platform used by hundreds of millions, reaching valuations north of US$25 billion.
- **Mike Cannon-Brookes** and **Scott Farquhar** bootstrapped Atlassian in 2002 using a credit card. They eventually grew it into a global software leader, valued (at the time of writing) at over US$50 billion.
- **Nick Molnar** and **Anthony Eisen** launched Afterpay in 2014, pairing bold consumer insight with seasoned governance. Just eight years later, the company was acquired by Block in a deal worth approximately US$29 billion.

This isn't just about starting a business. It's about accountability, perspective, and staying in the game.

Building wealth is a team sport. The right minds around you can open doors to better opportunities, smarter investments, and faster financial progress.[5]

You don't need speed. You need steady progress, together.

5 That's why I created the FG Community. It's one of the few spaces in Australia dedicated entirely to connecting people who want to achieve financial freedom. You can look up the FG Community online.

CHAPTER 5
WRITE IT DOWN, MAKE IT REAL

THE POWER OF WRITTEN GOALS

One thing that never fails to surprise me is how resistant people are to writing down their goals. They have dreams, ideas, and aspirations swirling in their minds, but ask them to put pen to paper, and suddenly, they hesitate. But the thing is: a goal that isn't written down isn't a goal at all, it's just a wish. Too often, people treat goals like new gym memberships, great in January, forgotten by February!

Writing crystallises thought. It transforms a vague desire into a clear commitment. And yet, this simple act, that takes just seconds and requires nothing more than a pen and paper, feels daunting to many. Perhaps it's because writing something down makes it real. It signals commitment. It means accountability.

Science explains why physically writing down a goal is so powerful: handwriting activates more of your brain than typing, boosting memory, focus, and goal-directed action. Neuroscience shows that when you write your goal, you're not just thinking it, you're wiring it in.[6]

Take it from me: you have everything to gain and nothing to lose. Writing down your goals is the easiest, most practical, and most powerful first step towards living the life you want.

The most successful people, from Olympic athletes to entrepreneurs, begin with written goals. Why? Because the act of writing forces clarity. It brings direction, urgency, and structure. Every great achievement begins with a focused objective.

6 Studies show that handwriting activates more neural pathways than typing, improving memory and cognitive engagement. Mangen, A., & Velay, J.-L. (2010). 'Digitizing Literacy: Reflections on the Haptics of Writing.' *Advances in Haptics*.

Without a clearly defined aim, we drift. Our energy gets scattered across trivial pursuits that don't move us forward. But once you define your aim and write it down, everything changes. Your actions gain focus. Your mind begins to filter distractions. You start aligning your efforts towards one meaningful target.

A written goal becomes a personal contract. It holds you accountable. It gives your ambition form, and it gives your mind a destination to work toward. Research backs this up: people who write down their goals are found to be significantly more likely to achieve them than those who don't. This isn't fluff, it's science.

A SIMPLE EXERCISE WITH LIFE-CHANGING RESULTS

Pick one goal, big or small, and write it down. Make it specific and clear. In that moment, you shift from dreaming to doing. You've taken your first real step towards making it happen.

Try this right now. Take 30 seconds, grab a piece of paper, and write down one clear goal for the next year. Don't write 'make more money.' Write 'Earn $100,000 by 31st December'. Don't write 'get fit'. Write 'lose 15 kilograms by my birthday'.

Then take a moment. Visualise yourself achieving it. What does it look like? How do you feel? What steps will you need to take?

In that simple act, you've planted a seed that, when watered with focus and action, will grow. Every major breakthrough in life and finance begins with this small, decisive act.

THE COMPOUND EFFECT OF WRITTEN GOALS

Here's the beautiful part: once you see your first written goal achieved, you'll want to do it again. And again. You'll become obsessed, not with hustle, but with clarity. Each win builds momentum.

Over time, what once felt impossible will become your new normal.

Written goals compound like climbing a mountain – each one brings you closer to the summit. And one day, you'll look back and see how far you've come, because you started with a simple decision to write it down.

One of the most powerful ways to connect your vision with action is by tracking your progress with a single, simple number I call your *Freedom Score*. You'll learn it properly in the *PLAN* section. For now, just remember what you wrote earlier: your living cost, your passive income, and the gap. That gap is what your Freedom Score is designed to shrink, step by step, without adding stress

Take 10–15 minutes to reflect and write down your answers to the questions below. Don't overthink it, just let your thoughts flow. This is your moment to define what freedom looks like for you.[7]

1. If money weren't an issue, how would you spend your time? *(Think about your ideal day, week, or life rhythm.)*

2. What are the top three things you want more of in life? *(E.g., Time? Travel? Security? Purpose? Family? Relationships?)*

7 You can get a Goals Sheet at www.rodnia.com.au.

3. What are you no longer willing to tolerate financially? *(E.g., Debt? Dependence? Stress? Living pay-to-pay?)*

4. When you imagine financial freedom, what emotions come up? *(E.g., Joy? Confidence? Peace? Excitement?)*

5. What's one bold 'freedom' goal you want to achieve in the next 12 months? *(It could be increasing income, reducing debt, building savings, investing, or lowering your cost of living. Make it SMART: Specific, Measurable, Achievable, Relevant, and Time-bound.)*

CHAPTER 6
YOU'RE NEVER TOO OLD; YOU'RE NEVER TOO YOUNG

THERE IS NO PERFECT AGE TO BEGIN

One of the biggest lies people believe about financial freedom is, 'It's too late for me', or at the other end of the spectrum, 'I'm too young, no one will take me seriously'.

But here's the truth: there is no perfect age to begin.

There's only the decision to begin, and that decision can change your entire life.

> The best time to start was yesterday. The second-best time is when you stop making excuses.

If you feel like you're too old to start building a life of financial independence, consider these examples:

- **Leonardo da Vinci** began painting the *Mona Lisa* at 51. Today, it's the most iconic artwork in the world. Imagine if he had said, 'It's too late. What's the point?'
- **Warren Buffett**, one of the greatest investors in history, made 99% of his wealth after the age of 50. His secret? Long-term thinking and patience, the very qualities that come with experience.
- **Colonel Sanders** didn't start franchising KFC until he was in his 60s. Before that, he had failed at multiple careers. Most people

that age are slowing down, but he was just getting started. By 73, his face was on buckets of chicken around the world.

These aren't outliers. They're powerful reminders that life doesn't follow a straight timeline. With the right mindset, the second half of life can be even better than the first.

If you are thinking: *I'm too inexperienced, I won't be taken seriously*, consider this: age doesn't equal authority. Clarity, action and courage do.

- **Steve Jobs** co-founded Apple at 21.
- **Melanie Perkins**, the Aussie founder of Canva, tested her design-platform idea while still at university, and by age 19 had started working on her startup full-time.
- **Moziah Bridges** began selling handmade bow ties at 9. By 11, he was on *Shark Tank*.

Your age doesn't limit you. *It empowers you.*

When you're young, you have time, creativity, and fewer obligations. You can afford to dream big, take bold risks, and recover fast. And when you show up prepared, passionate, and consistent, people notice.

So, whether you're 18 or 68, here's what you need to know: You are not too early. You are not too late. You are right on time. Financial freedom doesn't care how old you are. It doesn't care how long it's taken or how many mistakes you've made. It only cares about one thing:

Will you start now?

That's all it takes. One decision. One commitment. One step.

CHAPTER 7
THE SWEET TASTE OF LATER

THE POWER OF DELAYED GRATIFICATION

> “Now let me tell you an earth-shattering truth: you must pay the price for your freedom before you get to enjoy it.

And the only way to pay that price is by doing what you'd rather *not* do, until you've earned the right to do whatever you please. This is where delayed gratification comes in. It's the secret sauce, the quiet superpower. Sacrificing now, living below your means, saying 'not yet' when the world screams 'buy now'.

It's about understanding that every short-term decision has a long-term consequence, and that choosing the one your future self will thank you for takes planning, patience, and the guts to walk past the shiny stuff.

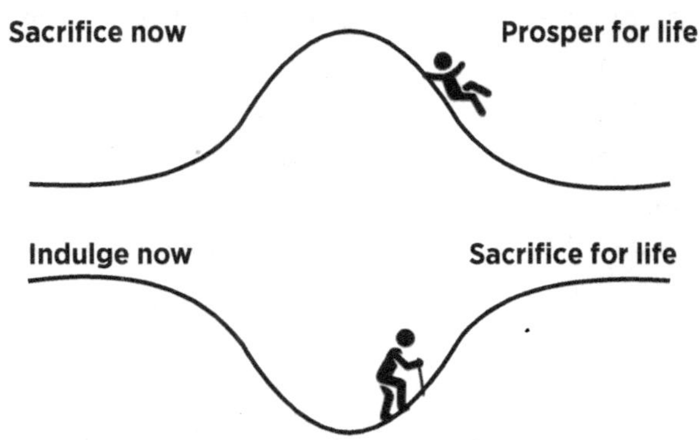

The concept of delayed gratification has been studied for decades, and one of the most famous experiments started with something sweet: marshmallows.

In the late 1960s, psychologist Walter Mischel ran a simple test with a group of children.

Each child was given a choice: eat **one** marshmallow now, or wait 15 minutes and get **two**.

The test was designed to measure the kids' ability to delay gratification, to say 'not yet' in exchange for something better down the line.

As you'd expect, some kids gobbled up their marshmallow the moment the researcher left the room. Others stared at the marshmallow, squirmed in their seats, covered their eyes, even sang songs to distract themselves.

But the ones who waited didn't just get two marshmallows, they got something much more valuable later in their lives.

Long-term follow-ups showed that those kids who could delay gratification tended to have better life outcomes: they had better grades at school, better overall health, lower levels of substance abuse, and greater career success. Later research found that the results were also influenced by family background and environment, but the core lesson remains: the ability to delay gratification gives you a powerful edge.

In other words: the marshmallow was just the beginning.

This lesson applies directly to personal finance. Just like those kids who waited for the second marshmallow, people who can delay gratification with their money, who choose to save, invest, and resist the sugar rush of impulse spending, tend to come out way ahead.

It's simple: say 'not now' to that shiny toy, and you're saying 'yes' to a financially free future. When you hold off on the instant wins and easy shortcuts, you create space for your money to grow, compound, and build real wealth.

Here's a rule I live by that makes it easier: whenever I feel the urge to buy something, I wait 24 hours. That one simple habit has saved me thousands by stopping shiny, short-lived purchases in their tracks. Once, I left a pair of sneakers in my online cart overnight. The next morning, the store emailed me: 'Still thinking about these?

Here's 20% off'. Yep, I was thinking about keeping my $200. So thanks, but no thanks.

Okay … you got me. *I did still buy them!* But hey, my 24-hour rule usually works pretty well.

But the point remains: delayed gratification isn't sexy. It doesn't give you a dopamine hit. But it moves the needle, every single time.

So, the choice is yours: Be like the kids who waited for that second marshmallow – practise delayed gratification. In investing, patience often gives you a better chance to build lasting wealth.

CHAPTER 8
UNCHAIN YOUR MIND

This part of the book isn't about getting everything right or holding fully formed ideas in your head. It's about noticing patterns, questioning assumptions, and allowing a few perspectives to quietly reshape how you see money. You'll need to make this shift before the PLAN part makes sense.

If something doesn't land straight away, that's completely normal. Some ideas do their work in the background and only click later. Just keep going.

BREAK FREE FROM INHERITED LIMITATIONS

We don't choose our first money beliefs, we inherit them. Remember how in the marshmallow test, later studies showed that family background and environment shaped the kids' decisions just as much as willpower? Well, the same is true for money.

Think about it. How many times have you heard someone say: 'I'd love to invest, but my dad always told me the share market is too risky.'

Or:

'Mum said someone she knew lost everything in shares.'

These ideas often come from parents or grandparents who lived through economic shocks, who are from generations shaped by very different rules. Baby Boomers grew up in a period of expanding consumer culture. Generation X came of age during recessions and market crashes, which taught many to be cautious with money.

This isn't about blaming our parents. They did the best they could with the knowledge they had. But if you're still operating under their belief systems without question, you might be unknowingly capping your potential. The ideas that served previous generations may not serve you today.

If financial freedom is your goal, you'll need to challenge inherited thinking. Replace fear with wisdom. And most importantly, trust your own judgment more than the warnings of those who never walked the path you're determined to follow.

DON'T FOLLOW THE CROWD

Let me ask you something: what if I told you I could teach you how to hunt an entire herd of buffalo, without a single weapon or tool?

Sounds like a tall tale, right?

In fact, I've taken a page out of the book of some Indigenous hunters in South America who've been doing exactly that for generations.

Here's how they do it.

No traps.

No weapons.

They apply pressure, guiding the herd towards the edge of a cliff until confusion and momentum take over. And once movement builds, the rest follow – because the conditions make it hard to do anything else.

Under pressure, even smart systems can behave in surprisingly irrational ways. In the right conditions – urgency, noise, and fear – individuals stop thinking independently and start following the crowd.

We humans like to think we're different. But we have our own version of the same pattern – not cliffs, but default paths we follow without questioning.

Have you ever changed lanes on the highway just because the cars ahead of you did, thinking they must be able to see something you can't? Or how about this: have you ever judged a restaurant's quality by how many people were already inside? As if a crowd automatically equals great food, rather than just great marketing (or a two-for-one schnitty night).

> “We follow crowds instinctively. And in finance, that instinct can be disastrous.

It’s the same herd mentality that fuels market bubbles and crashes. First, everyone piles in because ‘everyone else is getting rich’. Prices skyrocket. Then, at the first sign of panic, the same crowd bolts for the exits, just because ‘everyone else is selling’.

Originally, herd behaviour kept us safe. In the wild, moving with the group reduced your chances of being eaten. But in today’s markets, that instinct can drive you off a financial cliff, and right into the hands of those ready to take advantage at the bottom.

If everyone’s following the crowd, no one’s questioning the direction. That’s why achieving financial freedom requires ‘accurate thinking’. This is the ability to separate facts from opinions and think independently.

Always ask: where did this information come from? Is it fact? Or is it an assumption, or just someone else’s opinion?

YOUR MIND CAN BE A RISK

The biggest danger in investing isn’t the market; it’s your own mind. That’s why the approach in this book matters. It’s about thinking long-term, using principles grounded in philosophy, psychology, and strategy. You don’t need insider connections or a Wall Street degree. But you do need to understand the game you’re in, and play it with clarity, confidence, and purpose.

A zero-sum game

There’s a fixed amount of money in the market at any given time. When one person wins a trade, that money comes directly from another’s losses. The total doesn’t grow or shrink, it just shifts from hand to hand. For every winner, there’s a loser. This is called a zero-sum game: all the wins and losses added together equal zero.

Now imagine this: you bump into the world’s top poker champion, and he invites you to sit down for a few hands.

Do you jump in thinking, 'What a sucker! I am about to take his money?'

Of course not. You know how that story ends.

You wouldn't just lose, you'd be lucky to walk away with your shirt still on!

Yet this is exactly what many people do when they enter the share market, often without even realising it.

Who's on the other side of this deal?

Every time you buy a share or make a trade, it's worth asking: 'Who's on the other side of this deal?' Because often, that someone isn't a casual investor, it's a professional. The vast majority of money in the market is managed by institutions, super funds, mutual funds, hedge funds, investment banks, organisations with million-dollar research budgets, teams of analysts, and cutting-edge technology. They've weathered crashes, bubbles, booms, and busts.

They're not guessing, they're calculating. And if you are in a trade with them, they have made the opposite decision to you.

CHAPTER 9
SHARPEN THE BLADE

Every financial decision you make passes through the same filter: your mind. And while we like to think we're rational, objective, and in control, the reality is far messier. Our brains are wired with shortcuts, biases, and blind spots that quietly distort how we see risk, value, and opportunity. In this chapter, we'll uncover the hidden ways your thinking can mislead you – and, more importantly, how to outsmart it so you can make clearer, sharper, and more confident decisions.

CAN YOU TRUST WHAT YOU SEE?

Here's a little test. Take a look at the two centre circles in images A and B below. Which one seems bigger? Take a moment. Trust your instincts.

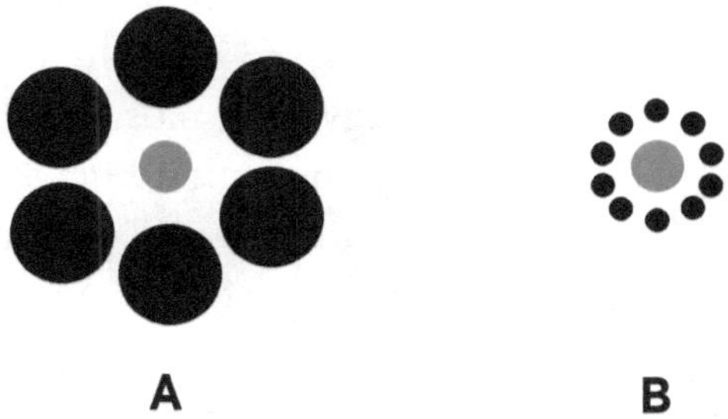

The Ebbinghaus Illusion

Got your answer?

Now here's the interesting thing: *they're exactly the same size.* No tricks. No Photoshop. The centre circles in A and B are completely identical.

So, what's going on?

This is the *Ebbinghaus Illusion* – a striking example of how your brain can mislead you without asking for permission. Because the surrounding shapes are different in size, your mind automatically skews its perception. One circle looks larger than the other, but in truth, there's no difference at all.

And here's the mind-bender: even after you *know* they're the same, they *still look* different. That's how deeply hardwired these mental shortcuts are.

> “Your brain isn't designed to see truth. It's designed to see patterns that feel useful, even when they're wrong.

This is more than just a visual trick. This is exactly how we misjudge value in finance: a house feels like a bargain because it's cheaper than the one next door, even if it's overpriced.

A share looks 'cheap' because it's down 30%, without looking at its earnings or future prospects.

You feel rich after a pay rise … until your friends start upgrading their cars and suddenly you feel poor again.

Perception isn't reality. But your brain often can't tell the difference. That's why you need more than instinct to make financial decisions. You need structure. You need strategy. And most of all, you need to keep an eye on the sneaky ways your own mind can trip you up.

If the circles in the Ebbinghaus Illusion still look different even after you *know* they're the same, are we just doomed to fall for every trick in the book?

Not so fast! *Awareness is your superpower.*

Sure, you can't delete these quirks of the mind; they're hardwired into your biology. But you *can* outsmart them. And when you combine awareness with specific strategies to counteract these biases, you gain an edge. You can begin to manage the impulsive part of your brain using the most rational part, the part that plans, reflects, and questions.

COGNITIVE BIASES: THE INVISIBLE ENEMIES OF WEALTH

One of the sneakiest ways our mind messes with our money is through what psychologists call the *anchoring bias*. This is where we unconsciously latch onto a specific number (a 'mental anchor') and use it as a reference point for all future decisions, even when it's no longer relevant.

Once you can spot these traps, the PLAN and DO parts of this book will become much easier to execute.

Anchoring bias: when your past frames your present

I've observed this in myself many times. When I have big chunks of cash sitting in my bank account, I start to see $1000 as a small, almost insignificant amount. A new gadget? A fancy dinner? Sure, why not? It's just a grand, right? You've got to live a little!

But when my cash reserves are low (usually because I've put everything to work in investments), that same $1000 suddenly feels like a monumental sum. I tighten up. I question every expense. I become really frugal, even stingy.

So, what has changed? Not the value of the money, just the context. My mind had anchored to a higher or lower baseline, and it distorted my perception of value.

Anchoring bias doesn't just affect spending. It can skew how we negotiate salaries, value investments, or set goals. And unless we become aware of it, we risk making decisions based not on what something is actually worth, but on the first number we happen to come across.

The antidote? Do your research. Understand the fair value of what you're buying *before* you see a price tag. Whether it's a car, a salary offer, or an investment property, knowing the true range of value ahead of time helps you avoid being unconsciously anchored by the first number you hear. In a world full of marketing spin and price manipulation, knowledge is the only anchor you can trust. And in the upcoming *DO* and *GEAR UP* parts of this book, I'll show you the exact tools and tactics to make sure you walk in prepared.

Confirmation bias: when your brain makes up its mind first

One of the most fascinating, and frankly terrifying, quirks of human psychology is a phenomenon called *confirmation bias*. This is when your brain makes up its mind first, then goes hunting for evidence to back it up. We don't really seek truth, we seek validation. Worse still, we often find exactly what we're looking for, especially in the age of the internet, where you can dig up 'evidence' to support just about *any* argument, no matter how absurd.

And here's what's wild about it: just knowing about confirmation bias doesn't protect you from it. Even the very scientists who discovered it are just as vulnerable to it in their everyday lives. That's how deeply hardwired this bias is. It's sneaky, it's stubborn, and it fools even the experts.

So ... what can we do?

HOW TO OURSMART YOUR BIASES

Because we can't switch off our biases, we need to *outsmart* them. My personal approach, and the one used in science for centuries, is to try to *disprove* what I believe, rather than trying to prove myself right. This is known as the scientific method. In science, you rarely prove something true. Instead, you show that the *opposite* is false. By eliminating the alternative, you strengthen the case for your original idea. It's not about being right, it's about ensuring you're *not wrong*.

I apply this to all of my big life decisions. Let's say I'm considering making a substantial investment in a share I really like. It looks promising. The numbers check out. My instinct says, *yes, go for it*. But before I act, I sit down and play the devil's advocate. I force myself to build a case *against* the investment. Then I'll go hunting for people who disagree: analysts, articles, forums, anyone pointing out flaws I might be blind to. I ask: *what could go wrong? What are they seeing that I'm not?*

If, after all that, I still believe in the investment, I move forward. But now I'm doing it with eyes wide open, not rose-coloured glasses. And that changes everything.

If you want to arm yourself against confirmation bias and other thinking traps, I highly recommend reading the brilliant little book

The Art of Thinking Clearly by Rolf Dobelli. It's an easy read and packed with real-world examples that will make you go, 'Ah, I do that too!'

If you're ready for something more advanced, dive into *Thinking, Fast and Slow* by Daniel Kahneman, the Nobel Prize–winning psychologist who helped lay the foundations of behavioural economics. It's dense but deeply rewarding, and it will forever change the way you think about thinking.

MY POTATOES AREN'T COOKED!

In the age of the internet, it's easy to quote a 'credible' source. It's even easier to misunderstand and misinterpret it, or to leave out the key bit of context that makes the story make sense.

Take this as an example: what if I told you there's a place in South America, called the Andes, where potatoes won't cook. You can boil them for hours, even days, and they'll still come out rock hard? Sounds ridiculous, right?

Well, I've got it on good authority: none other than Sir Charles Darwin himself. And no, I'm not even joking. I can point you straight to my source of evidence, Darwin's book *The Voyage of the Beagle.*

Okay, let me tell you the story!

During his famous expedition with the Beagle, Darwin and his crew made camp one evening high up in the Andes Mountains. After a long day of trekking, they lit a fire, filled a pot, and set some potatoes on to boil. The fire was hot. The water was bubbling. Everyone relaxed.

Hours passed. Night fell. The crew drifted off to sleep.

Now the fire had burned all night. The water had been boiling. But the potatoes? Still uncooked.

Everyone was really puzzled. But Darwin, being Darwin, started thinking it through.

He knew something the others didn't: At high altitudes, the boiling point of water drops. At sea level, water boils at 100°C.

But high up in the Andes? It boils at around 70°C. And that's nowhere near hot enough to cook a decent spud.

But the rest of the crew didn't know that. So, they did what people often do when they are confused: they guessed.

One blamed the cursed potatoes. Another figured they must've picked up some strange foreign variety. Someone else suggested the firewood was no good, or worse, mountain spirits had sabotaged the meal!

Darwin just smiled.

It wasn't the potatoes.

It wasn't the fire.

And it definitely wasn't the spirits.

It was physics.

The water boiled. But it didn't get hot enough to get the job done.

Just because the water's bubbling, doesn't mean the potatoes are cooking.

APPEARANCES DON'T TELL THE FULL STORY

When it comes to your finances, understanding the truth is crucial. If you don't understand the context, if you misread the conditions or lean on second-hand stories, you can end up making big decisions based on half-baked potatoes ... sorry, facts.

You might follow a hot tip, mimic someone else's strategy, or act on something that *sounds* right ... only to end up broke, confused, and wondering why things didn't work out.

> “It's not enough to see the bubbles; you need to know the temperature.

In money, just like in the Andes, what you don't know can leave you hungry.

So, don't settle for surface signs. Check the facts. Understand the mechanics. Because boiling isn't cooking, and noise isn't knowledge.

RISK VS GAMBLING

Taking calculated risks is an essential part of building wealth. In fact, success in any domain, whether in finance, business, or life, requires a level of boldness. But, as with everything in life, there's a fine line between being courageous and being foolhardy. The key difference lies in whether the risk is calculated or if you're merely gambling. And this will be a lifesaver when you get your hands dirty in the DO part.

The great German general Erwin Rommel, famously nicknamed the 'Desert Fox' for his brilliant tactics in World War II, offers a sharp analogy that captures this distinction perfectly. Rommel, a master strategist, understood the fine line between risk and gambling. He drew the line like this:

> Both risk and gamble involve an action with only a chance of success, a chance that is heightened by acting with boldness. The difference is that with risk, if you lose, you can recover: your reputation will suffer no long-term damage, your resources will not be depleted, and you can return to your original position with acceptable losses. With a gamble, on the other hand, defeat can lead to a slew of problems that are likely to spiral out of control. If you encounter difficulties in a gamble, it becomes harder to pull out, you realise that the stakes are too high; you cannot afford to lose. So, you try harder to rescue the situation, often making it worse and sinking deeper into the hole you cannot get out of. Taking risks is essential; gambling is foolhardy.

Rommel's insight isn't just about war. It's about life, and especially about money. A calculated risk is something you can bounce back from. Sure, it might sting, but it won't wipe you out. You still have the resources, financial, emotional, and mental, to regroup and go again.

A gamble, though? That's a different beast. That's betting the farm with no plan B. When it goes wrong, and it usually does, you don't just lose money. You lose peace of mind, opportunities, even your reputation.

That's the real difference: risks can teach you, gambles can break you. And that brings us to one of the oldest debates in wealth-building: diversify or concentrate?

CHAPTER 10
DIVERSIFY OR CONCENTRATE?

FINDING YOUR BALANCE

What we're about to cover in this chapter matters enormously when you get to the PLAN part.

Let me share the best piece of advice I ever received. It came at a time when I had just $100 to my name and no job. Every minute of every day, I scoured Gumtree, applying for anything and everything: cashier, desk clerk, labourer, delivery driver, even odd-sounding jobs. If it had an 'Apply Now' button, I clicked it. But the only thing that came back were rejection emails. Hundreds of them. Each one was a gut punch, another reminder that time, and money, were running out.

I remember riding the bus, looking around at strangers and thinking: *that guy has a job, this guy has a job.* As I walked through the shopping centre, I'd watch people at work and feel a pang of envy. I thought to myself, *I'd give anything to swap places with that cleaning lady; how lucky she is to have steady work.*

Then, by sheer luck, I ended up chatting with someone who changed everything for me. He said, 'Amir, you're zigzagging all over the place, spreading yourself too thin. If you're desperate, focus only on the two kinds of jobs that are easiest to get, cleaning or kitchen-hand. Pick one and go all in.'

That advice hit me like a lightning bolt.

I had always loved cooking, so I decided to go with kitchen-hand. Without wasting another second, I went to Officeworks and printed 300 résumés. Then I walked the streets of the city in Brisbane – every laneway, every restaurant strip – and handed them out one by one. No online applications. No waiting. Just footwork and unshakable determination.

Once the 300 résumés ran out, I printed another lot. By the time I was done, I had handed out over 500 résumés. And finally, *finally*, I landed a trial at a kitchen that turned into a job. And yes, it was scrubbing pots in a hot, chaotic kitchen, what we affectionately call a 'dish-pig' in the hospitality industry. But let me tell you, it was the most exhilarating feeling in the world. To this day, I still get goose-bumps thinking about it.

CONCENTRATE TO BUILD WEALTH, DIVERSIFY TO PRESERVE IT

I'm telling you the story of my dish-pigging days because that notion of concentrating on only the two most viable options saved my life.

In all my years of research, I am yet to come across a book or article that clearly articulates one of the most critical principles of wealth-building: *concentration and diversification are to be used at different stages of your financial journey.* The correct use of these tools can mean the difference between substantial wealth creation and mediocre returns.

The principle is simple: concentrate to build wealth; diversify to preserve it. These strategies have specific purposes and applying them in reverse will lead to subpar results.

In my role as a financial planner, much of my work revolves around retirement planning, which often follows this exact principle. During the accumulation phase, when individuals are actively building their wealth, it's common to take on more risk, focusing on opportunities that offer the potential for higher long-term returns. As people approach retirement, however, the goal shifts towards preserving wealth, with a more conservative approach to guard against losses.

THE WISDOM OF GREAT WEALTH BUILDERS

Let's now turn to three of the wealthiest men in history, who exemplified the power of concentrated wealth-building: Andrew Carnegie, John D. Rockefeller, and Warren Buffett.[8]

Andrew Carnegie: an absolute master of focus

Born into poverty in Scotland, Andrew Carnegie moved to America with his family and got his start earning just $1.20 a week in a factory. But he wasn't content with survival; he wanted more.

His first big break came when he invested in railroads. But his real fortune came from betting everything on one industry: steel. By focusing deeply, building efficiency through vertical integration, and scaling aggressively, Carnegie turned Carnegie Steel into the world's largest producer. When he sold it to J.P. Morgan in 1901 for what would be over $15 billion today, he became the richest man alive.

Carnegie's philosophy was to 'put all your eggs in one basket, and then watch that basket closely'. Focus wasn't just his motto. It was his strategy.

John D. Rockefeller: a paragon of concentrated effort

Born in modest conditions in 1839, John D. Rockefeller started out trading commodities. But in 1863, he zeroed in on a risky industry: oil. While others speculated wildly, Rockefeller played the long game.

By co-founding Standard Oil and controlling every step, from drilling to refining to transport, he built an empire that dominated the industry. His focus turned him into history's first billionaire, with a fortune worth over $400 billion in today's money.

Rockefeller could have spread himself thin. Instead, like Carnegie, he chose discipline and depth. The lesson? Wealth comes from concentrating on what you know best, not from scattering your bets.

---

8 Disclaimer: This section and the stories are shared for educational purposes only, to illustrate how some of history's wealth builders approached risk and focus. They are not a recommendation to follow the same strategies, or avoid diversification. Everyone's circumstances are different, and you should seek advice before making financial decisions.

Warren Buffett: the greatest investor of all time

No one has championed focused investing like Warren Buffett. Often called the greatest investor of all time, Buffett has long dismissed over-diversification, famously calling it 'protection against ignorance'. His view is: if you don't know what you're doing, scatter your bets. But if you do, focus.

Together with Charlie Munger, Buffett built Berkshire Hathaway by concentrating on a handful of high-quality businesses they understood deeply. Rather than owning hundreds of stocks, they invested big in a few, backed by research and conviction.

The results speak for themselves. Over nearly 60 years, Berkshire Hathaway's per-share market value has surged by over 5,500,000% since 1965. By comparison, the S&P 500, the benchmark for America's biggest 500 companies, rose about 39,000% over the same period.[9]

COMPOUNDING: THE POWER OF HIGHER RETURNS

One of the key reasons why concentration is so powerful as a wealth-building strategy is in the power of compounding. Let's break this down with an example.

If you invest $100,000 and it returns 3% per year, in 30 years, your portfolio will grow to just shy of $243,000. Not bad.

But if you focus your efforts on high-quality investments that generate a 15% return per year, that same $100,000 grows to over $6,620,000.

The difference between these outcomes is mind-blowing and explains why higher returns, even on small sums of capital, can be completely transformational.

Now, I'm not suggesting you should expect to generate a 15% return with ease; I'm just using this as an example to illustrate the power of compounding.

In the early stages of your financial journey, when your capital is small, diversifying too broadly dilutes your returns. Instead of having the capital to place meaningful bets on strong opportunities,

---

9 Based on CNBC reported data, 'Warren Buffett's Return Tally After 60 Years: 5,502,284%', 5 May 2025. Assumes all dividends are reinvested.

you scatter it across too many investments, many of which may be mediocre. The result is often subpar returns that could take decades to compound into meaningful wealth.

WHY CONCENTRATION WORKS BEST WITH SMALL CAPITAL

Charlie Munger, Buffett's partner, and my personal favourite investor, was a lifelong champion of focus. He often warned that excessive diversification guarantees average results. Buffett once said: 'I could make you 50% a year on $1 million'. The problem, he admitted, is that those same opportunities don't exist when you're managing billions.

That's the hidden advantage of starting small. With $5,000, you can back a niche opportunity that has real potential. With $5 million, you're forced to spread yourself thin. Smaller sums allow for nimbleness, concentration, and meaningful bets that bigger players can't make.

That's why, in the early stages of wealth-building, concentration can be such a powerful ally. It gives your seed capital the chance to grow faster, setting the foundation for everything that follows.

We'll put this into practice in the PLAN section.

Now let me show you what focus looks like in real life.

Meet Cass.

REAL PEOPLE, REAL SUCCESS STORIES

CASSANDRA

'From Zigzags to Train Tracks'

Cassandra has always been one of those people who just lights up a room. I've known her for years; we first met working in a commercial kitchen. While the rest of us were dragging ourselves through long shifts, she'd be buzzing around like a spark plug, making everyone laugh and keeping the energy up. Customers loved her, the staff adored her, and honestly … it was impossible not to.

But for a long time, there was one thing that kept holding her back financially: Cass was always zigzagging.

One week it was crypto. The next, real estate. Then maybe becoming a real estate agent. Or moving interstate. Or jumping into the next hot stock tip from someone at work. Her energy was contagious, but it was scattered, not focused.

Later, she moved into FIFO work and started earning serious money – something like half a million dollars in after-tax income over a three-year period. But still, nothing to show for it. Cash went out as fast as it came in.

I used to joke with her all the time: 'Cass, you're zigzagging again. You know what you need? You've got to get your plans on train tracks.'

The train tracks metaphor stuck. Because when you're on the tracks, you don't get pulled off course every time someone waves a shiny new idea in front of you. You stay the course. You build your plan and forge ahead.

Then came another turning point, an idea I'd shared with her, originally from Tony Robbins: complexity is the enemy of execution.

Once Cass embraced this concept, along with the train tracks mentality, everything changed. She stripped her plan down to something simple but powerful. Her newfound clarity made it possible to actually follow through.

She put together a clear plan of attack. She'd always dreamed of having her own place – private, secure, somewhere to call home. So the first stop on the new train was: buy my first home.

From that moment on, when people told her 'now's not the time to buy property' or 'you should invest in this instead', she just didn't listen. She stayed on track.

With that unshakable determination, Cass bought her first home – her foundation. Now she's got a clear path ahead: property number two, a growing share portfolio, and a future where passive income funds her freedom, not fleeting trends.

Cass now likes to describe her transformation like this: 'Focus is like holding a magnifying glass over a single point. The sun's rays are the same either way – scattered, they only warm. But focused on one spot, they burn through anything in their path.'

That's the power of focus. Cass didn't just dream about a better life – she laid down the tracks and drove her train forward.

INVEST IN WHAT YOU KNOW – OR LEARN UNTIL YOU DO

One of the golden rules of investing is simple: only put your money into what you truly understand. Warren Buffett summed it up perfectly: 'Risk comes from not knowing what you're doing.'

Investing blindly in areas or industries you have little knowledge of is akin to gambling. You wouldn't suddenly open a restaurant if you've spent your entire career in healthcare, would you? Yet, many people make similar mistakes in investing, diving into markets and businesses they don't understand, often with disastrous results.

Play to your strength

If you're going to buy property, it makes sense to choose an area you know well. Maybe it's your hometown, or a suburb where you've seen the schools, transport, and local economy evolve over years. That insider knowledge gives you an edge outsiders cannot match.

The same applies to business and shares. If you've spent decades in healthcare, you'll naturally understand the players, the trends, and the pain points, making you far better placed to judge the value of a healthcare company than someone guessing from the sidelines.

Learn before you leap

Of course, you don't have to limit yourself to industries you've already worked in, but you do need to do the work. If you're eyeing a tech start-up and your background is in retail, study the fundamentals. Understand the landscape, the competitors, the risks. Understanding must come before investing.

When you invest in areas you understand, you reduce risk. You can better anticipate shifts, spot opportunities, and avoid pitfalls.

Knowledge is the best protection against risk, but it doesn't have to come from you alone. When we learn together, we grow faster and make fewer mistakes.

STRONGER TOGETHER: OUTSMARTING BIAS AS A TEAM

No one has all the answers. The smartest investors don't go it alone; they surround themselves with people who challenge their thinking and fill in the gaps. That's why I've created a community for readers of this book: a Community where you can put your knowledge into practice alongside others on the same journey.

It's a space to form a *Gameplan Crew*, swap stories, share insights, and call out blind spots before they turn into costly mistakes. Your experience might spark someone else's breakthrough; their perspective might save you from a bad decision.

Need a devil's advocate to test your investment idea and combat confirmation bias? Curious how others handled the same challenge you're facing? That's what this community is for: sharpening each other's thinking and staying ahead in a fast-changing financial world.

If you'd like to connect with others on the same path, you can step inside the conversation at www.rodnia.com.au.

Or simply scan this QR code:

THINK One-Step Action

Write down your freedom goal.

Take five quiet minutes and use the goal-setting template in this part to write your number, your reason, and the life you want. Clarity beats motivation every time.

PART I RECAP

RESET YOUR MINDSET: MASTER THE INNER GAME TO WIN THE OUTER ONE

Every mindset shift you make strengthens your ability to grow your *Freedom Score* without self-sabotage. Thinking clearly today protects your score tomorrow.

Change your thinking, and your outcomes change with it. The wealth starts in the mind, long before it hits your bank account. Your mindset is the engine. Everything else is just fuel.

Before you can build wealth, you must train your mind to think like a wealth builder. This section laid the psychological foundation for your financial journey. We covered why success doesn't start with strategy. It starts with how you see yourself and what you believe is possible.

If you remember nothing else, remember this: you don't need to understand everything before you begin. The system will make sense as you use it.

KEY TAKEAWAYS

- **Self-belief + Imagination = Superpower:** Edison, Oprah, Ali, and Jobs didn't wait for permission. They envisioned the impossible, and then made it happen. You can too.
- **Roots before fruits:** Focus on becoming the kind of person who produces wealth, rather than chasing outcomes. Character compounds faster than cash.
- **Guard your mindset:** Be decisive. Silence doubt. Trust your vision, even when others don't. And beware of crabs in the bucket trying to pull you back.
- **Surround yourself with likeminded people:** Form a Gameplan Crew. Your tribe will shape your trajectory.
- **Clarity is power:** Write down your goals. Your brain needs clear instructions to deliver big results.

- **It's never too early or too late:** Whether you're 18 or 68, the best time to start is when you stop making excuses.
- **Discipline beats impulse:** Delayed gratification is the secret to exponential wealth.
- **Think independently:** Challenge inherited beliefs, watch for mental traps like anchoring and confirmation bias, and avoid herd mentality.
- **Know the game:** Understand the difference between a calculated risk and a reckless gamble. This knowledge will protect and empower you.

UP NEXT: PLAN

Congratulations! You've already done the hardest part: shifting how you think.

From here on, things get clearer, more practical, and more concrete.

In the next part, you'll go from mindset to the method of action. You'll learn how to design your path to financial freedom with clarity and purpose, just like an architect drafts a building before laying the first brick.

Don't think of this part as just theory, you're no longer simply reacting to money.

Instead, you're about to start mastering it.

Now, when you're ready to move from clarity to action, you'll find a tool waiting for you, one that maps the path forward no matter your starting point.

Keep in mind, you now hold the rarest advantage in today's financial world: not another strategy, but a new way of thinking.

Use it wisely, and everything changes. You're not just changing your finances. You're changing who you are.

Move forward from this moment with clarity, confidence, and purpose, and let your plan take shape.

Let's go.

PART II
PLAN

Build Your RICH Trifecta™

> **A note from the legal department**
>
> This part is general information and education only. It isn't personal financial advice and doesn't take into account your objectives, financial situation, or needs. It may include general discussion of asset classes, strategies, and borrowing. Before acting on anything in this book (including buying, selling, borrowing, or changing structures), consider getting advice from an AFS licensee or authorised representative. Past performance is not a reliable indicator of future performance. You are responsible for assessing whether any concept or strategy is appropriate for your circumstances.

WHAT TO BUILD AND HOW THE MACHINE WORKS

This part blends timeless wealth principles with unconventional insights drawn from real-life experience. You don't need to memorise or even remember everything in this section. PLAN is about seeing the *shape* of your strategy, not locking in details. Think of it as a map, not a contract.

You can always come back to refine things later. For now, clarity beats precision.

What follows is the second stage of the Freedom Framework, the strategic lens of planning. Here, we zoom out to chart your direction before diving into the how-to in the next part.

Most people think they have a money problem. But what they really have is a strategy gap.

If you don't have a clear system for building wealth, you're probably following someone else's plan.

And guess what?

Their plan doesn't serve you, unless your dream is to help them retire early!

This section reveals the wealth-building model I call the *RICH Trifecta*. It's not just about what you invest in, but *when, why, and how much*. It's about building a personal wealth engine that works for you in *real life*, not just on spreadsheets. Its job is simple: to build the assets that steadily increase your Freedom Score.

Think it sounds complicated?

It isn't. That's the beauty of it. You'll see.

KICK-OFF

Now that you've sharpened your money mindset, it's time to build a strategy. A practical, all-weather plan that can carry you through every financial season.

This isn't about reacting to every bump in the road. It's about creating a path so steady that you can move with confidence, no matter what life throws at you.

At this stage, we're still flying at 30,000 feet, looking at the big picture.

We're mapping your financial landscape before we zoom in on the finer details.

And hey, if you're already thinking, *this all sounds great ... but where on earth am I supposed to find the money to do all this investing?*

Relax! I used to think the same thing when we were broke.

Keep reading. The answer's in the pages ahead.

And no, it doesn't involve selling your furniture or giving up your morning coffee!

CHAPTER 11
THE RULES OF WEALTH THE RICH ALREADY KNOW

STRATEGY VS TACTICS: KNOW THE DIFFERENCE OR PAY THE PRICE

Before we go any further, let's clear up one of the biggest misconceptions in personal finance: the difference between strategy and tactics.

Think of it like this:

Strategy is your GPS. Tactics are your steering wheel.

One tells you where you're going.

The other helps you turn corners.

Most people mess this up. They chase tactics, buying trendy shares, flipping houses, jumping on the latest 'hot tip', all without a clear strategy. It's like throwing darts blindfolded and hoping one hits the bullseye … or at the very least, not your foot!

Strategy is the big picture: what you're trying to achieve, and why.

Tactics are the moves you make along the way.

The key is this: your strategy stays steady. Your tactics adapt.

What this looks like in real life

Your financial strategy is your grand plan. It might include investing in shares, property, and private business. That doesn't change just because interest rates nudge up or the media screams about another recession.

But your tactics? They better be nimble.

Say your strategy includes building wealth through real estate. Tactically, you might start with residential property. But if the market shifts or income returns tighten, you might pivot to commercial property. Or maybe you'll adjust your structure to something more tax-efficient.

Same strategy. Responsive tactics.

Or say you're investing in shares. During a market high, you might hang back. But during a crash? That's when you may find opportunities. Pull cash from your offset account (which we'll explore shortly) and buy quality companies at bargain prices. Tactical brilliance.

LESSONS FROM BABYLON

One of my favourite books about wealth is *The Richest Man in Babylon*.

Set in ancient times, it follows a wealthy man named Arkad who shares simple principles of money that have stood the test of time. Strip away the old language, and the message comes down to:

- **Pay yourself first** – set aside a portion of everything you earn. This is your foundation.
- **Put your money to work** – savings alone won't set you free. Invest it so it grows and produces income.
- **Seek guidance from those who've done it** – real experience beats hype every time.
- **Stick to what you understand** – confusion is expensive. Clarity is profitable. Stay in your lane.
- **Avoid shortcuts** – if it sounds too good to be true, it usually is.

That's it.

Thousands of years later, nothing has changed.

In today's world of ETFs, crypto, tax structures, and economic chaos, it's easy to feel overwhelmed. The pace of change, new laws, and new platforms can paralyse even the most enthusiastic investor.

This is where the old wisdom of Babylon meets the modern philosophy of *Freedom Gameplan*. Despite the decades between us, the principles outlined in that little book are as relevant as ever.

Those Babylonians didn't have Wi-Fi, Uber Eats, or TikTok, but somehow, they managed to figure out how money works better than half the 'experts' on YouTube.

But while the principles are timeless, the way we apply them has evolved. Today's world moves faster, offers more options, and demands a clearer system to navigate it all.

That's where the *RICH Trifecta* comes in.

CHAPTER 12
A MODERN WEALTH MODEL FOR REAL FREEDOM

HOW THE *RICH TRIFECTA* WORKS: THREE ASSETS, FOUR FILTERS, ONE MACHINE

Let's get something out of the way first.

RICH Trifecta™ might sound like a racing tip or a millionaire's catchphrase. But it's neither.

Yes, *trifecta* is a word you'll hear at the racetrack.

Yes, *rich* can conjure images of yachts and gold watches.

But in this context, '**RICH**' isn't a status symbol. It's a filter. A four-part lens to evaluate every financial decision you make:

Risk. Income. Capital. Hassle.

'**Trifecta**' isn't a bet. It's a strategy. A synergy of three core assets: **Property. Shares. Private business.**

Together, they form the foundation of real, lasting wealth. Not in isolation, but in concert.

Three assets. Four filters. One machine.

So how does it work in real life?

Let's start going through the four stages of wealth building and you'll see.

THE FOUR STAGES OF WEALTH BUILDING

The four stages of wealth-building are illustrated in the following flowcharts. You'll probably see yourself in one of them. Keep an eye out.

As you go through the below flowcharts, keep in mind that arrows show how the money flows, in and out.

And remember, you don't need to master all this today. All you need right now is a rough mental picture.

I promise that the details will fall into place naturally as you move forward.

Stage 1: The employment trap – trading time for money

Let's start with where most people are.

You go to work. You get paid. The money drops into your account. Then it's out again: rent, mortgage, bills, groceries, fuel. Maybe there's enough left for a holiday, a new laptop on Afterpay, or the latest iPhone on a plan. You get the idea.

That's the cycle:

Work → Pay day → Spend → Repeat.

Even if you are self-employed, if the business can't run without you you're still in the employment trap. You've just built yourself a job.

If that feels uncomfortably familiar, you're not alone. Most Aussies are stuck in Stage 1. But if you're reading this, you've already decided you won't stay here. So let's keep moving.

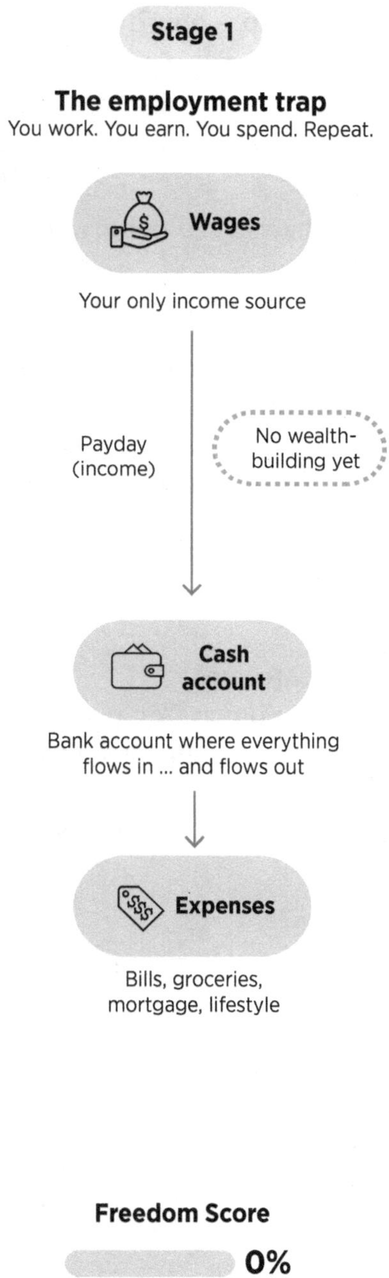
Stage 1
The employment trap
You work. You earn. You spend. Repeat.
Wages
Your only income source
Payday (income)
No wealth-building yet
Cash account
Bank account where everything flows in ... and flows out
Expenses
Bills, groceries, mortgage, lifestyle
Freedom Score
0%

Stage 2: The products trap – owning but not winning

This stage looks like progress on paper; there's some 'investing' happening. Maybe you have:

- an investment property that's negatively geared – and now it's chewing up income
- bought a handful of shares or ETFs because it 'seemed like a good idea'
- a hot tip or started a venture that ends in exhaustion.

This is the products trap: buying investments without a strategy. Cashflow gets tight, progress stalls, and there's no capacity to keep investing.

The biggest mistake people make is starting with products instead of starting with a plan.

They skip the goal.

They skip the mindset.

They skip the plan.

They buy things, not outcomes.

But you're not going to do that. You've already done the groundwork, you've clarified your goals, sharpened your mindset, and built a solid foundation. You THINK.

Now, you're ready to PLAN, and build something that actually works.

Stage 2

The products trap

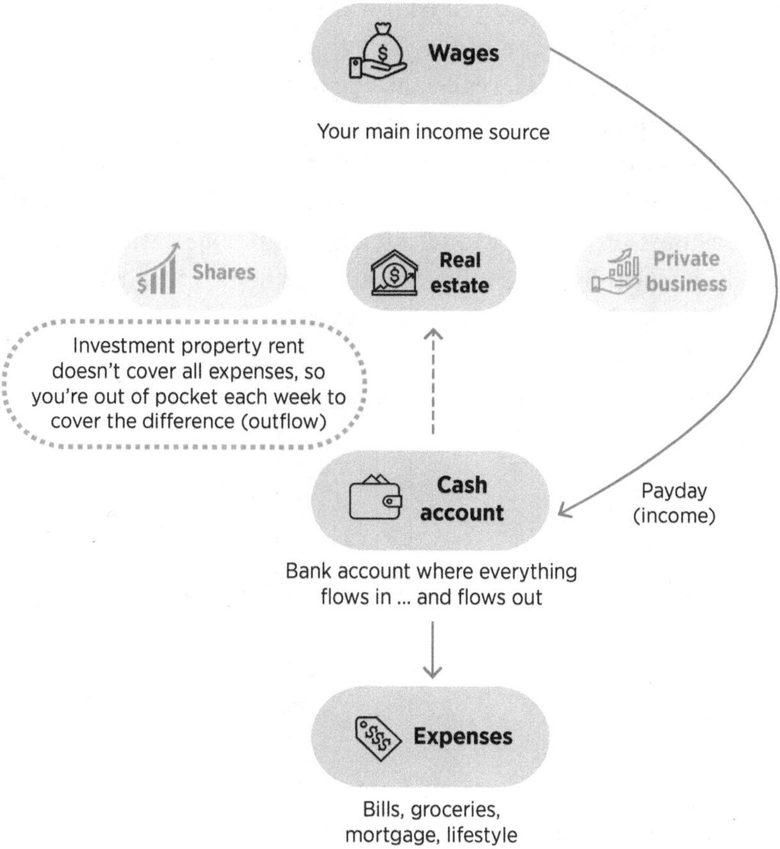

Freedom Score

0%

Stage 3: The fine-tuned machine – earning while you sleep

Here's where things get exciting.

You're still working, but now you're doing it with purpose. Your income is no longer disappearing into the black hole of expenses; a portion of your pay is being directed towards greasing the wheels of a machine you're building: the *RICH Trifecta.*

Three key assets: **shares, real estate, private business.**

Each one with its own structure and superpower.

Bit by bit, as you continue feeding your Trifecta Machine, each asset box in the below diagram starts to grow. Dividends. Rental income. Business profits start to trickle back into your cash account. And slowly, beautifully, your reliance on wages begins to shrink.

You're still working. But you're not working for survival, you're working to accelerate the build.

The gears are turning. The machine is in motion.

Stage 3

The fine-tuned machine

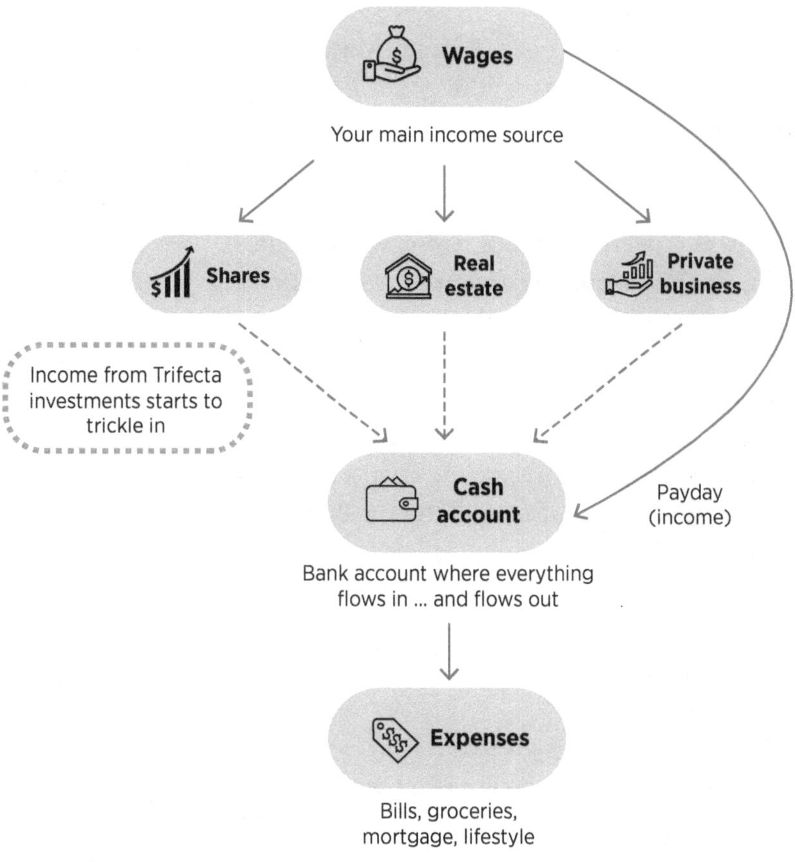

Freedom Score

20%

Stage 4: Life on your terms – the self-sustaining Trifecta

Now for the magic moment.

Drum roll, please!

You wake up one morning and realise something incredible: **you no longer need your job**.

Your investments in your Trifecta Machine are now generating enough income to cover everything: your mortgage, your bills, your holidays, your life.

The cash account fills itself automatically. It has become your *Hub Account* (more on this later).

Expenses? Covered without stress, without effort.

You're not just surviving anymore. You're thriving.

But this isn't only about balance. It's about how the three prongs of the machine amplify one another. When they work in harmony, something powerful starts to happen: each asset begins to support the others. You'll notice that idea labelled in the diagram, and we'll unpack it properly in the upcoming chapters.

Because here's the real magic: the machine doesn't just maintain your lifestyle.

It grows.

It reinvests.

It compounds.

It multiplies.

And what does all this give you?

One thing most people never get: **Choice**:

- The choice to work, or not.
- The choice to travel, build, rest, give, create.
- The choice to permanently clock off the wage cage.

That's the power of a well-oiled Trifecta Machine.

Stage 4

The self-sustaining TRIFECTA MACHINE

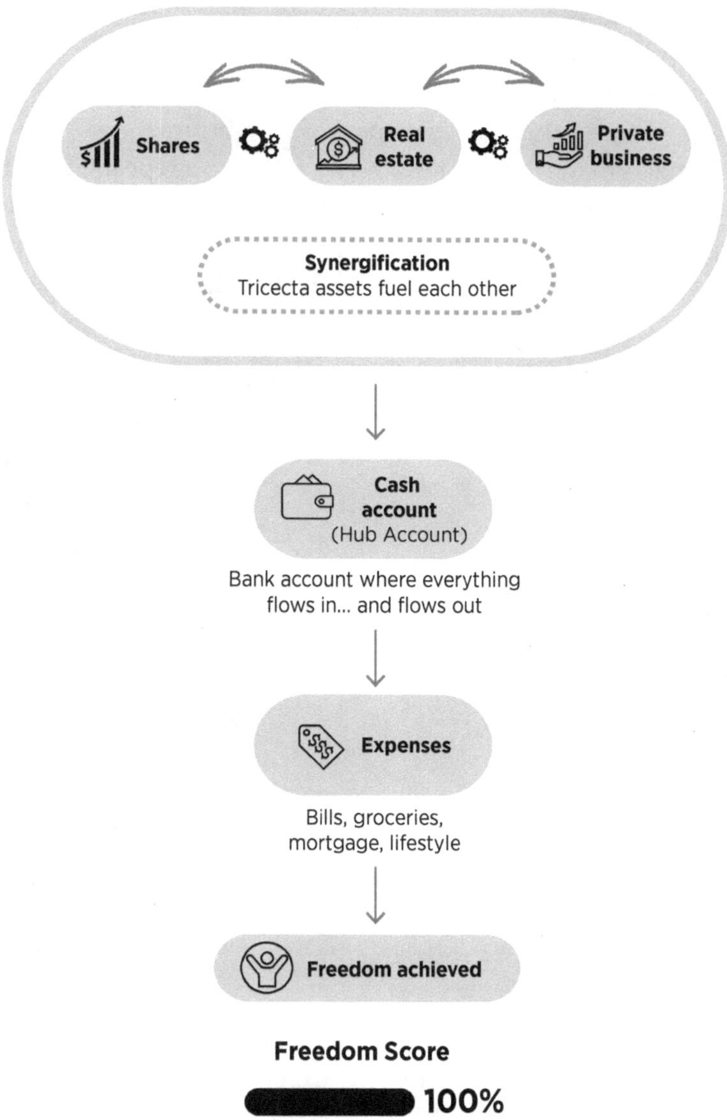

Where do you see yourself in the four stages? Share your journey and learn from others walking the same path in the FG Community.[10]

If you remember nothing else from what you've just read, remember this:

You're building a machine.

At first, it runs on your effort.

Over time, it runs on your assets.

The goal isn't to become an expert overnight.

The goal is to move from random investing to a repeatable system.

Next, I'll give you a simple way to measure your progress, so this all stops feeling abstract and starts feeling real. The order is simple: build the engine first, then learn the moves in the coming DO part.

10 Prefer a visual reminder? You can download a full-colour printable version of the *RICH Trifecta* for your office or vision board at www.rodnia.com.au.

CHAPTER 13
MEASURE WHAT MATTERS: YOUR FREEDOM SCORE

HOW WEALTH COMPOUNDS

Before we go any further, let's simplify the whole thing into one clean dashboard metric. You've probably heard the saying, 'What gets measured, gets managed'.

When you measure the right thing consistently, progress stops being accidental, and becomes inevitable.

We touched on the *Freedom Score*™ concept in the Intro and THINK parts. This is where you will learn how to apply this to your own life. If the *RICH Trifecta* is the engine, your *Freedom Score* is the dashboard. It tells you how close you are to escaping the wage cage and stepping into real freedom. If you remember only one metric from this book, make it this one. Because your Freedom Score tells you the truth most numbers hide.

The four stages of wealth-building we just went through aren't just about where your money flows, they're also about how close you are to freedom. That's why each stage includes a Freedom Score benchmark at the bottom. This is your north star.

Working out your Freedom Score is really simple:

Passive income ÷ Expenses × 100

That's it. Let's say your expenses are $50,000 per year. This is the total amount you need to live life on your terms. If your investments (such as dividends, cashflow positive property, business income) are bringing in $25,000 per year in passive income, your Freedom Score is 50%. Dead simple.

That means you're halfway there, and that's worth celebrating.

Because now you have a scoreboard for your life, not just your money.

Track it. Share it. Grow it.

The intended purpose of every strategy and tactic in this book is to simply help you think about ways to increase your Freedom Score without increasing stress.

Net worth and employment income can rise while your true freedom falls. But if your Freedom Score rises, that's where you will truly live free and reclaim time.

The Freedom Score Spectrum

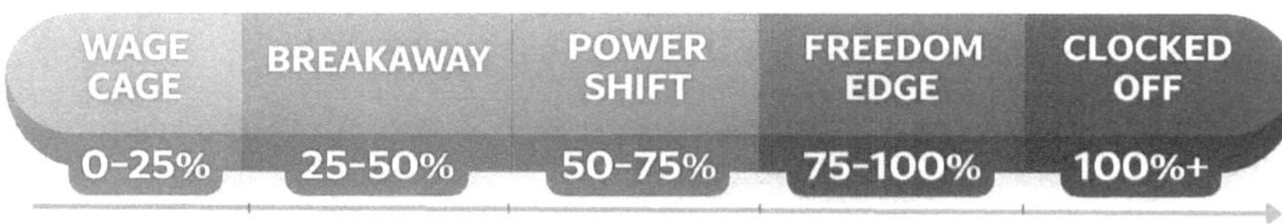

> “Net worth is vanity. Income is comfort. Freedom Score is time reclaimed.

Most Australians live in the Wage Cage.

Few ever reach Freedom Edge.

Almost nobody gets to Clocked Off.

Over time, smart financial decisions can move you closer to the right-hand side of the spectrum. Each time you increase passive income, reduce debt, or lower costs, your score ticks higher.

The goal? To reach 100%, and beyond. This is when money works for you, not the other way around.

Clocked Off doesn't mean you have to retire. It means you no longer *have* to work.

Instead, do the work that you love, spend more time with family, or do some volunteer work.

But *knowing* your score isn't enough. The real question is: how do you increase it faster, without working harder for longer?

That's where the real power of your machine begins to show.

CHAPTER 14
BUILDING YOUR MACHINE: FROM ACTIVE TO PASSIVE INCOME

This is where the machine stops being a collection of assets and starts becoming a Freedom Score accelerator. Every wealth journey starts with active income, meaning your wages. That's the seed.

At first, the Trifecta Machine is fragile. You must feed and reinvest it. Essentially, water and nurture it like you would with a young plant. Over time, like a seed growing into a tree, it becomes self-sustaining. Passive income flows. Compounding takes over. The machine begins to run itself.

This is the moment your assets start to *synergify*, working together to push up your *Freedom Score*, instead of working in separate silos.

This is the point where work shifts from survival to choice.

DEPTH CREATES BREAKTHROUGHS

Now imagine you own a plot of land, and underneath it lies a massive pocket of oil. But you've only got access to limited resources.

You could dig 100 shallow holes, each 10 metres deep, hoping one of them strikes oil.

Or …

You could do your research, hire an expert, identify the most promising spot, and drill in one spot 1000 metres deep.

Which one do you think would give you the better chance of striking oil?

The answer is obvious. And it's the same for how the *RICH Trifecta* works. Let me explain.

SYNERGIFICATION™: WHEN YOUR ASSETS TEAM UP

Everyone talks about diversification as a *defence* strategy, to protect you if one asset fails.

But what about *offence*?

Relying on diversification alone is like putting eleven soccer goalkeepers on the field. You might block every shot, but who's going to score?

Synergification flips the game. This is the strategy of using each asset class to power the next, creating a self-fuelling wealth engine. Property, shares, and business don't sit in silos; they play as a team, amplifying each other's power and driving momentum.

For example, if your shares surge and look overvalued, you can lock in gains and reallocate the money into a new business, a property opportunity, scaling your side hustle, or simply park it in your offset account to boost reserves and cut interest costs. Or maybe you use the income from each asset to fuel the next.

Below is what that may look like in practice. In each scenario, you're watching your assets *synergify*, each one powering the next in a self-fuelling loop.

Scenario 1: Equity ignites expansion[11]

You buy a $650K property – maybe it's your first home, or maybe it's an investment property. Five years later it's worth $850K. You refinance and pull out $100K in cash (I'll explain exactly how in the DO part, Tactic 4).

You then use that to:

- invest in dividend-paying ETFs (shares) that earn $2000 to $3000 per year in passive income
- launch a side hustle that earns $1000/month by year three.

One property fuels your share portfolio and business. That's a triple wealth engine. All without having to sell your property.

11 The following examples are simplified illustrations and do not represent recommendations. Strategies involving borrowing can significantly increase risk and are not suitable for many individuals.

Scenario 2: Dividends fund development

Your share portfolio pays $7000/year in dividends.

You channel that into:

- hiring a Virtual Assistant to scale your business; or
- paying down your mortgage, freeing up cashflow.

Now your shares are feeding your business or your property.

Scenario 3: Business powers the Trifecta Machine

Your side hustle has grown to $40K/year.

You use that income to:

- qualify for a second property loan; or
- increase your ongoing share investment program (more on this in part III).

In this scenario, the business isn't just a side gig. It's a fuel source for your entire machine.

That's *Synergification* in action: the whole becomes greater than the sum of its parts.

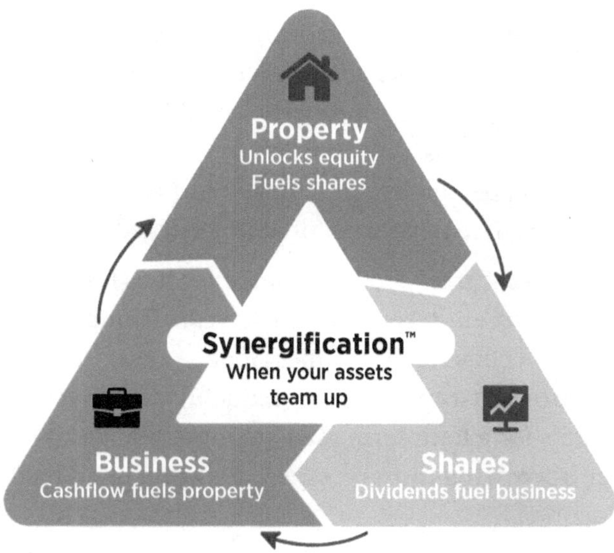

Each asset class is strong on its own. But when they're combined strategically, they become a powerhouse of compounding momentum.

> Diversification spreads. *Synergification* compounds.

Think about your own situation: which asset could you use to fuel the next? Once you identify that first spark, your whole machine begins to *synergify*. At first, slowly, then faster, until momentum takes over.

Synergification isn't about taking on more risk. It's about using existing resources more intelligently.

In the next section, we're going to unpack exactly how the *RICH Trifecta* works, in real-life steps.

I'm excited for you! Let's build your machine.

THE ENGINE BEHIND *SYNERGIFICATION*: CAPITAL ACCESS

So, what really makes the machine hum? Access to capital.

Wealth isn't just about what you own, it's about how quickly you can mobilise it when opportunity strikes. That's why real estate is so pivotal: it unlocks two levers other assets can't match.

Borrowing capacity and available equity

One of the greatest strategic advantages of owning real estate is the ability to borrow against your property's available equity, and to do so on very favourable terms.

Compared to personal loans, business loans, or margin loans (a loan against a share portfolio), property-backed finance offers:

- **Lower interest rates** – because banks see it as less risky.
- **Longer repayment terms** – up to 30 years, compared to 5 or 10 years for a personal or business loan.
- **Smaller monthly repayments** – reducing cashflow stress as repayments for a long-term loan are more manageable.
- **Greater borrowing limits** – especially when paired with a solid income.

But keep in mind, these features can make borrowing more accessible, but they also increase exposure to debt obligations and financial risk, particularly if income is disrupted or asset values fall.

The offset account (or redraw facility)

The offset account is one of the most underrated tools in personal finance. In the *RICH Trifecta*, it acts as a key pillar of your capital strategy.

Your offset is your capital reserve, cutting loan interest while giving you tax-free, instant access to cash when opportunity strikes. Its superpowers are:

- **Instant access to capital** – When opportunities pop up that require fast action (such as a sudden market crash, a distressed asset sale), you don't always have time to go through a full loan application. Having funds on standby means you can move fast.
- **No tax on earnings** – Unlike interest in a savings account, the 'return' (savings) with an offset is tax-free, because you're saving on loan interest rather than earning taxable income. Compared to a savings account, you will usually get a better interest rate for savings in an offset account.
- **Peace of mind** – It's your emergency parachute, helping you sleep better at night knowing you're covered for any unexpected setbacks.

These features mean that capital isn't locked. It flows. You can pull it from one part at its peak, and rotate it into another where value is stronger.

KEEPING YOUR WEALTH MACHINE IN BALANCE

Capital access transforms the *RICH Trifecta* from a static portfolio into a wealth machine that evolves, compounds, and gets stronger over time.

Because each component of your machine behaves differently, when one slows, another often shines. A share market crash doesn't always mean property is falling too, and business opportunities often pop up when other markets are quiet.

The combinations are endless, but the principles stay the same:

- harvest gains strategically
- reallocate where value is stronger
- keep your Trifecta compounding.

This is why capital (how freely your money can move) is one of the four RICH metrics: free-moving capital is what makes *Synergification* possible.

THE RICH METRICS: RISK, INCOME, CAPITAL AND HASSLE EXPLAINED

Now that you understand how the *RICH Trifecta* machine works, you need a simple and clear way to assess your investment choices.

That's where the *RICH* metrics come in: *Risk*, *Income*, *Capital*, and *Hassle*. The four key factors that guide how you build your wealth and assess investments. (Later in the *GEAR UP* part, we'll explore how to actually score different opportunities using this model, so you can compare them side by side and choose the right one for you.)

The table below illustrates the interaction of the RICH metrics with the Trifecta assets.[12] More stars is better (lower risk, higher income, lower capital required, lower hassle).[13]

RICH metrics

	Shares	Real estate	Private business
Risk	Medium ★★★☆☆	Low ★★★★☆	High ★★☆☆☆
Income potential	Moderate ★★★☆☆	Low to moderate ★★☆☆☆	High ★★★★★
Capital required	Low ★★★★★	High ★★☆☆☆	Low to moderate ★★★★☆
Hassle	Low ★★★★★	Moderate ★★★☆☆	High ★☆☆☆☆

12 You can download the printable colour copy at www.rodnia.com.au to accompany your *RICH Trifecta* chart.

13 These ratings are purely illustrative. They're here to help you understand the *RICH Trifecta* machine, not to tell you what to buy or recommend any specific asset class. You should always put your own thinking into the ratings.

Sure, there are plenty of other variables we could consider. But if you focus on these four, you'll have a simple yet powerful lens to evaluate any opportunity and run an efficient wealth machine.

> “ Most plans optimise money. RICH optimises freedom.

The RICH filters help you improve your Freedom Score in real life by giving you a tangible way of judging each investment.

THE FUN STORY OF HOW THE *RICH TRIFECTA* WAS BORN

Before we dive into the model, let me share a fun little story about how the RICH metrics came to life.

If you ever come to my house, chances are you'll have to survive *'the whiteboard ordeal!'*

I love explaining things on a whiteboard. So much so that I've been known to hijack dinner parties with impromptu finance lectures. Friends, family, unsuspecting guests … no one's safe.

One evening, I was in full whiteboard mode, passionately walking my father-in-law, Paul, and his partner Sarah through the wealth-building model I've shared in this book.

Back then, I listed the four key factors as: **Hassle, Income, Capital, and Risk.**

And I didn't even bother with an acronym: HICR!

Anyway, as I was scribbling away, Paul suddenly lit up.

'You know, Amir,' he said, 'if you rearranged those … it spells RICH.'

Boom. Mind blown.

In that moment, everything clicked. The model didn't just work, it finally had a name that captured what it was all about.

Simple. Sticky. And spot on.

That, my friends, is how the *RICH Trifecta*™ was born.

So, hats off to Paul for the golden insight. And a lifetime exemption from whiteboard duty.

(Just kidding, Paul. You know I physically *can't* help myself.)

Now, let's break down each element.

Risk

Risk is one of the most misunderstood concepts in all of investing. Most people think volatility is the enemy. Volatility is just ups and downs in price.

Please allow me to set the record straight: volatility is just noise. Risk is losing money you can't get back.

Picture this: a top-tier company's share drops 15% in a week. Is the business broken? Probably not. More likely, it's the market having a mood swing, reacting to headlines, hype, or fear. The fundamentals are still solid.

The real danger isn't the dip, it's what you do during the dip.

Sell in a panic? Buy without understanding? That's where the real risk lives.

And here's a mind-blowing fact: if you lose 50% of your money, you'll need a 100% gain just to get back to where you started. That's no easy mountain to climb.

So, what's the takeaway? Be bold, but be smart. Take calculated risks. Only the kind you can recover from if things go south.

We will dive deeper into this distinction between risk and volatility later in this part.

Income

Income (or yield) is crucial because *passive income* is our ultimate goal here. The magic of compounding lies in the reinvestment of this income to generate even more returns.

Let's say you invest $100,000, earning 5% a year.

If you take the income, you receive $5000 each year. But if you reinvest it, the following year you're earning 5% on $105,000. Then on $110,250. Then more again.

At first, the increase is barely noticeable. Over time, it becomes the entire story.

After 30 years, that original $100,000 grows to approximately $432,000. And the annual income? It's no longer $5000. It's now over $21,000 per year – without adding another dollar of your own money.

Capital

This is your seed money. It's the fuel that powers your financial engine.

You build it by saving, living below your means, and directing surplus cash towards assets. The more capital you grow, the more doors open. Larger deals unlock, with better leverage, and faster progress. Think of it as the foundation you're building on. The more disciplined you are at creating a surplus income, the faster you can grow your seed capital. Capital measures how much money is required for an investment and how easily it can be accessed (cashed out).

Hassle

This is all about how much time, effort, and stress an investment demands.

Some investments are simple and hands-off. Others are like getting a second job. And while high-hassle investments can sometimes deliver higher returns, you need to balance them with options that let you breathe.

After all, freedom is the goal, not burnout. Some investments are like a cruise-control road trip: easy, smooth, and you barely have to touch the wheel.

Others?

Ooh, they can be like babysitting a toddler hyped up on red cordial: noisy, unpredictable, and guaranteed to leave you questioning your life choices!

Take a breath.

If your brain feels like it just ate a whole buffet of new ideas, that's normal. Right now, you don't need detail. You just need orientation.

So here's the only question that matters: which stage am I in right now … and what would the next stage look like?

That's it. Don't overthink it. You're just mapping things out right now. We'll deal with the details later.

CHAPTER 15
THE THREE WEAPONS THE WEALTHY WIELD

BUILDING YOUR WEALTH ARSENAL

Each element of the *RICH Trifecta* Framework offers unique advantages depending on your goals, resources, and stage in life. The key is knowing which one to focus on, and *when* and *how* to balance them over time to build a wealth machine that runs smoothly and grows steadily.

Let's take a closer look at each prong of the model and how they align with the RICH metrics.

As you read, keep asking the question that matters most: how does this asset help move my Freedom Score?

As you explore the three asset classes in the *RICH Trifecta*, keep this in mind:

While I've provided general RICH guidelines for each asset type below, it's critical that you assess the RICHness of each specific investment on its own merits. For example, while real estate as a category may generally score low on risk, a particular property, say in a volatile area or with development issues, could be high-risk in practice.

Each opportunity must be run through the RICH filter individually. Don't rely on broad assumptions. The power of the *RICH Trifecta* lies in helping you make smart, case-by-case decisions.

In this part, you're seeing the *strategic* side of the *RICH Trifecta*. Later in the *GEAR UP* section, we'll bring it to life with real-world side-hustle examples and RICHness star ratings. This will give you a clear sense of how the model works in practice, and how you can apply it to your own opportunities.

REAL ESTATE: THE BEDROCK OF STABILITY

Real estate has historically been viewed as relatively stable over the long term, though it can still experience periods of decline. From feudal lords in medieval Europe to modern investors, land has symbolised stability, security, and status. Today, property ownership remains a defining factor in long-term success. It preserves wealth while creating a platform for growth and mobility.

For many Aussies, owning a home is the first major milestone, and often the foundation of their wealth.

Running property through the RICH Filter

Risk ★★★★☆: Historically, real estate is viewed as low-risk, especially in stable markets. Property prices may fluctuate, but they have increased over long periods. The ability to leverage financing (mortgages) can potentially magnify risk, or provide for amplified gains, all based on the quality of your decision. Real estate can be risky if you invest during over-inflated markets, or without first doing your homework.

Income potential ★★☆☆☆: Real estate can provide a steady income stream through rental properties. The income, however, is usually modest, especially after accounting for maintenance, property taxes, and management fees. For instance, in many residential markets, net rental yields (income after expenses) hover around 2% to 4%. While this may not seem high, it becomes much more attractive when you couple it with the potential for capital appreciation, if done right.

Capital required ★★☆☆☆: Real estate is a capital-intensive asset class. Buying property requires a substantial upfront investment, on the other hand, it is one of the few asset classes where access to bank lending can help people get their foot in the door. For example, if you buy a property with a 20% downpayment, you control the entire asset, but the bank finances 80% of it. This leverage can amplify your returns (and losses) on investment. If the property appreciates by 10%, your actual return on your equity can be far higher. We'll unpack this in detail when we get to Tactic 4: *Borrow against equity* in the *DO* section.

Hassle ★★★☆☆: Real estate requires more hands-on management than shares. You may need to deal with tenants, vacancy issues, property maintenance, and repairs. However, many investors outsource property management to reduce the hassle, making it more passive over time, albeit with the real estate agent's fee eating into the income yield.

Upsides:

- **Tangible asset:** Real estate is something you can see, touch, and feel, which provides comfort to many investors.
- **Leverage:** The ability to borrow against real estate has the potential to significantly boost returns.
- **Inflation hedge:** Property values historically tend to rise with inflation, providing a safeguard against the eroding purchasing power of money.

Downsides:

- **Illiquidity:** Real estate isn't as easily bought or sold as shares. If you need cash quickly, you can't always access the equity in a property without refinancing or selling. And let me tell you, trying to sell a house in a buyer's market is like running a sausage sizzle at a vegan festival. Lots of smiles, not many takers!
- **High transaction costs:** Buying and selling property comes with costs such as taxes, stamp duty, legal fees, and real estate agent commissions.
- **Ongoing costs:** Property comes with maintenance costs, land tax, and potential vacancies costs.

- **Leverage risk:** Borrowing can magnify gains, but it also magnifies losses. If property prices fall, your losses are amplified, and the bank still expects repayments.

SHARES: OWNING A PIECE OF THE ACTION

The share market is like a kid who has raided the lolly jar. Bouncing off the walls at first, but then crashing hard! Only the calm, long-term investors make it to bedtime with their sanity and wealth intact.

The share market has been creating wealth for centuries.

It all began in the 1600s in Amsterdam with the Dutch East India Company, widely considered the world's first publicly traded corporation. For the first time, everyday people could buy shares in a company and participate in its profits.

Since then, the share market has grown into one of the most popular and accessible ways to invest, offering ownership in companies across various industries, geographies, and sectors.

Owning shares in a company allows you to participate in its success through dividends and capital gains, all without needing to run a business yourself. That's why it works so well for our financial freedom purposes.

You can earn without having to lift a finger!

Running shares through the RICH Filter

Risk ★★★☆☆: Shares can range from low-risk (e.g., blue-chip companies) to high-risk (e.g., speculative startups or emerging markets). However, volatility is often mistaken for risk. Price fluctuations are a natural part of share market investing, but they are not inherently risky if you focus on long-term goals. Risk comes when you panic-sell, hype-buy, or invest in companies without understanding their fundamentals.

Income potential ★★★☆☆: Shares can provide dividends, a source of passive income. Dividends represent a portion of a company's profits paid out to shareholders. For example, a dividend yield of 6% on a $100,000 investment would give you $6000 in annual income. Dividends can compound if reinvested, boosting your returns over time.

Capital required ★★★★★: Shares offer the advantage of being accessible to investors with relatively small amounts of capital. You may be able to start investing in the share market with as little as a few hundred dollars. This accessibility makes shares particularly valuable in the early stages of wealth-building, where the goal is to grow small amounts of capital.

Hassle ★★★★★: Shares are much more hassle-free compared to real estate or private business. Once you own shares in a publicly listed company, you don't need to worry about managing the business, the company's directors handle that. This makes shares a great option for passive income seekers.

Upsides:

- **Liquidity:** Shares are highly liquid, meaning you can buy and sell them easily, giving you access to your money when needed.
- **Income potential:** Dividend-paying shares can offer a great stream of income.
- **Compounding:** Reinvesting dividends can dramatically increase your returns through compounding.

Downsides:

- **Volatility:** Share prices can swing wildly, and if you're forced to sell in a downturn, you could lock in permanent losses.
- **Market risk:** Even great companies can fall during tough markets. And bad companies? They might not get back up at all.
- **Emotional investing:** News cycles, market crashes, and hype can push you into costly mistakes if you're not grounded in a long-term view.

Why shares belong in your *RICH Trifecta*

Shares grow wealth in the background while you focus on work or business. They're flexible too, easy to cash in if an opportunity arises in property or business. That liquidity makes them the perfect counterbalance to property, which sits at the opposite end of the spectrum. And as your portfolio grows, dividends become meaningful income.

In short: shares compound both wealth and options. They're one of the most flexible tools for increasing your Freedom Score over time.

PRIVATE BUSINESS: THE FREEDOM ENGINE

Private business has been a core pillar of wealth creation for a long time. From the Industrial Revolution to the rise of Silicon Valley, entrepreneurs have built vast fortunes by taking risks, building businesses from the ground up, and creating value.

Starting a business is like riding a rollercoaster blindfolded. Exhilarating, terrifying, and occasionally nausea-inducing. But boy oh boy, the view at the top is worth it!

Unlike real estate or shares, where you invest in existing assets, private business offers something unique: *the ability to create an asset out of nothing.*

Running business through the RICH Filter

Risk ★★☆☆☆: Success hinges on your experience, industry knowledge, and execution. If you operate within your circle of competence, you dramatically reduce the risk.

Income potential ★★★★★: Private businesses offer high income potential. You control pricing, expenses, strategy, everything. Unlike shares, you're not waiting on a dividend declaration; you decide how and when the profits are used.

Capital required ★★★★☆: While you may need some capital to get started, many businesses can scale rapidly with reinvested profits or outside funding. The return on capital can be extraordinary.

Hassle ★☆☆☆☆: Let's be real, this is the most hands-on Trifecta component. You'll deal with staff, suppliers, customers, and the occasional fire to put out. But the hassle can be reduced by building the right systems and team (which we'll cover in the *DO* section).

Upsides:

- **Control:** You have direct control over the business's operations, strategies, and growth.
- **Income potential:** A successful business has the potential to generate more income than shares or real estate.
- **Growth opportunities:** Some businesses can scale quickly, increasing profits dramatically with additional capital.

Downsides:

- **Risk of failure:** Many small businesses fail within the first few years.
- **Time-intensive:** Running a business requires significant time, energy, and emotional investment.
- **Illiquidity:** Private businesses are often less liquid than shares, or even property, meaning it can take a long time to sell or exit.

The secret: work on the business, not just in it

To make private business truly powerful, your mission is to create something that runs without you. Build systems. Hire great people. Step back. The less your business depends on you, the more valuable, and hassle-free, it becomes.[14]

This transformation does two big things:

- it reduces your time commitment
- it makes the business far more appealing (and profitable) to potential buyers.

14 Now, if you're wondering, 'Okay, but how exactly do I do that?', that's a great question. I've included a dedicated section on this in the *Bonus Material*. You can get a free copy at: www.rodnia.com.au. Or simply scan the QR code.

Private business is a wealth accelerator

Look around. Everything in your life, from the coffee mug you're holding to the phone in your pocket, started as someone's idea. These ideas became companies. These companies create wealth.

Every great company had humble beginnings.

- **Apple** began in Steve Jobs's garage.
- **Canva** began as a tiny yearbook-design idea founded by a Perth student, Melanie Perkins. Today, it's worth over $25 billion and used by millions worldwide.
- **Atlassian**, started by two Sydney uni mates, Mike Cannon-Brookes and Scott Farquhar, with a $10,000 credit card, grew into a software powerhouse worth over $60 billion.
- **Amazon** started in Jeff Bezos's spare room.
- **Nike** was launched from the trunk of Phil Knight's car.

None of these founders had millions to start with. What they had was vision, grit, and the courage to act.

Why business beats almost everything else:

- **Create something from nothing:** Unlike shares or property, you're not buying a finished product, you're building one. The potential upside can be significant.
- **Compounding growth:** A well-run business can scale exponentially.
- **Flexibility:** You can pivot, improve, or completely reinvent the business.
- **Ultimate leverage:** You control capital, income, operations, and your future.

And once your business becomes self-sustaining, it's no longer just a job. It's an engine for long-term wealth.

> “Remember: the goal isn't just building assets. It's closing the gap on your Freedom Score.

Private business isn't for everyone. But for those willing to learn, lead, and take smart risks, it can be the most powerful wealth-building tool of all. A business isn't just income. Done right, it can be a powerful lever for improving your Freedom Score.

Let's meet Dan. His story is what happens when a business stops being a job and becomes an engine.

REAL PEOPLE, REAL SUCCESS STORIES

DANIEL

'Skills can be learned. Determination can't.'

Dan is one of those people you just know is going to go places the moment you speak to him.

Originally trained as a lawyer, he quickly realised that the legal world didn't align with his deeper aspiration to help people in a more meaningful way. So, he took a leap into a completely different field: recruitment.

There, he found purpose. He helped countless candidates land roles that were perfect for them, many of whom never thought their dream job was even possible. But after a few years, Dan found himself feeling restless again. He'd done well, made great money, and built a strong reputation, but deep down, he knew he was capable of much more.

And so, he made another leap – this time even bigger.

He resigned from his well-paying job as a recruiter and started his own business as a mortgage broker. During his time in recruitment, he'd helped many brokers find new roles and had always found the work intriguing. Helping people buy their first home, handing over the keys to their dream, felt exciting and deeply aligned with his mission of helping others.

So, he backed himself. Everyone around him thought he'd lost his mind, stepping into a field where he had zero experience and starting a business from scratch. But Dan knew better. He's the kind of person for whom experience is no barrier. He works with such intensity and focus that something which might take others years to master, he conquers in months.

Plus, having that beard can't hurt, right?!

Today, Dan has helped countless people secure their dream homes. And in the process, he's built a business of real, tangible value – the kind of business someone would happily pay good money to buy.

He's done what so many great entrepreneurs do: he created a valuable asset from nothing. A business with heart, purpose, and momentum. Today, when people in his community think about getting a loan, there's one name they remember: 'The Bearded Broker!'

CONCENTRATE TO BUILD, DIVERSIFY TO PRESERVE

As you know by now, the beauty of the *RICH Trifecta* Framework lies in its three-pronged approach: real estate, shares, and private business, which complement and strengthen one another. Each asset class has its pros and cons, but together they form a powerful, resilient, and *synergified* strategy.

In the accumulation and growth phase, you're not trying to juggle all three at once. Instead, you focus your capital where it will work the hardest. That might mean doubling down on shares during a market dip or channelling energy into building your business. Real estate often enters the picture through the purchase of your first home, a stable, leverageable base that supports your next move.

But as you approach financial freedom, the strategy evolves. This is when the magic of the *RICH Trifecta* truly shines. You shift from concentrated growth to diversified preservation. Your wealth begins to spread more evenly across all three components, not out of obligation to 'balance' your portfolio in the traditional sense, but because each asset now plays a unique, reinforcing role.

> **“ In the early days, you concentrate to build. Later, you diversify to preserve.**

As we explored in the THINK part, this is more than a clever phrase. It's a cornerstone of wealth strategy.

By the time income is flowing from all three arms of your Trifecta, you're not just financially stable, you're financially free. You've mastered not just the mechanics of investing, but also the timing, discipline, and flexibility needed to thrive in any market.

> Conventional wisdom says to diversify early, like dumping all the ingredients in a pot and hoping for the best. The *RICH Trifecta*™ is more like a gourmet dish: you add the right ingredients, at the right time, in the right order, creating something refined, balanced, and exceptional. Bon appétit!

This strategy is a blueprint. It shows the flow of capital across time and serves as a guide for your wealth journey. Instead of diluting your efforts by diversifying too broadly too soon, you purposefully deploy capital where it has the most impact, then gradually expand into other areas.

Okay, now for the exciting part. Let's map your way forward and find your next move.

CHAPTER 16
MAPPING YOUR WAY FORWARD

Alright, well done! You've taken in a lot so far.

Let's zoom out for a bird's-eye view and map out the road from debt to financial freedom. One way to think about the journey might look like this:

- **Acquire quality assets.** Many people build wealth by acquiring assets like real estate or shares, which may appreciate over time. Consider whether borrowing to invest would be appropriate. This is like planting seeds in fertile soil.
- **Consolidate your position.** As your assets grow in value, begin consolidating your holdings. This means selling off some assets to strengthen your position, utilising the *RICH Trifecta* Framework. It's like thinning out the garden, removing the weeds, and nurturing the healthiest plants.
- **Eliminate debt.** As your capital grows, start paying down your debt. This is the pruning phase, cutting away any dead weight so your financial garden can flourish.
- **Enjoy the harvest.** With little to no debt and a robust portfolio of high-quality assets, you're now in a position to live off the income generated by your investments. It's time to sit back, relax, and enjoy the fruits of your labour. You have arrived!

You're not just hopping from one asset to another willy-nilly; you're following a carefully planned sequence. Timing and rhythm are everything.

MAP YOUR NEXT MOVE: THE FREEDOM MAP™

Ah yes. The 'map' I teased back in the *THINK* section?

You've just found it.

Now, I want to give it to you straight. When you first glance at the Freedom Map, your brain might go, 'Whoa, that's a lot'. And that's okay!

But let me tell you: this isn't just a pretty picture. It's a tool for clarity, designed to turn the strategy we've covered into your next real-world move. Think of it like unfolding a guide for a road trip; you don't need to follow every road at once. Just focus on the next turn.

Here's how to use the Freedom Map:

Step 1: Start at the '**Start Here**' point.

Step 2: Explore one path at a time.

Step 3: Circle where you are now (own a home/have surplus cashflow/etc.).

Step 4: Go to the relevant section (DO/GEAR UP/Bonus).

Step 5: Revisit during your *Freedom Ritual* (more on this later).

Each step invites you to pause, reflect, and consider a next move to build momentum. Let your eyes scan the Freedom Map, and you'll see: it's just a series of simple, thoughtful decisions.

Adapt it.

Make it yours.

By the time you become familiar with it, I promise you will come to love it! For now, just glance over it and familiarise yourself with how the pieces fit together. Some of the potential steps you'll see here will be explored in more depth in the upcoming parts: *DO* and *GEAR UP*. If any of the terms in this map feel new, The Freedom Gameplan Glossary at the back of the book is your quick decoder.

The Freedom Map is also printed in full colour on the inside fold-out cover of this book.

And remember, the goal isn't perfection, it's progress.[15]

15 Disclaimer: This is not personal advice. It's a general framework. Always consider your individual circumstances or seek professional advice before making decisions.

FREEDOM MAP: EXAMPLE PATHWAYS

This map is a general education tool, not personal financial advice.
Your path depends on your own circumstances[16]

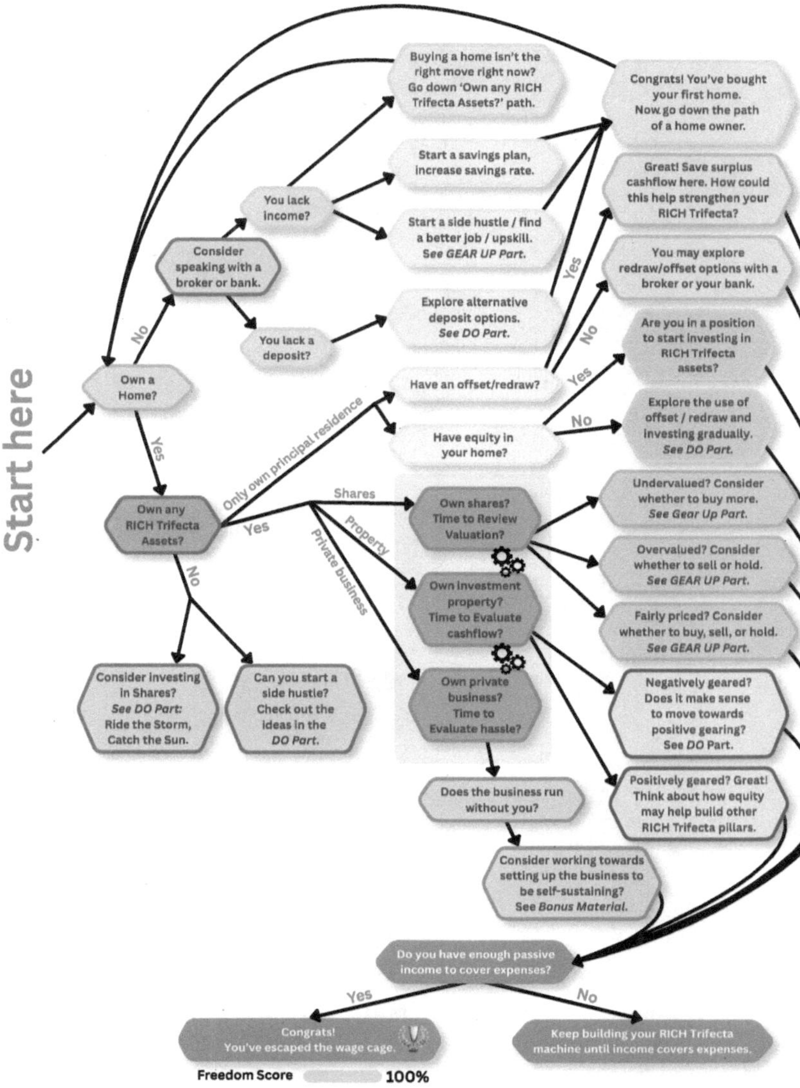

16 This map is a simplified illustration of common pathways only, not a step-by-step plan or prescribed strategy. There is no single correct path and outcomes depend on individual circumstances. Borrowing can increase both returns and risks. You should seek advice from a licensed financial adviser before acting on any information in this diagram.

CHAPTER 17
TAME THE BEASTS BEFORE THEY BITE

DEBT: A POWERFUL TOOL (WHEN USED RIGHT)

The great Greek mathematician and astronomer Archimedes famously said, 'Give me a long enough lever and a place to stand, and I shall move the world'.

Well, I say: 'Give me borrowing power and the right assets, and I might just move myself out of financial slavery!'

Sure, I say that with a wink. But there's truth behind the humour. Debt, or more precisely, credit, is one of the financial world's greatest lever. It's how fortunes are built. When you borrow to buy assets, it's called *leverage*. And like any levers, it can lift you or crush you.

Let's set something straight upfront: *This isn't advice*. I'm not telling you to go out and borrow money. My goal here is education. Whether you love debt or fear it, understanding how it works is essential in today's economy.

Unfortunately, debt has gotten a bad rap. And no wonder – misused, it *can* wreck lives. Ask anyone who lived through the 2008 Global Financial Crisis. But that's not the tool's fault. A chainsaw can prune a tree or level a forest. It all depends on the hands that wield it.

> “ Debt can be a burden ... or a breakthrough. It depends on whether you use it, or it uses you.

Here's a fun stat for you: only about 10% of the world's money is real.

The remaining 90%? Pure credit, digital IOUs flowing through the banking system.

We're all basically playing Monopoly, just with real houses, real money, and slightly worse attitudes.

Horrifying?

Not really.

This system functions because we believe in it. As long as borrowers repay their debts, and lenders trust the system, the economy hums along. But trouble brews when that trust breaks down.

The double-edged sword of credit

Leverage reduces your margin for error. Before borrowing to invest, consider your cashflow stability, risk tolerance, and capacity to absorb loss.

If the asset drops in value or stops producing income, the debt doesn't take a break. Repayments keep coming, magnifying capital losses and putting pressure on your cash flow. And even when income is flowing in from the asset, this can be reduced or disrupted. That's why a repayment buffer isn't optional, it's essential.

In some cases, if asset values fall significantly, investors can end up owing more than the asset is worth. This is known as negative equity. Combined with ongoing repayment, this can force difficult decisions, including selling at a loss or holding a stressed position for extended periods. Leverage is not suitable for everyone and requires careful consideration of risk tolerance, income stability, and financial buffers.

To understand why this matters on a broader scale, it helps to zoom out and look at how credit behaves across entire economies.

Ray Dalio, one of the world's most successful investors, has studied how credit drives and derails economies. His books *The Changing World Order* and *Big Debt Crises* pull back the curtain on how borrowing fuels growth … and how it sometimes crashes the party.

Here's the core idea: Credit allows us to borrow from tomorrow to invest in today. Used wisely, this forward-looking mechanism creates jobs, builds infrastructure, and boosts productivity. If businesses had to rely solely on savings, progress would be slow, and innovation would stall. Imagine if you had to save the full price of a home before buying – you'd be saving for decades.

Credit is baked into the economy's DNA. And so is flow. Think about it: your *income* is someone else's *expense*. Your *debt* (mortgage) is your bank's *asset*. Your spending is the local café's *income*.

It is all interconnected.

The trick is to get the flow right, where your assets generate income, and your income isn't all going to someone else's assets.

Used correctly, credit lets you acquire assets, like investment property, shares, or businesses that can generate income.

But don't let the tool make you reckless. As Dalio explains, debt cycles follow a predictable pattern:

1. In the early stages, credit fuels real growth.
2. Then optimism sets in, and people borrow more.
3. Eventually, borrowing exceeds productive use, and trouble begins.

This is when the shiny car shows up in the driveway before the wealth is real. You start believing your own hype: 'I'm doing well, why not treat myself?' But if that credit is funding consumption instead of income-producing assets, it becomes a ticking time bomb.

Eventually, repayments outpace earnings. Defaults (payment failures) rise. Lenders tighten. Spending slows. Asset prices drop. The spiral begins, and if it's bad enough, it ends in recession or crisis. We've seen it before. We'll see it again.

That's the **double-edged sword of credit**. It can fund progress, or create collapse. The challenge for you lies in using it *productively*.

So, what's the takeaway?

Credit isn't evil. It's essential.

Debt isn't a villain. It's a tool.

But the person holding the tool? That's where the responsibility lies.

GOOD DEBT VS BAD DEBT

If you're serious about building long-term wealth, one of the most important distinctions to understand is the difference between good debt and bad debt.

Good debt is like a loyal employee. It works for you, helps grow your wealth, and eventually pays for itself.

Bad debt is more like a flashy mate in a Gucci tracksuit. He's broke, overcaffeinated, and texting you at 2 am with, 'Hey, can you spot me rent?' Fun at first. Regretful by sunrise.

Let's break it down with some examples to help you see the mechanics for yourself.

Good debt

Think of someone who borrows money to buy an investment property. The rent covers some (if not a big portion) of the mortgage, and the property grows in value over time. In some cases, they may even end up selling and downsizing, paying out the mortgage and pocketing the difference.

That's good debt in action: borrowing not just for the sake of owning something, but to build a future income stream. In this scenario, the debt produces income *and* increases net worth.

Bad debt

Now picture a shiny new BMW bought on credit. It looks great. It feels powerful. But it starts losing value the moment it leaves the lot. Meanwhile, the monthly repayments don't budge. Add in maintenance, insurance, and interest, and you've got a costly commitment for an asset that's depreciating faster than a dropped iPhone.

Some people are still making repayments years later, on a car they no longer drive or can't even repair. That's bad debt: money going out without anything valuable staying behind.

But of course, these labels are simplified concepts. Whether a debt is 'good' or 'bad' depends entirely on your personal circumstances, goals, and risk tolerance.

INVESTMENT VERSUS CONSUMPTION

Here's a generally sound way to understand debt:

- **Debt for investment:** Commonly used to acquire assets that may generate income or appreciate in value, such as property, an investment portfolio, or a business.

- **Debt for consumption:** Typically used to purchase items that decline in value over time, such as cars, luxury goods, holidays, or electronics.[17]

And here's another key principle: the numbers have to make sense.

> "If a debt-funded investment isn't generating enough income to comfortably cover repayments, it could be more risk than reward.

The same goes for poor investment decisions: when things go wrong, debt doesn't disappear. It magnifies the loss, leaving you with the burden but not the asset.

In the end, debt is a tool. Nothing more, nothing less. Used wisely, it can fast-track financial progress. Used recklessly, it can do the opposite.

So before taking on new debt, ask yourself: Is this a lever that will lift me up, or a weight that will drag me down?[18]

> **Expert tip:** A margin loan is a specific type of loan that allows investors to borrow against a share portfolio. Margin loans are a high-risk tool. Without deep understanding or expert advice, they can magnify losses significantly and are generally unsuitable for most investors.

---

17 Disclaimer: This section is intended for educational purposes only and does not constitute personal financial advice. Please consider your own financial circumstances or seek guidance from a licensed professional before making financial decisions.

18 Extra credit: Ray Dalio's Economic Machine. If you're a visual learner or love a good analogy, check out Ray Dalio's excellent short video here: www.youtube.com/watch?v=PHe0bXAIuk0

CHAPTER 18
UNDERSTANDING INTEREST RATES AND INFLATION

First, a quick word on why we're examining this now: the DO part is where you'll start taking real steps, and I want those steps to hold up in the real world.

Anyone can follow tactics when the economy is calm. But if you understand interest rates and inflation, you won't get knocked off course every time the headlines get dramatic. This is you upgrading from 'hoping it works' to 'knowing what you're doing'.

So, let's talk about two economic forces that can quietly make or break your financial future. These aren't just things economists argue about on TV. They are the levers that shape everything from your rent or mortgage repayments to your grocery bill, and they're deeply tied to how you use debt to build wealth.

INTEREST RATES: THE ECONOMY'S VOLUME DIAL

At its core, an interest rate is just the price of borrowing money. And when rates are low, it's like happy hour for borrowers: cheap loans, booming investments, and rising asset prices.

This is when people load up on property, shares, new businesses, you name it. Debt grows. Confidence grows. Asset prices fly. It's all sunshine and rainbows … until the clouds roll in.

Because cheap money also fuels risky behaviour. When borrowing is easy, people borrow more than they should. That's when asset bubbles start forming. Houses are suddenly worth a million bucks on paper, and the share market looks like it's had too many energy drinks.

But rates don't stay low forever.

When the RBA starts lifting rates to cool things down, borrowing becomes more expensive. People tighten their belts. Investors sell off assets. Businesses cut costs. That high-flying economy starts to glide back down to Earth. And over-leveraged folks feel the bump the hardest.

If you're using debt as part of your approach, you've got to be ready for this cycle. Low rates are your friend. High rates? That's when your plan needs to hold strong.

INFLATION: THE SILENT THIEF

Let's talk inflation. Most people only think of it when prices go up on milk, rent, or their weekend takeaway. But inflation is much sneakier than that. It quietly erodes the value of your money over time.

Here's how it works: the more money in circulation, the less each dollar can buy. Too much money chasing too few goods means rising prices. And when governments print heaps of money to patch problems, the balance tilts.

And this isn't just theory, it's history.

Back in the 1860s during the American Civil War, the Confederate side needed money. So, what did they do? They started printing it, fast. At first, it seemed clever. But with no gold or silver backing their currency, value plummeted. People needed a wheelbarrow of notes just to buy lunch.

Then came the twist: Union forces captured the Confederate printing presses in Columbia. Suddenly, the printing stopped … and inflation cooled.

The lesson?

Too much money creates too little value.

During the COVID pandemic, central banks across the globe hit 'print' on an industrial scale. In Australia, the Reserve Bank pumped over $300 billion into the economy. It was necessary at the time: individually and as a country we were in survival mode.

But all that cash flooded the economy while production had hit pause. Demand skyrocketed, supply couldn't keep up, and voilà, inflation exploded.

In 2022, inflation in Australia hit 7.8%, the highest in over 30 years. To fight it, the RBA lifted the cash rate repeatedly, taking it from 0.10% to 4.35%. Mortgage repayments soared. Rents jumped. Groceries? Don't even ask. This pattern occurred worldwide.

Was all this preventable? Not entirely. But you can be prepared next time.

WHAT IT MEANS FOR YOU: READING THE SIGNS

You don't need a PhD to spot economic shifts. Here's a practical way to read the room:

- **Inflation is rising?** Expect interest rates to follow. Brace yourself for tighter cashflow.
- **Social or economic crisis brewing?** Think COVID, trouble in the Middle East, bushfires, Robodebt, housing crunch. When governments panic, they often print money. That sparks inflation … and rate hikes soon after.
- **Inflation is cooling?** Central banks usually cut rates, which can boost share prices and property values again.

Understanding the cycle can help you make more informed choices.[19]

Use fixed vs variable rates to see what's coming[20]

Want a shortcut to reading the market?

Look at the gap between fixed and variable home loan rates.

When **fixed rates are higher**, that can suggest banks are pricing in future rate increases.

When **fixed rates are lower**, that can suggest they're expecting rates to come down.

It's not bulletproof, but it's one of the clearest signals available. You can study this by looking up the fixed and variable interest rates for a few major banks.

19 Disclaimer: This section is for general educational purposes only and is not financial advice. Please seek professional guidance before making financial decisions.
20 This is not a prescription and is only intended for education purposes.

Fixed vs variable home loan rates
What banks expect

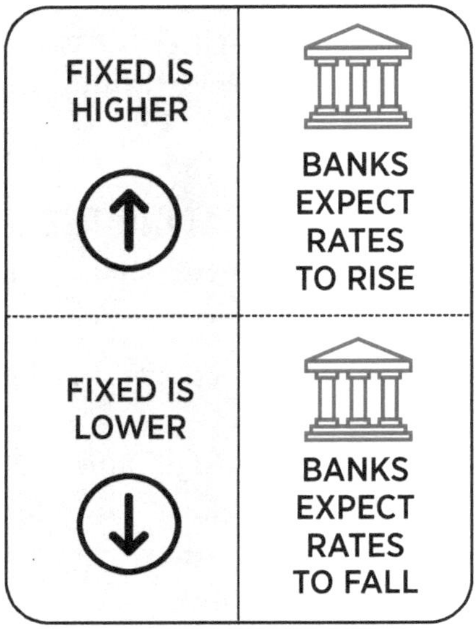

Tip: Fixed rates reflect the bank's expectations of future rate changes

If you're ever refinancing or considering a purchase, take a look at that rate gap. It might help you better understand the environment, assess risks, or explore options with more confidence. It can also be helpful to pay attention to whether that gap has been widening or closing.

- **If the gap has been widening**, it can mean something is changing in the background, like growing signs that rates could move in one direction more than the other.
- **If the gap has been shrinking**, it can mean things are settling down and the outlook is becoming less dramatic.

It's not a crystal ball, but watching that gap (and whether it's stretching or tightening) can help you get a clearer sense of the interest-rate mood.

FINAL WORD: KNOW THE GAME YOU'RE PLAYING

Inflation and interest rates are like the weather of the economy. You don't control them, but you can dress accordingly. Watch the forecasts. Read the signals. Consider how you might adapt.

Because wealth doesn't just go to the smartest or the strongest. It goes to those who are prepared when the winds change.

You're doing great, my friend.

Most people never learn this stuff, and that's exactly why they keep repeating the same money mistakes in every cycle. And here's the best part: once you understand these levers, the DO section becomes 10 times easier.

CHAPTER 19
RISK VS VOLATILITY

DON'T CONFUSE THE TWO

Let me let you in on a little secret: **volatility is not risk**. And if you treat it like it is, you're going to make some mighty expensive mistakes.

Volatility is just the market doing what the market does. It's like a toddler on a trampoline, up one day, down the next, and occasionally throwing a tantrum. But does that mean the trampoline is broken?

This chapter isn't here to slow you down.

It's here to stop you from sabotaging yourself later, right at the moment you start executing.

> "The biggest wealth-killer isn't lack of knowledge. It's emotional decisions under pressure.

Volatility is movement. It's normal. It's expected. If you've invested in solid, well-researched assets and you have a clear long-term plan, a bumpy ride shouldn't scare you. The only people who get hurt on a rollercoaster are the ones who don't strap in.

Now, real risk? That's a whole different beast.

Risk is what happens when you bet the farm on a hot tip from your barber's cousin. It's buying what you don't understand, with money you don't have, on the hope that the market will make you rich by Friday. That's not strategy, that's gambling in a suit.

You don't lose money because of volatility. You lose it because you panic, you sell low, you follow the herd, or you stretch yourself too thin.

The damage doesn't come from the storm. It comes from poor navigation.

THE BALANCE BETWEEN COURAGE AND DISCIPLINE

If you want to build real wealth, get comfortable with a little uncertainty. You don't climb a mountain by hugging the base. You've got to move upward, one deliberate step at a time.

Too cautious? You'll move so slowly you'll never get there. Too reckless? You'll fall off the edge before you hit your first milestone. The key is courage guided by wisdom. Boldness with brakes.

You want to take smart risks – calculated, measured, and aligned with your strategy.

So, ask yourself: do I understand this investment?

Am I prepared for a downturn without losing my cool?

Does this move bring me closer to my goals, or just scratch an emotional itch?

Because at the end of the day, the riskiest thing you can do … is never take a risk at all.

CHAPTER 20
NOTHING LASTS FOREVER

Here's one truth you *must* tattoo onto your financial brain: *nothing lasts forever*.

Markets shift. Trends die. What built your wealth yesterday could wreck it tomorrow.

If you want lasting success, stop chasing 'forever' strategies and start building your ability to **adapt**.

If your financial plan is still stuck in yesterday's playbook, it's time for an upgrade.

Let me show you what happens when these needed upgrades don't happen in time:

- **Lehman Brothers bank:** 158 years old. Survived world wars, depressions, recessions. Then collapsed almost overnight in 2008. Why? They ignored the warning signs.
- **Nokia:** Ruled the mobile phone world. Then the iPhone arrived. Nokia dug in its heels, and the world moved on.

The lesson? Complacency kills.

Even brilliant strategies will die if you don't evolve with the world around you.

EVOLVING WITH THE WORLD AROUND YOU

Like any living system, your wealth strategy needs to change over time – moving through stages of birth, growth, maturity, decline, and reinvention. If you lock yourself into one approach and refuse to adapt, you risk becoming the next cautionary tale.

So, what should you do?

1. Run a regular strategy health check

Ask yourself:

'Is this still working?'

'Am I operating in *today's* market, or stuck in yesterday's rules?'

Do it yearly. Or anytime the winds shift.

2. Create 'pivot triggers'

Set conditions ahead of time that signal it's time to shift gears. For example:

- rental yield drops below 3%
- business income stalls for six months
- shares are overvalued.

Don't wait for a crisis. Build a plan for change before you need it.

3. Study failures, not just successes

Blockbuster didn't fail because of Netflix. It failed because it didn't pivot.

Ask yourself: 'Is any part of my portfolio starting to look like yesterday's hero?'

* * *

Don't get stuck – get strategic.

Revisit your approach often. Stay aware of what's changing. And when needed, pivot decisively – even if your current plan feels 'safe'.

> “Adaptation isn't just survival. It's what sets you apart in an unpredictable world.

LET'S TAKE THIS BABY FOR A SPIN

Now, I get it. You've been introduced to a few shiny new ideas: *RICH Trifecta*, Freedom Score, Freedom Framework, Freedom Ritual … it might feel like a lot to take in.

But trust me, it's very simple.

Picture your Freedom Framework journey as driving a custom-built, high-performance freedom vehicle. You're in control, and these are your *core freedom drivers*:

- **The *RICH Trifecta*** is your engine, the true powerhouse. It's what actually builds your wealth through real estate, shares, and private business working together.
- **The Freedom Score** is your dashboard. It tells you how close you are to freedom – your clearest measure of progress.

These are your *supporting systems*. They're there to help the ride run at its best:

- **The Freedom Ritual** (coming in part III) is your wheels in motion. A powerful habit that keeps you checking in, learning, and improving each week. It doesn't create freedom, but it keeps you moving towards it.
- **The Hub Account** (coming in part III) is your fuel tank. It's a simple way to ensure your cashflow is efficient, clean, and always working in your favour.

At its heart, this is simple: build with the *RICH Trifecta*, track it with your *Freedom Score*, and let the rest support you on the ride.

Alright. You've got a solid understanding of strategy. You now understand the machine, the dashboard, and the weather conditions that can mess with your momentum.

That means you're ready for the fun part.

Next comes DO.

That's where we take this plan off the whiteboard and into real life, with practical moves you can actually execute, whether you're starting from scratch or you have already driven halfway up the mountain.

Let's get tactical.

FREEDOM FRAMEWORK

THINK → PLAN → DO → GEAR UP

Drive your way to financial independence

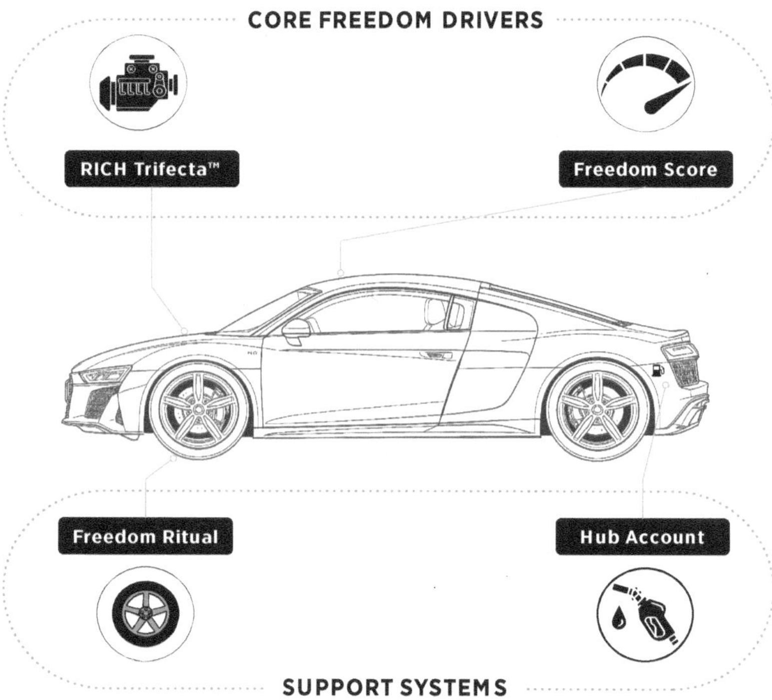

Every part plays a role.
Together, they drive your financial freedom.

Scan the QR code for a printable copy.

PLAN One-Step Action

Print your Freedom Map from this part and put it on your wall.

Then spend a few minutes studying the map. Reflect on what your next move may look like. You can download a printable full colour version of this map at www.rodnia.com.au. Or scan the below QR code.

PART II RECAP

LOCK IN YOUR STRATEGY – BUILD THE MASTER PLAN THAT KEEPS YOU ON COURSE

Most finance books teach you how to get rich.

This book teaches you how to measure freedom.

Because when you track your *Freedom Score*, every financial decision becomes clear.

Does it increase the score … or move you further away?

Your strategy determines how efficiently your *Freedom Score* compounds. A scattered strategy produces scattered results. A focused strategy builds freedom.

Wealth isn't won. It's engineered.

In this part, you discovered that strategy is your long-term game plan. It's how you decide what matters, what to say yes to, and when to walk away. With a clear plan, you stop chasing fads and start building momentum.

KEY TAKEAWAYS

- **Strategy drives outcomes:** Tactics without strategy is just noise. Strategy makes your actions compound.
- **The *RICH Trifecta* Framework** ties together real estate, shares, and business into a unified wealth engine.
- **The RICH Metrics** (Risk, Income, Capital, Hassle) help you assess any opportunity with clarity.
- **Wealth-building is a system, not a scramble:** Build assets that fund each other and reduce dependency on any single income stream.

- **You must evolve:** From working for money to managing money to multiplying money. Your current stage defines your next move.

UP NEXT: DO

Now that you've designed your big-picture strategy, it's time to zoom in and take action. In the next part, you'll dive into the *how*, the proven tactics that everyday Australians are using to grow wealth through property, shares, and business.

Most people stop at diversification. But you're not most people. You're building a wealth engine powered by *Synergification*, where each move strengthens the next, and the whole becomes greater than the sum of its parts.

You've drafted the blueprint.

Now it's time to turn the key.

Dive into the next part now. This is where your blueprint becomes reality.

Along the way, you'll learn practical steps, clever workarounds, and underrated tools that give you the edge, no matter where you're starting from.

So let's get tactical.

Here's where your journey hits momentum.

PART III
DO
Tactics That Work

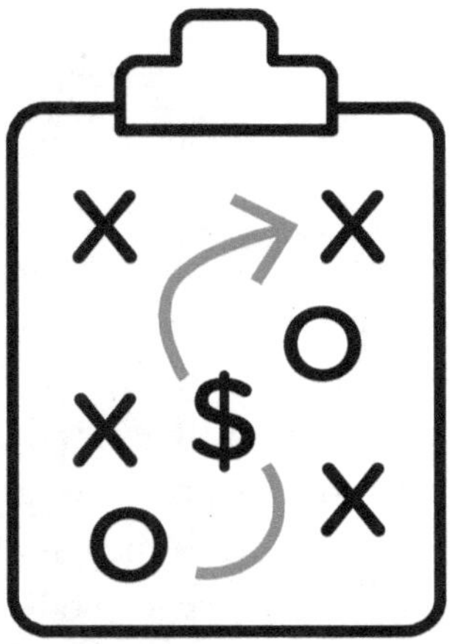

> **Another note from the legal department**
>
> This part is general information and education only. It isn't personal financial advice and doesn't take into account your objectives, financial situation, or needs. The following tactics are examples of how financial strategies may be applied in different situations. The suitability of any approach depends on your personal circumstances, financial position, and risk tolerance. Some strategies discussed may involve leverage, tax considerations, or changes to existing structures, which can increase risk and may not be suitable for all individuals. This section includes general examples and frameworks that may not be suitable for your circumstances and should not be relied upon as a substitute for personal advice. Before acting on anything in this book (including buying, selling, borrowing, or changing structures), consider getting advice from an AFS licensee or authorised representative. Past performance is not a reliable indicator of future performance.

HOW THE LEVERS WORK

Welcome to the action zone. DO is where the Freedom Framework gets tactical. With your mindset clear and strategy set, it's time to shift gears, descending from the bird's-eye view to the ground-level. Here lie the finer details and practical levers that can help turn vision into action. Every tactic in this part has the same purpose: to potentially increase your Freedom Score, either by lifting passive income, lowering expenses, or improving your capital position.

Before we get into it, I'd like to point out that this section is intentionally modular. You are not expected to do everything here. Each tactic stands on its own. Some will be perfect for your situation right now. Others won't be. One well-chosen action, applied consistently, will take you further than 10 half-finished plans.

Everything in this part connects to one of the three categories in your Freedom Map:

- property.
- shares.
- business.

If you've printed your Freedom Map, keep it nearby as you read.

In PLAN we explored the overarching RICH characteristics of each Trifecta pillar. In DO, you'll see RICH Ratings™ attached to some tactics. These aren't rankings or prescriptions. They're lenses. A way to quickly assess how a move behaves across Risk, Income, Capital, and Hassle. Later in GEAR UP, we will also use the RICH Rating for some specific ideas and investments.

As you know by now, tactics change. They evolve. What works today might not work tomorrow. That's just the nature of the game.

But don't worry. I've done my best to hand-pick practical, commonly used tactics that have been applied across different market conditions over time. Not fads. Not gimmicks. Real, practical tools that'll be around for a while.

Ready? Let's dive in.

KICK-OFF: WHAT YOU'RE ABOUT TO DISCOVER

This is the part where things get tactical. I'll show you:

- what the available options are to buy your first home with little deposit[21]
- a method to flip a cashflow-negative investment property into a weekly money-maker, without lifting a hammer or laying a single tile, using a little-known tactic
- a smarter way to think about super and mortgage reduction
- how to double the value of your side hustle without doubling your time.

---

21 Entering the market earlier can be powerful, but it also means taking on a larger loan with less margin for error. You should ensure you can comfortably afford repayments not just at today's rates, but if rates rise materially.

These real-world tactics are designed to give you an edge. They won't just save you money. They'll change the way you see money. I want you to also know that the concepts in this section build on the risk, debt, and strategy principles covered earlier. If you've skipped those sections, it's worth revisiting them before applying any of these ideas.

START YOUR WEEKLY FREEDOM RITUAL

One last thing before we dive into the tactics: there's one thing that determines whether any of them actually work long-term. It's not intelligence. It's not motivation. It's **repetition with reflection**. That's what the Freedom Ritual is designed to lock in.

You'll see this weekly habit again at the end of this part, because it's the thread that ties everything together. It has three simple steps:

1. **Act** – Try one idea from this book. Doesn't matter how big or small. Just start. Then review its impact on your *Freedom Score*.
2. **Reflect** – What worked? What didn't? What surprised you? Log it in your *Decision Log* (you'll find the template for this at the end of this part). Glance at your *Freedom Map* to spark your imagination.
3. **Share** – Post your story in the Freedom Gameplan Community, share with your partner, or a trusted friend. Help someone else. Spark a conversation. Tell people about your experience.

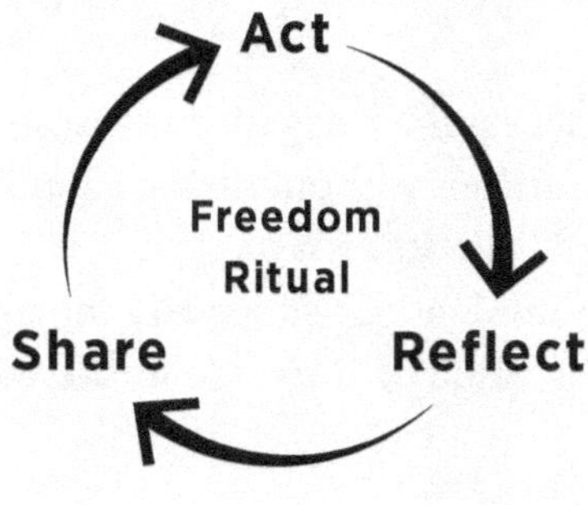

Then repeat. Again. And again. That's how mastery is built. That's how freedom is achieved, one baby step at a time.

HOW TO USE THIS PART

Not every tactic in this part will apply to you right now. Some are quick wins for those who are starting out. Others are more advanced moves for seasoned wealth builders. To help you navigate, I have labelled each tactic with a level:

- **Foundation level** – Simple steps to get you started.
- **Intermediate** – For when you've built some momentum.
- **Advanced** – Higher-level strategies for experienced players.

You'll also see a '**Best For**' label to help you zero in on what's relevant to your situation right now without having to first read the full tactic to decide.

You're not expected to use every tactic immediately. Start by exploring the ones that align with your current goals:

- **First home buyers** → Start with Property: Foundation Tactics
- **Existing homeowners** → Start with Property: Intermediate Tactics
- **Keen to invest in shares** → Start with Shares: All Levels Tactics
- **Income feels capped** → Start with Business: Foundation Tactics
- **Time-poor or overwhelmed** → Start with the Clever Moves

This is a playbook, not a to-do list. Come back as your *Freedom Score* grows. What might feel too hard today could be the exact power move you need six months from now.

Look for this icon

Some tactics, however, are *must-reads*. No matter where you are in your journey. You'll see them marked with the icon above. Each section also begins with a short must-read introduction. It sets the strategy. The tactics do the execution. These are the fundamentals that build lasting wealth.

You can skip around. Just make sure you don't skip the *must-reads*. You can use the Tactics Directory on the next page to orient yourself and your tactics. The real power comes when these tactics start working together in a *synergified* fashion.

DO: TACTICS DIRECTORY

Property

PROPERTY POWER PLAYS INTRO MUST READ

- F TACTIC 1: Buy your first home
- F+I TACTIC 2: Win by walking away – outsmarting the auction trap
- F+I TACTIC 3: Negotiate like a pro – your playbook for property deals
- I TACTIC 4: Borrow against equity – a path to fund your next investment
- AL TACTIC 5: Offset account – the interest assassin MUST READ
- F TACTIC 6: The Hub Account – from scattered to streamlined MUST READ
- I TACTIC 7: The RICH Reset – shifting towards positive cashflow

Shares

SHARE MARKET PLAYS INTRO MUST READ

- AL TACTIC 8: Dollar Cost Averaging – how to ride the waves calmly
- AL TACTIC 9: Crash Investing – navigating market panic
- AL TACTIC 10: Harvesting shares for steady dividend income
- AL TACTIC 11: Ride the storm, catch the sun – your all-weather investing plan MUST READ

Business

BUSINESS PLAYS INTRO MUST READ

- F+I TACTIC 12: Start a smart, flexible side hustle
- I+A TACTIC 13: Build a hassle-free business (from day one)
- A TACTIC 14: Buy an established business – skip the startup pain

Clever Moves

- AL TACTIC 15: Get a helping hand MUST READ
- AL TACTIC 16: A smarter way to balance super and your mortgage
- AL TACTIC 17: The Decision Log – your secret weapon for better choices MUST READ
- AL TACTIC 18: Your Freedom Ritual MUST READ
- AL TACTIC 19: Day trading – why even the smartest monkey can lose

F Foundational | I Intermediate | A Advanced | AL All levels | MUST READ Must read tactic

CHAPTER 21
REAL ESTATE TACTICS: MAKING PROPERTY WORK FOR YOU

We already explored the power of real estate in the *PLAN* part, how it's been a cornerstone of wealth from ancient Babylon to modern Australia. Here in the DO zone, we'll focus less on why property works, and more on how to make it work for you in the modern age.

That said, let's quickly recap the key idea.

Real estate isn't just about bricks and mortar. When used strategically, property can help you:

- create reliable income through rent
- access equity for other investments
- shield yourself from inflation over time.

It offers stability, scalability, and flexibility. Especially when paired with smart tactics like offset accounts and equity recycling (all of which we'll get into shortly).

WHY PROPERTY IS EASIER TO UNDERSTAND (AND WHY THAT MATTERS)

One of the best things about property is this: you don't need a finance degree to make sense of it.

Compared to shares, bonds, or complex financial instruments, real estate is refreshingly straightforward. You don't have to decode balance sheets or analyse quarterly earnings reports. You just need a good eye for value and a bit of common sense.

Here's what makes property such a practical asset to work with:

- **You can see it. Walk it. Inspect it. Insure it.** Real estate is tangible. That alone makes it easier to trust than some shares that may disappear in a bad tweet, or crypto that tanks on a rumour.
- **Location still rules.** Think proximity to schools, transport, shops, parks, and low crime rates. A beachfront view will always beat a view of a smokestack. If it feels like a great place to live or rent, chances are others will think so too.
- **You can judge with your own eyes.** Drive around the neighbourhood. Is it clean? Are people walking dogs, pushing strollers, sipping overpriced lattes from local cafés? That's usually a good sign.

Yes, property values rise and fall. But demand for homes doesn't usually disappear overnight, which makes well-located real estate fairly resilient.

I'll tell you exactly what to look for, and avoid, step by step in the *GEAR UP* part.

Now, you might be thinking: *if property's this good, why not just put everything into real estate and skip the rest?*

Great question. Yes, property is a powerful engine for wealth, but it's not the whole vehicle. Here's why it's not perfect:

- **It's slow to cash in.** You can't sell your house with a click. Selling real estate takes time; weeks, months, sometimes longer.
- **It's a long-term game.** This isn't a quick flip. Think of property like a committed relationship. Not a Tinder swipe.
- **It incurs significant costs.** You'll have to pay stamp duty to buy, real estate agent fees to sell, legal fees, title registration fees, upkeep, and more.

That's exactly why equity recycling – borrowing against your property to invest elsewhere – can be so powerful. Rather than selling, you hold long-term, unlock the value, and reinvest it into shares, private business, or another property. That's how you make real estate work within your *RICH Trifecta* strategy.

Let's get into it.

TACTIC 1: Buy your first home

Level: *Foundation Level.*
Best for: *Renters considering their first home.*

If you already own your home, congrats! Skip ahead to Tactic 2.

But if you're renting, this can be one of the foundational wealth steps.

People often say, 'I don't want to buy a house and pay $1,000,000 in interest over 30 years!'

Sure, but have you seen what rent costs over 30 years? That's like buying a Ferrari … for your landlord.

Buying your first home isn't just a lifestyle choice. It's your foundation upon which other tactics in this book can be built on.

WHY IT WORKS

- **Leverage:** Once you're in, you can borrow against your equity to invest in other assets (explained in upcoming tactics).
- **Forced savings:** Mortgage repayments usually include principal. That's money you're saving, without having to think about it.
- **Capital growth:** Property values, over long periods of time, tend to go up. And when they do, you win.

Based on long-term data, median home values have risen by roughly 412% for the past 25 years.[22]

If you had bought a home for $800,000 in 1995, it could now be worth around $4.14 million.

Yes, you might have paid $1 million[23] in interest over the life of the loan, but your total cost would still be under $1.8 million for an asset now worth more than double that.

THE HIDDEN BONUS: FREEDOM, COMFORT, AND PRIDE

Owning your own home isn't just a financial win. It's a personal joy.

22 www.aussie.com.au/content/dam/aussie/documents/home-loans/aussie_25_years_report.pdf

23 Assuming 6.5% median interest rate for the period.

You can paint the walls lime green if you like. Knock out a wall. Plant a veggie garden. Hang art wherever you want. There's no landlord telling you what you can or can't do.

It's not just a house, it's *your home.*

And that pride of ownership? That feeling of security? That's priceless.

DON'T LET THE FEAR MONGERS GET TO YOU

You've probably heard these online:

'Only idiots buy a house to live in – you'll pay triple in interest!'

'Now you have to pay rates and insurance too – your landlord used to do that!'

Well, let me ask you this: If you're paying off someone's mortgage, wouldn't you rather it be your own?

Social media's full of opinions from people who've never owned a property. But here's the truth: your landlord isn't losing sleep over those rates and insurance premiums ... because you're covering them.

Although renting can still be a good solution for some, depending on flexibility, lifestyle, and financial position, the issue is that it doesn't support wealth building. For many Australians, owning a home can become a foundation for long-term wealth building.

You can keep renting and help your landlord build wealth ...

Or you can own your home and start building your own.

Financial freedom starts with a solid foundation.

And that foundation, for most Australians, is their first home.

When this may not be suitable:

- If your income is unstable or you're not confident you can comfortably meet repayments.
- If you value flexibility and may need to move locations in the short to medium term.
- If you have high-interest debt or limited savings buffers.
- If your personal or career situation is uncertain.

What could go wrong:

- Property values can fall, especially in the short term.
- Interest rates can rise, increasing repayment pressure.

- Unexpected costs (repairs, rates, insurance) can strain cashflow.
- Being forced to sell during a downturn can lock in losses.

HOW BUYING A HOME REALLY WORKS

I've had many conversations with people who want to buy their first home, and I've noticed a common thread: because they've never done this before, the whole thing feels like trying to assemble IKEA furniture without the instructions! They don't really know the steps involved.

But don't worry, I've got your back my friend!

Here's a quick map of the journey, from handshake to house keys.

Keep in mind this is a general guide. Your exact journey may vary depending on your situation, the seller, and the contract. But for most buyers, these are the key milestones.

Once you've found a place you like, it goes like this:

From handshake to house keys
The house buying roadmap

Negotiate	Sign contract	Conditional period	Unconditional period	Settlement day
This is where you and the seller shake hands (figuratively) on the deal. Key points to negotiate are: **Price** **Settlement period** (e.g., 30 days) **Conditional period** (e.g., 14 days) **Special conditions** (e.g., seller to provide pool safety certificate)	You'll sign a contract of sale. Before doing this, get your conveyancer or solicitor to check it and make sure important clauses are included (like finance and building and pest inspection). At this stage, you usually pay a small deposit.	This is your safety window. Arrange a building and pest inspection and confirm finance approval with your bank. If something goes wrong (e.g., the inspection reveals major issues or the bank won't approve your loan), you may be able to cancel the contract without losing your deposit.	Once the conditional period ends, the contract becomes 'unconditional'. That means you're locked in. If you pull out now, you risk heavy financial penalties – so only get here once you're 100% confident.	This is the finish line. Your bank transfers the money to the seller, the property officially becomes yours, and you collect the keys to your new home. Celebration day!

Let's tackle the biggest hurdle most first-home buyers face: saving a deposit.

FAMILY GUARANTOR: YOUR SECRET WEAPON

Level: *Foundation Level.*
Best for: *First-home buyers with good credit, good jobs, and a relative who's willing to help.*

Let me guess, you're pumped to buy a home, but there's just one problem: 'How on earth am I supposed to save a 20% deposit when property prices are this high?!'

I've heard this so many times I can practically hear you say it. And you're not wrong. Saving for a deposit today can feel like trying to fill a bathtub with a teaspoon.

But what if I told you ... you might not need a deposit at all?

Yep. Zero. Zilch. Nada.

All you need is a 'yes' to two simple questions:

- Do your parents (or a close family member) own their home outright, or at least have a decent chunk of equity?
- Do they like you (said with a wink!)?

If the answer is yes, then they may be able to go guarantor on your loan, allowing you to buy a home *without* the traditional 20% deposit.

A guarantor loan allows someone, usually a parent or sibling, to use the equity in their property as additional security on your loan. It doesn't mean they give you cash. It means they vouch for part of your loan, typically up to 20%.

Here's what that unlocks for you:

- **No Lender's Mortgage Insurance (LMI)** – This alone could save you tens of thousands.
- **Faster entry to the market** – You get to buy now, not in eight years after living on instant noodles.
- **The guarantor's risk is limited** – They're only backing part of the loan, not all of it.
- **The guarantee can be released over time** – Once your property grows or you pay down the loan, the guarantee can be removed.

The guarantor becomes liable if you miss loan repayments *and* the home is sold at a loss.[24] But even then, only for the portion they guaranteed. That's why it's called **limited security**.

Many believe that if you miss a payment, your parents are immediately on the hook for everything. Not necessarily true. Here's how it really works.

The bank will come to you first. Only if you keep missing loan repayments and the home is sold at a loss would your guarantor be asked to cover the guaranteed portion.

Even then, it's usually no more than 20% of the loan, not the whole amount.

Only if you repeatedly miss repayments, and your home is sold for less than what you paid for it, will your guarantor's property be at risk. But even then, they may have the option to cover the shortfall out of their own pocket.

In most cases, if you're responsible with your repayments, your guarantor will not be called upon.

Let's have a look at an example.

Emily is 28, has a stable job, and wants to buy a $600,000 home.

She can afford the repayments, but doesn't have the $120,000 deposit needed to avoid LMI.

Her parents own their home outright and offer to guarantee the 20% using their equity.

Emily borrows the full $600,000.

Her parents back the 20% ($120,000) using their home's equity.

She avoids LMI, saving $10,000 upfront.[25]

Her parents don't pay a cent, and Emily covers all repayments.

In a few years, once she's built enough equity, the guarantee is released.

Result?

Emily gets into the market years earlier, avoids LMI, gets a better interest rate, and her parents help without giving her cash.

---

24 Before entering into a guarantor arrangement, both parties should consider obtaining independent legal and financial advice, as this structure can expose the guarantor's property to risk if repayments are not met.

25 Actual savings depend on property value and lender policies.

Being a guarantor is a generous gesture, but not a reckless one, as long as you can meet your loan repayments. For you, the borrower, this is a good opportunity to get a foothold in the property market without waiting a decade to save for a deposit.

For your family? It's a powerful way to help you without having to fork over cold, hard cash.

If you're lucky enough to have support, don't feel guilty. Feel grateful. Ask for help and make the most of it. If you've got someone who believes in you, and owns a property, this can be a pathway into the market earlier than traditional saving methods.

But like anything involving debt, there's risk. Make sure both sides are comfortable and clear on what could happen before jumping in.

When this may not be suitable:

- If either party is uncomfortable with the financial or emotional risk.
- If the borrower's income is stretched or uncertain.
- If the guarantor may need access to their equity in the near future.
- If family relationships could be impacted by financial stress.

What could go wrong:

- The guarantor may be required to cover losses if the loan cannot be repaid.
- Property values falling could increase risk.
- Financial stress can strain or damage relationships.
- The guarantee may remain in place longer than expected.

Now, let me show you what this looks like in real life.

Meet Estelle and Rob's family.

REAL PEOPLE, REAL SUCCESS STORIES

ESTELLE & ROB

'A house is made of walls and beams; a home is built with love and dreams.'

Estelle and Rob had always dreamed of owning their own home – a place to raise their three kids, plant a veggie patch, maybe put a trampoline in the backyard, and add a pool for endless summer splashes. A place that was theirs – no more asking permission to hang a picture or drill a hook into the wall.

They both had solid incomes. But saving a couple of hundred thousand dollars for a deposit isn't exactly easy when you've got three kids and all the costs that come with raising a family. Still, Estelle isn't the kind of person who lets opportunity pass her by.

When she discovered the Family Guarantor Loan tactic we've just explored, her eyes lit up like she'd cracked some secret code. She marched over to her dad's house and pitched the idea, half expecting a long, cautious conversation. Instead, without missing a beat, her dad said, 'Yeah, I trust you. Let's do it.'

Game. On.

With her dad's support locked in, they worked with a great broker, found the right lender, and before long, they'd landed on a place they loved. They used the negotiating tactic shared later in this section to secure a fair deal for their family.

They eventually bought their home at a great price. Now, Estelle and Rob enjoy the freedom and security of a home they truly own. No more landlord tantrums. No more moving on someone else's timeline. No more awkward emails about 'unauthorised hooks in the wall'.

Just a backyard full of laughter, a veggie patch that's a work in progress, and three kids who think the pool is the best thing ever. A place to grow, build memories, and finally put down roots.

Well done, Estelle and Rob.

Expert tip: Before you walk into your local bank branch, consider this: a mortgage broker can do the shopping around for you, often for free. Most brokers are paid a commission by the lender, so you usually won't be out of pocket.

A good broker won't just find you a sharp rate, they'll help match you with a lender who's actually willing to approve your application. That can make all the difference.

But just like mechanics and hairdressers, some brokers are brilliant, and others … not so much. Ask for referrals, check reviews, and make sure you've got someone who's got your back, not just your business.

FIRST HOME GUARANTEE SCHEME: LEVEL UP WITHOUT THE 20% DEPOSIT

Level: *Foundation Level.*
Best for: *Renters ready to build a foundation.*

If you're thinking, 'But I don't have anyone to guarantee my loan,' – don't worry, you're not out of the game yet.

That's where the First Home Guarantee (FHG) comes in.[26]

No parents? No problem. Let the government be your guarantor instead.[27]

At least they can be useful for once, right?

Instead of leaning on Mum and Dad, this scheme lets you lean on Uncle Canberra. And he won't raid your fridge or ask when you're getting married. Win–win.

This government scheme lets eligible buyers get into their first home with just a 5% deposit. The government guarantees the remaining 15%, which means no LMI. That's a potential $10,000+ saving right there.[28]

Why it matters

Normally, if you don't have a 20% deposit, the bank slaps you with LMI to 'cover their risk' (not yours).

Translation?

You pay thousands just for the *privilege* of borrowing money. But under the FHG, the government steps in and says, 'We'll back you.' So instead of watching house prices race ahead while you save, you get in early, *without the LMI handbrake.*

---

26 Disclaimer: This is general information and does not consider your personal circumstances. These examples are illustrative only. Always seek advice from a licensed financial adviser.

27 Like any scheme, eligibility rules, caps, and conditions apply and should be checked carefully.

28 Actual savings depend on property value and lender policies. Eligibility is subject to rules and future changes. This is general information, not personal advice.

How it works: a tale of two buyers

Below is a numerical example to explain how it may work. So, take it as just that, an example and not forecasts or expected outcomes.

1. **Sarah (uses the FHG)**
   Buys a $600,000 home.
   Saves just a 5% deposit = $30,000.
   No LMI, buys years earlier.
2. **James (saves 20% the old-fashioned way)**
   Needs $120,000 deposit to buy a $600,000 home.
   Spends over five years renting while saving.
   By then? House prices have gone up, again.

Sarah's riding the property wave while James is still waxing his board.

Who can apply?

- Australian citizens or permanent residents aged 18 or over.
- First-home buyers or those who haven't owned property in Australia in the past 10 years.
- Applicants intending to live in the purchased property (owner-occupiers).
- Property purchase price within the state-specific cap.

What's the catch?

Bigger loan equals bigger repayments (you're borrowing 95%). And you still need to qualify; the bank will assess your income, expenses, and credit score.

But here's the thing: these aren't deal-breakers. If you wait years to save the 'perfect deposit', property prices might climb higher than any interest you'd have paid on a bigger loan.

Final thought

If you qualify, it's a good potential way to enter the market sooner. It saves you from years of rent and regret. Just make sure you're ready for the responsibility, mortgage repayments, rates, maintenance – the grown-up stuff that comes with owning a home.

If saving 20% feels impossible, this scheme may provide an alternative pathway. Use it wisely, and you could be unlocking your front door sooner than you ever thought possible.

When this may not be suitable:

- If you're not confident managing a higher loan with a smaller deposit.
- If your income is tight or sensitive to rate increases.
- If you prefer a larger equity buffer for peace of mind.
- If you don't meet eligibility criteria or expect them to change.

What could go wrong:

- Higher loan size increases repayment pressure.
- Limited equity buffer if property prices fall.
- Policy or eligibility changes could impact access.
- Borrowing at your limit can reduce financial flexibility.

SUPERCHARGE YOUR DEPOSIT: FIRST HOME SUPER SAVER SCHEME

Level: *Foundation Level.*
Best for: *First-home buyers (especially employed PAYG earners) wanting to supercharge their savings.*

Buying your first home is a major milestone, but let's be real: saving a deposit can feel like trying to scale Everest in thongs. Luckily, there's a hidden weapon in the super system that hardly anyone talks about: the *First Home Super Saver Scheme* (FHSSS).[29] This scheme can help to improve outcomes for eligible savers.

What is it?

The FHSSS lets you use your super fund as a high-powered savings tool. Instead of stashing your deposit in a low-interest bank account,

29 Disclaimer: Eligibility for these schemes depends on individual circumstances and government policy. This is a general explanation only and does not take into account contribution caps, tax implications, or eligibility rules specific to your situation. Always check the latest requirements or speak to a financial adviser. This is general information and not personal financial advice.

you could make voluntary contributions into your super (up to $15,000 per year, maxing out at $50,000 total per individual, under current rules).

When you're ready to buy your first home, you can withdraw those contributions plus earnings, all taxed at a lower rate than if you had saved the same money outside of super. That means more of your money ends up in your deposit, less goes to the taxman.

Why this matters

Even if you're already eligible for a no-deposit strategy (like using a guarantor loan or the FHG), FHSSS is still worth doing to supercharge your savings.

Here's why:

- Pay less tax overall while you save.
- Withdraw more than you'd otherwise save.
- Use it for purchase costs or to lower your loan.

And the real kicker?

You can double the benefit if you're buying with a partner.

Two people, one clever strategy

Let's say you and your partner each contribute $15,000 into super towards the end of the financial year in late May/early June (through salary sacrifice or personal deductible contributions). That's $30,000 total.

You then repeat this in July, which means it'll be in the new financial year. Let's now assume:

- you each earn around $60,000 per year
- your marginal tax rate is 32% (including Medicare).

The result?

The combined tax saving for this simplified scenario could be around $9100 compared to saving outside super. But of course, the actual outcome will vary depending on income, contribution timing, and individual tax circumstances. This is a simplified example, and actual outcomes will vary based on tax rates, contribution timing, and the rules at the time.[30]

Instead of slugging it out for years trying to save in your personal bank account, you've now got a deposit boost and a head start, in just one move.

Expert tip: This strategy may work best towards the end of the financial year when contributions and withdrawals align. Time it right, and you could save two years' worth of tax in just a few months.

How to get started

- Confirm you're eligible (first-home buyer, intend to live in the property for at least 6 months).
- Ring your super fund and ask if they allow withdrawals for FHSSS.
- Set up voluntary contributions into your super (either salary sacrifice or personal deductible).
- Apply for a FHSSS determination via your MyGov account when you are ready to withdraw.
- Withdraw funds when you're ready to purchase.
- Use towards your deposit or buying costs.

Use the Tool: You can access the free FHSSS calculator and estimate how much more you may be able to save by using this tactic at www.rodnia.com.au or scan the below QR code:

30 Assumes 5% deemed earnings applicable in super. 15% tax in super. Withdrawals are taxed at your marginal rate less a 30% tax offset. The information included in this section and the examples are illustrative only and are intended as an education tool. This is general information and does not consider your personal circumstances. Always seek advice from a licensed financial adviser.

Bottom line

You've got a turbo-charged savings vehicle sitting right under your nose. And with this scheme, you get to drive it straight to your first home. Use it wisely, and you might just beat the market to your front door.

When this may not be suitable:

- If you may need access to the funds before buying.
- If your income is low and tax benefits are minimal.
- If you're unsure about contribution limits or rules.
- If your timeline to purchase is uncertain.

What could go wrong:

- Funds are locked in super until withdrawal conditions are met.
- Investment returns inside super are not guaranteed.
- Legislative or tax rules may change.
- Poor timing could reduce expected benefits.

RENT IT FIRST, LIVE IN IT LATER: STRATEGY UNLOCKED

Level: *Foundation Level.*
Best for: *Renters ready to build a foundation.*

You've found a tidy little place. It's not your dream home, but it's a foot in the door. And let's be honest, *any* foot in today's market is a win.

But then the bank throws cold water on your plans: 'Sorry, you don't earn enough.'

Now, before you throw your hands up and walk away, here's a tactic that just might save the day.

Consider buying the property as an investment first. Move in later.

Yep. You can rent it out first to boost your borrowing power, then make it your home once you're in a better financial position.

How it works

When you buy a property as an investment, lenders may include a portion of expected rental income in your borrowing assessment.

Rental income may be considered by lenders when assessing borrowing capacity.[31]

Then after a few years, or once you've built some equity or your income's increased, you move in and make it yours.

Why this works

- Rental income boosts borrowing power: The rent helps cover some of the loan repayments and expenses, and that makes you look a lot better on paper.
- You start building equity earlier: While others are still saving, you're already riding the property wave.
- Ideal if you live with parents at home or with a partner: Keep living expenses low while your tenant helps pay the mortgage.
- Great for high-price areas: A smart workaround when you're otherwise unbale to enter the market.

But there's a catch (or two)

There are a couple of goodies you'll miss out on by going the investment-first route:

- FHSSS: Only available if you *live* in the property first.
- Stamp duty exemptions or other concessions: These only apply to homes you occupy, investments don't get the red-carpet treatment. So, the property will end up costing you more, and the concession will be lost permanently.

Final word

If you're hitting a wall with the banks, this is a clever way to squeeze through a side door. It's not for everyone, but for the right buyer, it's a golden workaround.

Think of it like dating the property before you marry it.

Let it pay the bills first, then move in and fall in love later.

---

31 Subject to their policies and buffers.

And just keep in mind: lender rules, tax treatment, and your own situation all play a big role here. What works for one person might not work for another.

When this may not be suitable:

- If you prefer to rely on first-home buyer concessions.
- If you don't want landlord responsibilities.
- If rental income assumptions are uncertain.
- If your borrowing capacity is already stretched.

What could go wrong:

- Rental income may be lower than expected.
- You lose access to certain grants or concessions.
- Vacancy periods can impact cashflow.
- Unexpected costs (repairs, tenants, management) can arise.

INDIGENOUS BUSINESS AUSTRALIA: A POWERFUL, UNTAPPED RESOURCE

***Level:** Foundation Level.*
***Best for:** First Nations renters ready to buy their first home.*

Indigenous Business Australia (IBA) is a government-backed initiative designed to support First Nations people who might otherwise be locked out of homeownership. Through subsidised home loans and tailored support, IBA helps turn 'maybe one day' into 'move-in day'.

What makes IBA loans different?

Unlike traditional banks, IBA understands that standard lending criteria don't work for everyone. That's why their loans are structured to support, not exclude.

Here's what sets IBA apart:

- Lower deposits required: You won't need the usual 20% up front.
- Tailored education and guidance: You won't be left figuring it out alone. IBA works with you every step of the way.

Example

Daniel, 32, had been renting for years while raising a young family. He had a solid job but patchy credit and limited savings. That's two strikes with most banks.

But when Daniel applied through IBA, everything changed. He qualified, even without a big deposit. His repayments were about the same as what he'd been paying in rent.

Within months, he had the keys to his own home.

Something he once thought was impossible became a reality, just because he took a different path.

Who can apply?

To qualify for an IBA home loan, you must identify as a First Nations person.

Loans are mainly for first-home buyers, though IBA can sometimes help in other situations (check with them directly). Only one partner in a couple needs to meet the First Nations eligibility criteria.

> **Expert tip**: Many people think these programs are too good to be true or that they won't qualify. Don't rule yourself out, check directly with IBA. You might be much closer than you think.

How to apply

Visit iba.gov.au to learn more and check your eligibility. You'll find everything from eligibility checklists to how the process works.

Final thought

Owning a home is more than just real estate. It's about security, stability, and financial empowerment.

If you or someone you know is of First Nations background and ready to take that first step, don't overlook this powerful opportunity. IBA may be able to help make your first home a reality, not a dream deferred.

When this may not be suitable:

- If you prefer broader lender choice or flexibility.
- If property limits don't align with your goals.
- If you're seeking faster approval timelines.
- If repayment capacity is tight.

What could go wrong:

- Higher borrowing with lower deposit increases risk.
- Loan terms may be more restrictive.
- Delays in approval or processing.
- Financial pressure if circumstances change.

Expert tip: P&I vs I/O repayments (and why it matters)

When you borrow money for property, you'll usually pick between two types of loan repayments:

1. **Principal & Interest (P&I):** Each payment chips away at your loan balance (the principal) *and* pays off the interest. Over time, your debt shrinks, your equity grows, and you move closer to owning the property outright.
2. **Interest-Only (I/O):** You're just paying the interest. The loan balance stays put. It's cheaper upfront, but you're not paying down the loan.

Here's the kicker: I/O loans usually come with higher interest rates. So, you might pay less now, but you'll pay more in the long-run. Use I/O loans wisely. They're a tool, not a ticket to easy money. If you're not careful, they'll cost more than they save.

TACTIC 2: Win by walking away – outsmarting the auction trap

Level: *Foundation to Intermediate.*
Best for: *Property buyers who want to avoid expensive mistakes.*

This one is more about what *not* to do.

Bidding at auction is like speed dating with your life savings on the line. Fast, emotional, and often followed by a serious case of buyer's remorse.

Now, let me tell you about one of the most fascinating, and downright horrifying, psychology experiments I know of.

It reveals exactly why smart people do dumb things when the pressure's on ... and why auctions are a playground for irrational decisions.

An economist walks into a room with a group of students and pulls out a crisp $20 note. He says, 'We're going to auction this off. Highest bidder wins the $20. But here's the twist: the second-highest bidder also has to pay their bid ... and gets nothing.'

It starts off innocently. Someone bids a dollar. Another offers two. A few laughs ripple through the room.

But then it gets serious. The bidding hits $19, then $20. Surely it stops there?

Nope.

The person who bid $19 is now staring down a guaranteed $19 loss. So, they bid $21, just to lose less. The $20 bidder fires back with $22. The cycle continues. In some cases, people have bid up to $50, for a $20 bill.

Why? Because humans are deeply *loss averse*. We hate losing more than we like winning. Once we're invested, emotionally or financially, we'll do almost anything to avoid admitting defeat, even if it means losing more.

This is an experiment first demonstrated by economist Martin Shubik, and later popularised by the Noble Prize winner Dr Daniel Kahneman. In his brilliant book, *Thinking, Fast and Slow*, Kahneman uses this experiment to explain why auctions can turn otherwise rational people into irrational bidders. Once your emotions take over, logic leaves the building.

Now … imagine that same scenario, but instead of a $20 note, you're bidding on a $1 million home.

THE HIGH-STAKES VERSION: PROPERTY AUCTIONS

The auctioneer is up front, commanding the scene with smooth patter and dramatic pauses. The crowd's tense. You've already toured the house, imagined your furniture in the living room, maybe even pictured your kids playing in the yard.

You want it.

Bidding starts. You join in. You're not just buying a house now, you're in a competition. You've emotionally committed. And before you know it, you're paying $1.1 million for a home that was listed at $800,000.

Sound extreme? It happens every weekend across the country.

Auctioneers are masters at their craft. I'll hire one the moment I want to sell a property. But as a buyer, you're stepping into a game wired to trip every psychological circuit you've got.

And the danger doesn't end when the hammer falls.

The trapdoor: unconditional contracts

Here's what many people don't know or fully grasp: *at an auction, the contract becomes unconditional the moment you win.*

That means no 'subject to finance' clause. No 'subject to building and pest'. No wiggle room. No 'outs'. It's instant commitment, and you're legally bound.

In a private sale, you'd get time to inspect the home properly, confirm your bank's support, and protect yourself with contract conditions. But at auction? It's all-in, right now.

Let's say you win the auction. You're ecstatic. But then you find out the 'independent' building inspection was done by the real estate agent's Uncle Bill. Or worse, your lender pulls back, and the finance falls through. Maybe the property didn't value up. Maybe your pre-approval wasn't ironclad.

Now you're in deep.

You can't walk away without severe consequences. You could lose your deposit, tens of thousands of dollars, and be sued for damages if the property later sells for less. That's not just a bad day. That could financially wreck your life.

Little upside, much downside

Let's call it for what it is: buying property at auction is a one-sided deal. The seller gets all the upside, competitive tension, emotional bidders, high price. You, the buyer, take on all the risk. You pay more and get fewer protections.

If you're a seller, auctions are brilliant. But if you're buying? You're betting your financial future in a game designed to make you overpay.

Unless you're paying cash, have done every inspection with your own people, have bulletproof finance, and have ice in your veins, stay away.

Also, rules vary by state and territory; always check with your local regulator.

In the auction game, 'winning' can be the most expensive mistake you ever make.

When this may not be suitable:

- If you're in a market where most properties sell via auction.
- If you're well-prepared with strong finance and due diligence completed.
- If you're comfortable making fast, unconditional decisions.

What could go wrong:

- You may miss out on desirable properties.
- Prices may rise while you wait for alternative opportunities.
- You could overcorrect and become too cautious.

TACTIC 3: Negotiate like a pro – your playbook for property deals

Level: *Foundation to Intermediate.*
Best for: *Those who want to turn the seller's agent into their personal negotiator.*

One of the biggest psychological traps in property buying is the anchoring effect. This is a cognitive bias where we fixate on the first price we hear and use it as a reference point for all future decisions.

For example: if the agent floats $850,000 as the asking price, your brain latches onto that number like Velcro. Suddenly, $830,000 feels like a bargain. Even if the property's fair value is closer to $780,000.

If you assess value before viewing, you set your own benchmark rather than being influenced by the agent's pricing tactics.

This is why you should always research a property's value before inspecting it, not after. This shields you from emotional decision-making and gives you control in negotiations. We will cover the research tools in the GEAR UP part, but for now, let's focus on your negotiating game.

YOUR GUIDE TO PROPERTY NEGOTIATION: A FOOLPROOF STRATEGY

Real estate agents are highly skilled negotiators. They do this every day, multiple times. No matter how good you think you are at negotiating, I promise you will be outmatched by these seasoned professionals. So, the best way to get an edge is to develop your own systematic approach.

Here's a step-by-step guide to negotiating property like a pro.

1. Play it cool during the inspection

Talk as little as possible and remain somewhat aloof, without being rude.

Don't spend too long at the inspection. If the price is right, you can always arrange a second visit later. Don't waste time hunting for hidden structural issues – you'll have a building and pest inspection in the contract.

Agents watch your reactions; don't show too much enthusiasm about a property.

Expert tip: Make sure you call your building and pest inspector after you have read their written report. Specifically ask them, 'Is the property worth buying?' on the phone. Because of legal restraints imposed by law, inspectors' reports may be overly legalistic in their language as they look to protect themselves against any liabilities. So, you can often get a more straightforward answer from them on the phone.

2. Make your first offer firmly and strategically

Call the agent after leaving and say: 'We're interested in the property and would like to make an offer of $X.'

Consider starting a few percentage points below the price you think is reasonable, regardless of the asking price.

Expect pushback. Agents will often act surprised, irritated, or claim there are higher offers. Listen respectfully, but don't let this sway your decision too much.

Ask that your offer is put to the seller. Agents are normally required to submit all written offers.

3. Reading the agent's response

If after the initial offer the agent completely dismisses your offer without room for discussion, you probably lowballed too hard.

If they push you to increase your offer, they likely don't have strong competing buyers. This is a sign you have room to negotiate.

4. Decide on a strategic price cap beforehand

If the agent pushes for continuous increases, set a clear limit.

Example: You start at $750,000 → The agent counters $800,000 → You go to $780,000 → STOP.

Constantly increasing sends a signal that you can be pressured. Once you've reached your cap, stand firm.

5. The closing move: reverse the pressure

If negotiations stall, call the agent the next day and say: 'We're also interested in another property with a similar price. The seller has given us two hours to make a final decision. We'd prefer yours, but at the end of the day, either property works for us. If your seller agrees to our price, we're ready to sign today.'

This flips the power dynamic. Now the seller and agent feel pressure to close the deal.

Agents are motivated to make the transaction happen, which often means they'll work to bring the seller towards your offer, essentially helping your case.

FINAL STEPS BEFORE SIGNING THE CONTRACT

Engage a conveyancer before you start serious property hunting.

Once you've agreed on a price, contact your conveyancer or solicitor to go through the contract before you sign, to include these key clauses:

- Building and pest inspection: This protects you from hidden defects.
- Finance clause: Allows you to back out if financing falls through.
- Any other conditions necessary: Cover off anything else like a pool safety certificate or required repairs.

When this may not be suitable:

- In highly competitive markets where speed matters more than negotiation.
- If you're not confident assessing fair value.
- If delaying risks losing the opportunity.

What could go wrong:

- Misjudging value can cost you the deal.
- Over-negotiating can push sellers away.
- Emotional decisions can override strategy.

TACTIC 4: Borrow against equity – a path to fund your next investment

Level: *Intermediate.*
Best for: *Homeowners with existing built-up equity.*

> Before we get into it, I have to tell you that this strategy involves borrowing and increases financial risk. It may not be suitable for many people. Whether it is appropriate depends on your income stability, risk tolerance, and financial structure.

Now let's talk about one of the most overlooked, but powerful, weapons in your wealth-building arsenal: your home equity.

If you already own a home, you might be sitting on a financial launchpad without even realising it. This tactic allows you to buy an investment property *without saving up for a new deposit*. That's right. This can reduce the need to save a separate cash deposit, but it also means taking on additional debt secured against your existing home.[32]

And this, my friend, is why your first financial milestone can be owning a home. Not just for the warm fuzzies of homeownership, but because of what that home can unlock later.

Now, most people have heard of 'using equity', but when I sit down with them, most of them admit they don't really know *how* it works. So, let's break it down simply.

WHAT IS EQUITY (AND WHAT CAN YOU USE)?

Equity = What your home is worth *minus* what you still owe.

Usable equity = The portion above 20% of your home's value that most banks will actually lend against.

32 This strategy comes with real risk. If property values fall or your financial position changes, using equity can amplify losses and increase financial pressure.

Example

- Home value: $1,000,000
- Outstanding mortgage: $600,000
- Total equity: $400,000
- Available equity: $200,000

(Because the bank keeps a 20% safety buffer = $200,000)

Now, let's say you want to buy an investment property worth $800,000.

You'd typically need a $160,000 deposit (20%).

But thanks to your $200,000 usable equity, the bank may lend you the full amount:[33]

- $160,000 secured against your current home
- $640,000 against the new property.

So, there you go. You now understand the basics of equity borrowing. But remember, if property values fall, your available equity can shrink quickly, reducing flexibility and increasing risk.

> **Quick tip:** Lenders will still check that you can afford the new loan. It's not a free-for-all, but if the numbers stack up, this can be one way to build wealth, depending on your circumstances.

So, next time you hear someone say, 'How do people keep buying more property?', you'll know a thing or two about how it works.

HOW HOME EQUITY CAN FUEL THE *RICH TRIFECTA*

Let's look at another example to break this further down.

Say your home is now worth $800,000 and your mortgage is $500,000.

- The bank will lend up to 80% of $800,000 = $640,000.
- You owe $500,000.
- So, your usable equity is $140,000.

33 Subject to lender assessment, including serviceability and lending criteria.

That's $140,000 of available equity. Then maybe you use $80,000 of this to:[34]

- cover the deposit for an investment property
- fund the *shares* arm of your *RICH Trifecta*; or
- invest in your own business.

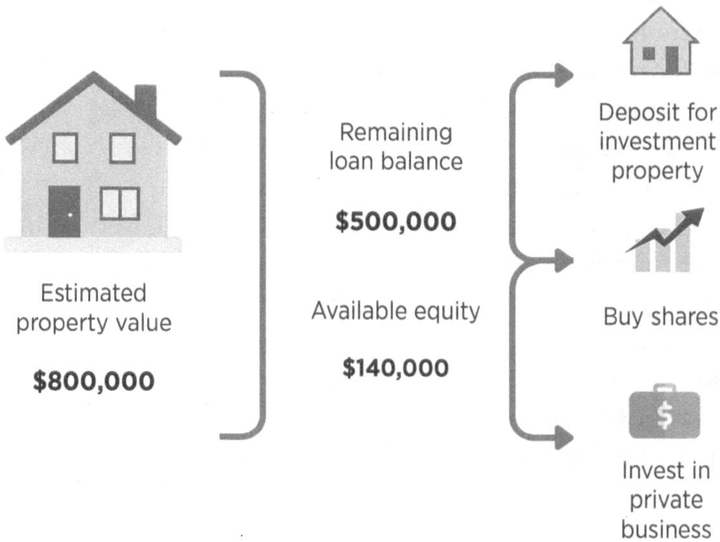

You're using your home, an asset you already own, to add more income-producing assets in your *RICH Trifecta* engine.

Now, here's the trade-off: you're using your home as security, which means you're taking on more risk. If things go well, it can accelerate your progress. But if they don't, you're still on the hook for the debt.

That's why this strategy only works when the numbers are solid and you've got buffers in place.

Otherwise, your primary residence could be at risk because your home is used as security.

34 Disclaimer: This example is included for education purposes only. Higher Loan to Valuation Ratio (LVR) borrowing strategies, and gearing in general, may incur significantly bigger risks. You should not act on any of this information without first considering your own circumstances and seeking advice.

THE TWO KINDS OF RETURNS

You've probably heard of *ROI (Return on Investment)*. But let me introduce you to its lesser-known, less commonly discussed cousin: *ROE (Return on Equity)*.

And don't worry if those sound like finance-speak. You don't even need to know these terms to get the concept. You'll get it crystal clear in just a moment.

Let's look at a hypothetical example.[35] Before I show you this example, it's important to understand this represents a strong out-come. Results like this aren't typical, but this is a useful way to show how leverage can change things.

Imagine you purchase a property for $410,000. You contribute $5,000 of your own money as part of the deposit and associated costs, with the balance funded through a mortgage.

Fast forward ten years, and that property doubles in value to $820,000. A tidy $410,000 value increase. After subtracting setup costs, that's a $405,000 profit on paper.

Let's do the basic math most people would use:

> Return on Investment (ROI) = Total gain ($410,000) ÷ Initial cost ($410,000) = 100%

That's a 100% total return over ten years, which is roughly 7% per year.

Not bad, right?

But here's the interesting part ...

In this hypothetical scenario, you didn't put in $410,000.

You only put in $5000 of your own money at the start, and covered the rest through a loan. Let's say over the ten years, you had some cashflow losses to cover expenses and the interest on the loan, totalling $30,000. This brings the total out-of-pocket capital to $35,000.

---

35 Assumes an annual rent of $20,800, with yearly expenses including insurance ($1,000), loan interest ($16,200), maintenance ($2,000), rates ($3,000), and agent fees ($1,602), totalling $23,802. This results in a net loss of $3,002 per year, or $30,020 over ten years. Combined with the initial $5,000 cash outlay, total personal outlay was $35,020, resulting in a $405,000 capital gain and a Return on Equity (ROE) of approximately 1,157%. This is general information and does not consider your personal circumstances. Always seek advice from a licensed financial adviser.

So, what was the actual return on your money?

Return on Equity (ROE) = $405,000 gain ÷ $35,000 out-of-pocket investment = 1157% in this specific hypothetical scenario

The jaw dropping difference between the two numbers (100% vs 1157%) works as a clear explanation of the concept: the difference between Return on Investment (ROI) and Return on Equity (ROE). This number looks extraordinary, because it's driven by leverage.

And it also goes the other way. If prices had fallen instead of risen, leverage would have amplified the losses just as dramatically. In some cases, this can mean losing your initial capital while still being responsible for the debt.

For example, if the property had fallen by 20% instead of rising, the initial capital could have been wiped out. But you would still be left with the debt.

This is the double-edged sword of debt: it can lift or crush you as we explored in the PLAN part.

That's why understanding leverage matters so much. Before using debt in any investment strategy, it's important to think about your income stability, cashflow buffers, ability to absorb setbacks, and whether the risks involved are appropriate for your situation.

The mathematics of leverage can look exciting on paper. But real life is rarely as smooth as a spreadsheet.

HOW IT WORKS: LEVERAGE

As you know by now, property allows you to access lending like almost nothing else.

That's why the difference between ROI and ROE (100% vs 1157%) is so significant. It's not just about how much your asset grows, it's about how little of your own money you need to use to control that asset.

Now, buying a house with only a small upfront contribution isn't typical. But as we've already explored in previous tactics, with the right structures, it can be done. Tactics like guarantor loans, government schemes, and equity financing can get you into the market sooner than you might think.

That's the real power of the *RICH Trifecta*:

- Property gives you leverage.
- Leverage builds capital.
- Capital unlocks opportunity.

No crystal ball. No guarantees. Just a disciplined strategy that can work when used prudently. But of course, outcomes can vary significantly depending on timing, market conditions and individual circumstances. This type of tactic can amplify both gains and losses and may not be suitable for all borrowers. Think of this as a lens, not a strategy. It helps you understand how leverage changes both returns and risk.

When this may not be suitable:

- If your income cannot comfortably support additional debt.
- If you have low risk tolerance or limited buffers.
- If your strategy relies heavily on short-term market performance.
- If you're not comfortable using your home as security.

What could go wrong:

- Losses are amplified if property values fall.
- Your home may be at risk if repayments cannot be met. In extreme scenarios, this can result in the forced sale of your home.
- Interest rate rises can strain cashflow.
- Investments may underperform or fail.

RICH Rating[36]

Risk ★★★☆☆: More debt means bigger swings, good or bad.

Income ★★☆☆☆: Often tight on cashflow at the start.

Capital ★★★★☆: Careful leverage can accelerate long-term growth.

Hassle ★★★★☆: Simple loan admin but ongoing tenant management.

---

36 These RICH Ratings are general educational illustrations only. They do not take into account your personal objectives, financial situation, or needs, and are not a recommendation. Always consider your own circumstances and, where appropriate, seek professional advice before acting.

TACTIC 5: Offset account – the interest assassin

MUST READ

Level: *Foundation to Advanced (all levels).*
Best for: *Homeowners who want their cash to work smarter.*

Let me introduce you to one of the smartest (and most underrated) tools in your financial arsenal: *the offset account.*

Most offset accounts look like a regular everyday transaction account, direct debits, online banking, card access, the works. But here's the twist: every dollar you park in it offsets the balance of your home loan. And that's where the magic happens.

Let's break it down with an example.

You have a $500,000 mortgage.

You also have $100,000 sitting in your offset account.

The bank only charges you interest on the difference of $400,000.

That means if your interest rate is 5%, you're saving $5000 a year in interest, just by letting your money sit there. That's $5000 that goes straight towards reducing your loan. No extra effort, no fancy tricks. Just smart structure.

> **Expert tip:** Offsets can cost extra. A 'redraw facility', usually built into your loan, saves the same interest, often fee-free. If you don't need daily flexibility, redraw can be the smarter, cheaper choice. Ask your bank or mortgage broker about this.

WHY IT WORKS SO WELL

Here's a question: How do banks afford those marble floors and free pens?

Easy.

Say the bank pays you 3% on your savings … and charges you 6% on your loan. That 3% difference? That's their profit, also known as the spread.

But with an offset account, you flip the script. Instead of earning 3% interest in a savings account (and then paying tax on it), you save 5% interest on your mortgage, and that saving is tax-free.

That's right. No tax. Just savings.

It's the same dollars, but suddenly they've switched teams!

When this may not be suitable:

- If you consistently spend rather than retain savings.
- If alternative investments better suit your long-term goals.
- If fees outweigh the benefits for your situation.
- If you don't maintain a meaningful balance.

What could go wrong:

- Savings benefits disappear if the balance drops.
- Higher loan costs may reduce overall benefit.
- Opportunity cost if funds could earn higher returns elsewhere.
- Overconfidence in 'safe' returns can limit growth.

A TACTICAL WEAPON IN THE *RICH TRIFECTA*

In the *RICH Trifecta* Framework, your offset account isn't just a savings hack, it acts as a flexible tactical reserve.

You can:

- park your cash to reduce interest
- keep it instantly accessible for deployment into new opportunities
- avoid locking it away or exposing it to risk
- earn a better 'effective return' than most savings accounts will ever offer.

But the *real* magic doesn't just come from where your money sits. It also comes from how your money flows.

RICH Rating

Risk ★★★★☆: Low risk. Same as cash in the bank.

Income ★★☆☆☆: Saves interest. No income.

Capital ★★★★★: Accessible, but relies on discipline.

Hassle ★★★★★: Simple, with minor setup.

Expert tip: Offset accounts are powerful, until your balance hits the size of your loan. If your mortgage is $300K and your offset has $350K, that extra $50K is dead money: not cutting interest, not earning returns. Once you've maxed the offset, put surplus cash to work, into investments, a savings account, or the other parts of your *RICH Trifecta*.

TACTIC 6: The Hub Account – from scattered to streamlined

MUST READ

Level: *Foundation.*
Best for: *Those who want clarity and control with their cashflow.*

If you've been using a multi-account system, one for bills, one for spending, one for tax, one for holidays, you're not alone. I used to do the same many years ago. And I completely understand why people love it. It makes sense. It feels reassuring that your commitments are covered.

For many, it's a fantastic starting point. It gives them peace of mind.

And in the early stages of your financial journey, it works well.

But over time, first in my own life, and later in the lives of clients, I noticed a pattern: the more accounts people had, the harder it became to track progress. Instead of clarity, money becomes scattered and harder to manage.

That's when I shifted to what I now call the *Hub Account*.

THE HUB ACCOUNT: ONE ACCOUNT; FULL COMMAND

This is a shift from micro-managing to mastery.

Instead of dividing your money into different pots, you channel everything through a single, powerful hub.

Whether that's an offset account or a high-interest savings account (more on that in a moment), this one change can transform your relationship with money.

Here's how it works:

1. One account for everything

All income flows into the Hub Account.

Salary. Side hussle income. Rental income. Bonuses. Everything.

This is the account that tells you the truth. One balance. One number. One source of clarity.

Think of the Hub Account as your vault, not your wallet.

The hub is where your money lives and works. No second guessing, no balancing acts, no forgotten accounts with money sitting idle.

But day-to-day spending doesn't need to happen directly from it.

In practice, I suggest adding one simple protection layer. From your Hub Account, you fund a separate spending account or credit card. Ideally, this sits with a different bank so if your login is compromised online, the scammers can't get access to your Hub Account. This is the card you use for groceries, petrol, coffees, subscriptions, and everyday life.

Think of it like this: the Hub Account is where your money lives and compounds. The spending account or card is where your money pays for stuff.

The flow looks like this:

- All income flows into the Hub Account.
- Once a month, or as needed, you transfer a set amount to your spending account or clear your credit card.
- All daily expenses happen from that secondary account.

This can help reduce exposure if a transaction account is compromised.

If a card gets skimmed, a login gets compromised, or you fall victim to a scam, only a small, controlled balance is exposed. Not your entire financial engine.

2. Use your offset (if you have one)

If you own property, this is your golden engine.

Every dollar in your offset works around the clock to reduce your mortgage interest, without generating taxable income.

That's a nice, compounding return.

3. If you don't have an offset (yet)

That's perfectly okay.

Use your highest-interest, lowest-fee account as your Hub Account.

It should be flexible, easy to transact from, and earning the best return available.

Sometimes, savings accounts don't allow you to transact and have to be linked to a transaction account. That's okay too. Just park everything in the high-interest savings account and transfer whatever you need out of that when you need it. Just check the account rules to make sure you don't miss out of interest by doing this.

When you eventually purchase a home and open an offset, you'll already have the right behaviours in place, just with a more powerful engine behind them.

WHY IT WORKS SO WELL

- **Clarity:** You always know exactly where you stand. One glance tells you your surplus, your buffer, and your progress.
- **Momentum:** Watching one strong account grow is motivating. It builds psychological ownership.
- **Efficiency:** No more idle money scattered across multiple accounts. You have one system working hard in the background.
- **Protection:** Your main balance stays insulated from everyday transaction risk.

Expert tip: Got both a home loan and an investment loan? Park your spare cash in the offset linked to your home loan. Why? Investment loan interest is tax-deductible. Home loan interest isn't, so it costs more in after-tax dollars. Offset the non-deductible debt first, whenever possible.

BUCKETS ARE A GOOD START

The bucket system is a great start. It gives peace of mind and keeps money 'set aside'. But buckets are just the beginning.

When you're ready to level up, the Hub Account is the upgrade. It's not about splitting money to avoid mistakes, it's about unifying money to drive growth. With everything flowing through one place, you gain clarity, momentum, and control.

That's why in the Stage 4 *RICH Trifecta* chart, back in the *PLAN* part, there's only one cash account shown. It's deliberate.

Unify your flow. Concentrate your force. Command your money.

When this may not be suitable:

- If you rely on structured budgeting systems to stay disciplined.
- If you struggle with impulse spending.
- If you prefer clear separation of funds for different goals.

What could go wrong:

- Overspending without clear boundaries.
- Reduced visibility on specific goals if not tracked separately.
- Security risks if not structured properly.
- Poor discipline can undo the benefits.

RICH Rating

Risk ★★★★★: Reduces debt. Keeps cash under control.

Income ★★☆☆☆: No income stream, just interest saved.

Capital ★★★★★: Fully accessible. No lock-ins.

Hassle ★★★★★: Simple setup. Set and forget.

TACTIC 7: The RICH Reset – shifting towards positive cashflow

Level: *Intermediate.*
Best for: *Investment property owners 2 to 10 years into a loan wanting better cashflow.*

Before we dive into this little-known tactic, let's clear the air on one of the noisiest, and most misunderstood, topics in Aussie property investing: *negative gearing.*

Gearing means borrowing. Easy.

Okay so here's the quick truth:

- Negative gearing = losing money
- Positive gearing = making money

Simple, right?

Yet between YouTube hype, social media clickbait, and backyard barbie chatter, this truth gets twisted. I've had clients genuinely disappointed their investment was *positively* geared, because someone convinced them that losing money was the goal.

If your dream is to lose money, don't bother with property. Buy a boat, throw a wedding, or back your mate's meme coin – you'll lose faster, and at least have a better story to tell.

SO WHY THE CONFUSION?

Negative gearing sounds sexy because of the tax deductions. And yes, they can help, but only if you're earning enough taxable income. No income equals no tax, which means no deduction.

And remember: deductions aren't dollar-for-dollar. If you lose $1000 and you're on a 32% tax rate, you're still out $680 in real cash.

That's why the endgame should be *positive gearing*. A property that pays you, not bleeds you.

And this is where one approach I often use comes in. I call it the *RICH Reset*.

Expert tip: Negative gearing isn't set in stone. Other countries, including the UK, US, Canada, and New Zealand, have modified, restricted, or phased out parts of their negative gearing rules in recent decades.

Australia could do the same. Tax policies shift with politics and economic conditions, and deductions that exist today might not be around tomorrow. That's why you should never build your entire plan on a tax rule. Instead, focus on fundamentals like cashflow, capital growth, and solid investment principles – the things that stand the test of time.

THE OVERLOOKED TACTIC: RESET THE LOAN, LET TIME DO THE WORK

This is an interesting one. I don't claim to have invented it, it's simply using how loans already work, but I've never seen anyone explain or apply it in this particular way. I first thought of it as a solution for my own personal purposes, and I've been using it ever since. Let me show you how it works.

When you first take out a mortgage, it's usually a 30-year P&I loan. As time passes, your balance shrinks, but repayments stay the same, unless interest rates shift.

Here's the idea: every few years, the loan can be reset back to 30 years.

By stretching the term, repayments fall. Meanwhile, rents usually creep up thanks to inflation and market growth.

The result?

Income starts to catchup to expenses, and your property edges towards positive cashflow sooner.

Why it works

Normally investors ignore the principal portion of their P&I loan when assessing property cashflow. And sure, it's technically 'forced savings', not an expense, so it makes sense.

But *cashflow is cashflow*. If you're out of pocket each month, you have less capacity to put that money to good use elsewhere, regardless of where that money's going.

Some investors use I/O loans to avoid this, but I generally think this is not the best option.

Why? Because I/O loans come with higher interest rates. And you're not paying down the loan – you're delaying the inevitable repayments. When the I/O term ends (normally 5 to 10 years), you get a massive surge in your repayments.

While there are cases where I/O loans may make sense, like short-term holding strategies or advanced structuring, for many investors, they can create challenges if not managed carefully, particularly when repayments increase after the interest-only period ends.

Consider if sticking with P&I works for you, pay down the loan steadily, and then use the RICH Reset when you need a boost in cashflow.

Just time and tactics

This isn't a loophole. It's simply smart use of how loans work.

- No need to jack up rents above market.
- No need to renovate or refinance into exotic products.
- Just let time do its thing, and give it a nudge with one tactical reset.

When it comes to wealth, positive cashflow is king, and this move may help you get there sooner.

Let's run an example calculation:[37]

- **Loan size:** $800,000
- **Interest rate:** 5%
- **After two years:** Loan balance = ~$776,000
- **Remaining term:** 28 years → Monthly repayment (P&I) $4,295

Now, here's the RICH Reset move:

- **Reset the loan term back to 30 years:** New repayment ~$4168/month
- **Immediate outgoings reduction:** ~$127/month (about $1524 per year) less in outgoings

That reduction in outgoings alone potentially pushes the property towards positive cashflow several years earlier in this example than if you left the loan as is. Although this depends on interest rates, rental income, and individual loan terms.

The charts overleaf show the difference.

---

37 Assumes property value $1 million, 80% LVR, rental yield 4%, rental expenses equal to 25% rental yield, P&I loan, inflation of 2.5%, annual rental increase of 3%. Loan is reset 6 times every 2 years starting year 3 at 5% flat interest rate. Model assumes simplified annualised calculations. Although annualised amortisation differs from actual monthly amortisation, both scenarios are modelled *identically*, so the relative comparison remains valid.

The RICH Reset tactic employed

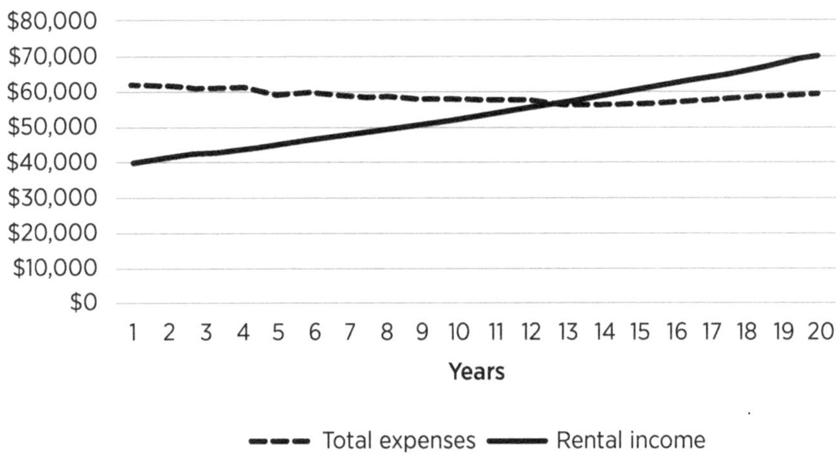

Maintaining the loan as is on P&I

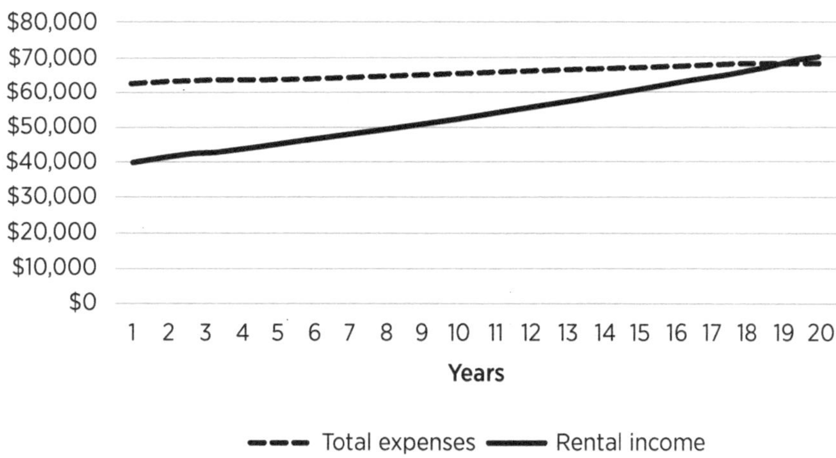

Without the RICH Reset, repayments stay locked at about $4295/month for the remaining 28 years (assuming no interest rate changes).

With the reset, repayments drop to around $4168/month. That's roughly $127 per month, or $1524 per year, freed up in cashflow.[38]

Now, there is a trade-off here. Resetting the loan can mean paying more interest over time and staying in debt longer.

The tactic only works if you use the freed-up cashflow wisely, not spend it.

Done right, it can improve flexibility and accelerate your position. Done poorly, it can slow you down.

In theory, if the freed-up cashflow is consistently directed towards reducing debt (such as via an offset account), the long-term impact may be reduced. But as I said, this depends entirely on discipline and execution.

Here's the key: the earlier positive cashflow counteracts with this, it buys you flexibility, breathing space, and capital you can actually put to work elsewhere.

The freed-up funds could be:

- parked in your offset account (same net effect as extra repayments)
- used to pay down non-deductible debt (like your home loan)
- channelled into your *RICH Trifecta* machine.
- simply used to cover living costs while you grow a business or reduce work hours.

Of course, changes in interest rates can also impact outcomes, as rising rates may offset or reduce the cashflow benefits of this approach. And if not managed carefully, repeatedly extending loan terms can result in carrying debt much longer than intended and paying substantially

---

38 This example assumes refinancing or loan restructuring is available, with no material fees and no interest rate change.

The example figures in this section are simplified and rounded for clarity. Tax implications (such as the deductibility of interest expenses and the effect on taxable income) have not been included in the example but may influence the real-world impact of this strategy depending on your personal circumstances. The 'six years faster' estimate is based on when rental income overtakes loan repayments and holding costs under moderate inflation, constant interest rates, and rental growth assumptions. This tactic is intended as a conceptual tool to spark discussion, not as financial advice. Always consult a qualified adviser or loan professional to determine suitability for your situation.

more interest over time, potentially delaying financial independence rather than accelerating it.

WHY TIMING BEATS TOTALS

The critical insight is: it's not about the lifetime interest cost, it's about *timing*. By becoming positively geared earlier, your property shifts from a financial drain to a self-sustaining asset. And once it pays for itself, that cashflow fuels the rest of your *RICH Trifecta* machine.

Like everything in *Freedom Gameplan*, this isn't a one-size-fits-all tactic. It's a tool in your financial toolbox, powerful when used well, but not always the right move.

Here's a general guide of when this works well:

- If you have a mortgage on an investment property and principal residence at the same time.
- If you want to free up cashflow for investment purposes elsewhere in your *RICH Trifecta* machine.
- If you anticipate that in future years you may no longer have much taxable income and so being negatively geared provides no tax advantage.
- If you want the investment property to be self-sustaining, so it's not a burden on your cashflow and gives you peace of mind.

Keep in mind, depending on your age, circumstances, and lender policy, some banks may not offer a full 30-year reset (or at all), especially as you approach retirement. Resetting a loan term also extends the repayment period, which increases total interest costs and prolongs exposure to debt.

Refinancing or restructuring a loan can be a smart move, but only when it genuinely fits your situation. Before making changes, speak with your lender, a licensed mortgage broker, or another appropriately qualified professional so you understand the costs, risks, and trade-offs.

And remember: the magic isn't just in property, it's in how your property, shares, and business moves *synergify* into a machine greater than the sum of its parts.

When this may not be suitable:

- If your goal is to eliminate debt as quickly as possible.
- If you lack discipline to use freed-up cashflow effectively.
- If you're close to retirement or restricted by lender policies.
- If interest rates are expected to rise significantly.

What could go wrong:

- Paying significantly more interest over time.
- Staying in debt longer than planned.
- Cashflow gains being spent rather than invested.
- Reduced benefit if rates rise.

RICH Rating

Risk ★★★☆☆: You need to be disciplined with the freed-up cashflow.

Income ★★★★☆: Designed to improve your cashflow.

Capital ★★☆☆☆: Somewhat capital neutral; without discipline you can be worse off.

Hassle ★★★★☆: Some paperwork and good discipline required.

CHAPTER 22
SHARE MARKET TACTICS: INVEST WITHOUT LOSING YOUR SHIRT

With all the noise around the share market – charts flashing red and green, talking heads shouting predictions, prices changing by the second – it's no wonder people become overwhelmed. But let me share a timeless truth that cuts through the distractions: *every share code represents a real business.*

Behind every symbol is a company, real people, real products, real challenges, real profits (or losses). And when you truly grasp that, everything changes.

You stop seeing the share market as a casino and start treating it for what it is: a marketplace of businesses looking for part-owners.

TWO PATHS, ONE DESTINATION

Once you understand that timeless truth, there are two smart ways you could consider for investing:

- **Active investing** – If you've got the skills to evaluate businesses, dive into individual shares.
- **Passive investing** – If you don't, no worries. Use well-managed ETFs or managed funds (I'll explain what these are in the GEAR UP part) that spread your money across quality businesses.

Either way, you're buying part-ownership in real companies, not glued to trading apps watching every blip.

And remember, every financial decision you make can be tested with one question:

Does this increase my Freedom Score?

Let's bring this to life: the café example

Let's say you're a chef. You've worked in kitchens your whole life, and now you're thinking of buying a little café of your own.

What do you do?

Well, you do what any sensible investor would do. You look at the numbers. Right?

- First, you watch the place for a while to see how many people walk in the door each day.
- You look at what they order, meals, coffees, muffins on the go.
- Then you estimate the annual sales based on your observations. Let's say you work out the place turns over $300,000 a year.
- Next, you estimate the expenses. Staff wages, rent, supplies, insurance. Let's say those total $200,000.
- That leaves $100,000 in profit.
- Then you poke your head into the kitchen, have a little stickybeak, and spot an oven, a grill, a couple of fridges, and a solid espresso machine. You tally it up in your head and figure the gear's worth about $20,000.

So, you think to yourself: 'Alright, this place has $100,000 a year in profit, has $20,000 in gear, looks tidy, good foot traffic, nice vibe … I reckon it's worth around $120,000 as a business.'

Armed with this info, you approach the owner, let's call him *Blokeman*, to strike a deal. Now, three scenarios could unfold:

- **Scenario 1:** Blokeman wants $1,000,000.
  You laugh in his face, say 'good luck', and walk out, fast. It's not even worth negotiating. Either he's had a knock to the head, or he thinks *you* have!

- **Scenario 2:** Blokeman wants $150,000.
  Now we're talking. It's a bit more than your estimated value, but not outrageous. You know the café's got solid potential, great location, good coffee, loyal customers. So, you negotiate, maybe

settle at $130,000. You pay a little more than you planned, but it still makes sense. You can see the growth potential.

- **Scenario 3:** Blokeman's in trouble. Owes some Yakuza serious coin. He says, 'Mate, I need $50,000 fast.'
  You nearly drop your latte. 'Deal!' you say, shaking his hand before he can change his mind. You just scored a great business at less than half your estimated fair value.

And here's the point: the exact same principles apply when buying shares in a company.

Some are overpriced. Some are fairly priced. And some are underpriced. But you've got to know how to tell which is which.

The only difference is: instead of buying the whole business, you're buying a piece of it. A *share*.

But here's the catch ...

Valuing a local café may be easy. Valuing global giants like Tesla or CSL? That's another beast entirely. Most people don't know how to do this. But here's the real problem: *they think they do.*

And so, they gamble, buying shares based on vibes, headlines, or hot tips from Cousin Greg.

That's not investing. That's just roulette in a smart-looking suit.

So what's the smart move?

A smarter way to approach this is to look at a mix of independent research, company announcements, annual reports, and other reliable sources.

Some investors lean on third-party research tools or brokerage research platforms to help cut through the noise. I'll walk you through how these work in the GEAR UP part.

Think of them as a guide, not a decision-maker. They don't replace your judgement, your own research, or proper advice.

Now before we go deeper, let's draw a hard line in the sand.

INVESTING VS SPECULATING: KNOW THE DIFFERENCE OR PAY THE PRICE

Everyone loves to quote Warren Buffett: 'Be fearful when others are greedy ... '. And I love it too.

But rarely anyone mentions the man behind Buffett's wisdom, Benjamin Graham.

Graham was Buffett's mentor, and together with David Dodd, in 1934 he wrote the share market investing bible *Security Analysis*. In it, he gave us what I consider one of the greatest mental filters of all time. It goes like this: 'An investment operation is one which, upon thorough analysis, promises safety of principal and a satisfactory return. Operations not meeting these requirements are speculative.'

Read that again. Let it soak in. Then tattoo it on your forehead, backwards, so you can see it in the mirror every morning!

Okay, let's break it down into simple language:

- **Thorough analysis:** Not 'my Cousin Greg said it'll go up'.
- **Safety of principal:** If it crashes, will you be toast?
- **Satisfactory return:** Will it do the job?

If it fails even one of those, it's not investing. It's speculating. Full stop.

Most people are speculators wearing an investor's hat. Don't be that person.

If you can't do the deep analysis yourself, use tools that can. The goal isn't to prove you're smart. It's to stack the odds in your favour.

It WILL go down

Here's a hard truth: your shares will abso-freaking-lutely drop at times.

It's not a bug in the system. It *is* the system. That's how markets work.

The key to surviving downturns isn't trying to avoid them; it's structuring your investments so that you're never forced to sell when things get rough. Markets don't crash because of one event. The 'trigger' (a war, recession, tweet, scandal, whatever) just lights the fuse. The real cause is usually the same: prices climbing too far above fair value for too long.

Most people confuse the symptom with the cause.

Investing isn't about always being right. It's about being prepared for when things go wrong. Treat the market like a business. Stick to timeless principles. Use quality research. And always, *always*, know whether you're investing ... or just guessing.

Because one builds wealth.

The other builds disappointment.

And you, my friend, didn't come here to be disappointed.

A PRACTICAL GUIDE TO PORTFOLIO ALLOCATION

Traditionally, portfolio allocation, meaning how much of your money you put into each investment option, has been based on your attitude to risk. Conservative investors load up on defensive assets like bonds and cash. Aggressive investors swing for the fences with growth assets like shares and property. Balanced investors normally go half and half.

But I want to offer you a more practical way of thinking about it, based on time horizon rather than just your nerves.

Instead of asking: 'How much risk am I comfortable with?'

Ask instead: 'When will I need this money?'

Because that question changes everything.

If you base your investments on when you'll actually need the funds, you can sidestep panic during downturns and keep your money working smarter.

The time-based allocation framework

Here's a rough guide on how to match your money to your timeline:[39]

- **Short term (0–1 year).** Planning to use the money soon, say for a home deposit or a big purchase? You can't afford to ride short-term price fluctuations. Focus on safety over returns.

  Potential allocation: 20% growth / 80% defensive. Or just park it in a high-interest savings account (or your offset). Preservation is king in this case.

- **Medium term (1–3 years).** You want some growth but still might need the money, or at least a portion of it.

  Think balance – you want upside without being forced to lock in losses if the market dips. **Potential allocation:** 50% growth / 50% defensive.

39 Disclaimer: These allocations are only examples of potential approaches and are illustrative only. This is general information and does not consider your personal circumstances. Always seek advice from a licensed financial adviser.

- **Long term (3–5 years).** You've got breathing room. This means you can afford more risk.

  Yes, markets will wobble, but history says they bounce back. You can afford to ride it out. **Potential allocation:** 70% growth / 30% defensive.

- **Very long term (5+ years).** This is money you won't touch for a very long time, maybe decades. Perfect for compounding returns.

  Potential allocation: Consider 90% growth / 10% defensive, or even going all-in on growth (100%). Let the market do its thing, regardless of how much it fluctuates.

UNDERSTANDING FAIR VALUE AND MARGIN OF SAFETY

If there's one golden rule in investing, it's this: don't lose money.

Obvious? Sure. But in the heat of a bull market or the buzz of a trending share, even seasoned investors forget it. That's where the concepts of 'fair value' and 'margin of safety' step in. They're your financial seatbelt and airbag combo.

What is fair value, really?

Fair value is the true worth of a company based on its actual business, not the hype, not the headlines. We're talking cold, hard fundamentals: revenue, earnings, assets, debt, growth potential. Just like the café example.

Remember how I mentioned that you could use research provided by professionals? One example is third-party analyst research from providers such as Morningstar.[40] These providers publish their own estimates and opinions based on company information, financial modelling, and other research inputs. Those estimates are not facts, guarantees, or recommendations. They are simply one lens among many.

Let's say the analyst tells you that the share ABC has a fair value of $100 per share. That's what they believe the business is worth, based on logic, not market mood swings. It is simply one input that can be weighed against price, fundamentals, and your own judgement.

---

40 These tools are examples only and not endorsements. There are many alternatives available.

Enter the margin of safety

Now let's say that same share is trading for $70. That $30 gap? That's your margin of safety. It's your built-in cushion if things don't go exactly to plan.

Because let's face it, no one's crystal ball works perfectly, and surprises happen. Growth slows. Interest rates spike. CEOs resign. A margin of safety gives you room to be *human* in your investing.[41]

This means you're buying the business at a discount, with less downside risk and more upside potential. That's smart investing, not wishful thinking.

A bit of timeless wisdom

Ben Graham (Buffett's mentor) coined the term 'margin of safety', and Warren Buffett ran with it all the way to billionaire status. As the Oracle of Omaha himself says:

'Price is what you pay. Value is what you get.'

Don't chase shiny objects. Chase value. And always leave yourself a margin of safety.

Look at the chart below. It shows the simple relationship between market price, fair value, and why the margin of safety matters.

Price to fair value threats and opportunities

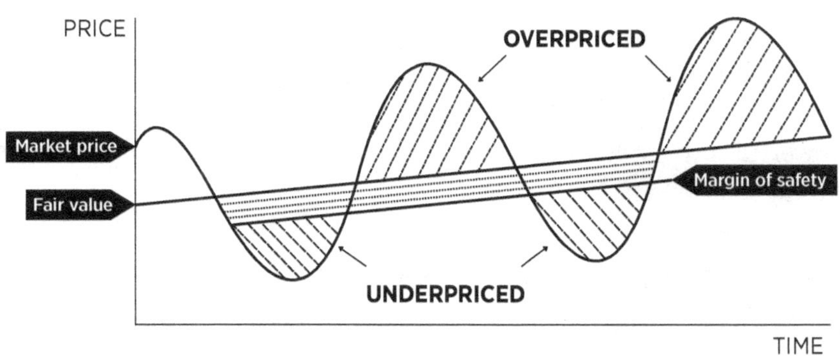

Illustrative concept diagram, not based on market data

41 Disclaimer: This is general information and does not consider your personal circumstances. This example is illustrative only, and not a suggestion of the mentioned share. Always seek advice from a licensed financial adviser.

In the GEAR UP part, I will explain how some investors read third-party research tools to compare market price with analysts' estimates.

> The next few tactics are where we build your share investing superpower, step-by-step. They might feel a little technical at times, but stick with me. It's all laying the groundwork for something powerful: the all-weather investment plan. This is a simple, flexible tactic you'll wish you'd known years ago. Trust me, it'll all click. Let's build the foundation first, then bring it all together.

TACTIC 8: Dollar Cost Averaging – how to ride the waves calmly

Level: *Foundation to Advanced (all levels).*
Best for: *Steady wealth builders in any market.*

One of the biggest mental roadblocks that stops people from investing in shares is the fear of getting the timing wrong.

'Is now the right time?'

'What if the market crashes right after I invest?'

'What if prices are already too high?'

These are perfectly normal questions, and ones even professional investors wrestle with. But here's the truth: no one can consistently time the market, not even the experts. That's why one of the most powerful, proven approaches for long-term investors is *Dollar Cost Averaging* (DCA).

WHAT IS DOLLAR COST AVERAGING?

DCA is a tactic where you invest a fixed amount of money at regular intervals (say, monthly or fortnightly), regardless of whether the market is going up, down, or sideways. This also works well whether you have a passive or active style of investing.

Let's say you invest $500 on the first day of each month into the same ETF or shares. Some months the price will be higher, and your money will buy you fewer units. Other months the price will be lower, and you'll buy more. Over time, your purchase price averages out, reducing the impact of short-term price fluctuation.

Why DCA works so well in volatile markets

When the market is volatile or is rallying, it's often difficult to tell if you're getting in at a good time. Investing a lump sum can feel risky. But DCA keeps you in the game without having to guess.

It reduces the temptation to try to time the market.

It helps you invest consistently, even during market dips.

It protects you from dumping all your cash at the market peak.

Most importantly, it helps you build the habit of investing, just like a direct debit into your future self. You don't need to be a share market genius. Just be consistent. Think of DCA like a gym membership for your portfolio – you might not see abs overnight, but one day you'll wake up and your net worth will be flexing.

But what about when the market crashes?

Ah, now this is where we flip our approach on its head. When the market tanks and everything's on sale, that's when lump sum investing can shine. Think of it as a store-wide clearance: quality assets at bargain prices. If you've kept capital handy in your offset account or via equity, you'll be ready to act.

So, the simple rule of thumb is:

- Rising or volatile market → stick with DCA
- Falling or crashing market → consider lump sums

We'll unpack all this much further soon.

When this may not be suitable:

- If transaction costs materially impact returns.
- If you struggle with consistency.

What could go wrong:

- Underperformance in rising markets.
- Continued losses in falling markets.
- Emotional decisions disrupting the plan.
- Inconsistent investing reduces effectiveness.

RICH Rating

Risk ★★★☆☆: Still market-exposed, but lowers the risk of a costly timing mistake.

Income ★★★☆☆: Potential dividends. But more about long-term growth than income.

Capital ★★★★★: You can start small and build steadily.

Hassle ★★★★★: Automate it and move on with your life.

Expert tip: You can set up an automated DCA plan through low-cost investment platforms. You'll be amazed how a few hundred dollars invested regularly can snowball into serious wealth over time. There is a step-by-step guide on exactly how to do this in the GEAR UP part. So, keep reading.

TACTIC 9: Crash Investing – navigating market panic

Level: *Foundation to advanced (all levels).*
Best for: *Disciplined investors who want to take advantage of lower prices during periods of market stress.*

WHY CRASHES CREATE OPPORTUNITY

Investing after a market crash is like buying sunscreen in winter; it's cheaper now, but come summer, you'll be glad you stocked up!

If you've been following the steps in this book, market crashes won't feel like disasters. They'll feel like opportunities. In fact, they might just turn out to be some of the most valuable opportunities over time.[42]

People always think I'm a bit strange because I *get excited* when the market crashes! While everyone else is panicking and running for the hills, I'm rubbing my hands together whispering, 'Ooooh yeah …'

Call me weird, but I call it being ready.

42 But remember, downturns can be prolonged and unpredictable, and not all investments recover in the same way or timeframe.

You see my friend, I've been waiting for this. My debt is strategic, my cash is liquid, and while the crowd's freaking out, I'm cool as a cucumber. That's the power of being crash-ready.

And that's exactly why the offset account in the *RICH Trifecta* Framework matters so much. It gives you instant access to capital – locked, loaded, and ready to go the moment shares go on sale.

Let me walk you through a hypothetical scenario that's similar to something I've explored in the past. It shows how dividend income, franking credits, and long-term growth can work together, when conditions line up and discipline is maintained.

WHY WAITING CAN BE WISER

Here's a powerful truth that most people overlook: as I explained in the *PLAN* part, when an investment falls 20%, it doesn't just need to rise 20% to recover. It needs to rise 25%, because the recovery is calculated from a smaller base.

For example, if a share drops from $20 to $16 (a 20% drop), a 20% gain only gets you to $19.20, still short. You'd need a 25% gain to get back to $20.

And the deeper the fall, the steeper the climb. If a share drops 50%, it needs to double (a 100% gain!) just to break even. Ouch!

This is one of my favourite things to explain – people's jaws always drop when they get it!

That's why *when* you invest can be just as important as *what* you invest in.

When you invest during a market upswing, you're competing for smaller gains and higher risks. But when you invest during a crash, when prices are beaten down and everyone else is panicking, you're buying future growth at a discount.

And here's what makes the *RICH Trifecta* so smart: while you wait, your capital isn't sitting idle. It can be:

- reducing your home loan interest in your offset account
- working inside your business
- standing by, ready to pounce.

Now let's look at the 2008 Global Financial Crisis (GFC) as an example.

CRASH-TESTED: FOUR DIFFERENT JOURNEYS THROUGH THE GFC

To show you how powerful the Crash Investing tactic can be, let's walk through four different investor scenarios during the 2008 GFC, all using actual market data.[43]

Scenario 1: Getting swept up by FOMO[44] – buying high, sinking low

- **Start April 2005:** You invest $100,000 after watching the market rise for a few years. Everyone else is making money. You don't want to miss out.
- **October 2007:** Your portfolio grows +37% to **$136,669**. You feel excited about possible continued future growth.
- **September 2008:** The GFC crash arrives and escalates quickly.
- By **February 2009** your portfolio goes down 49% from the October 2007 high to **$69,295**.
- **August 2010:** You're still down, but slowly recovering. Now at nearly –2%, which means you have **$98,256**.
- **January 2013:** Finally, you're up again: +36% to **$135,988**.
- **Time to recovery:** 5+ years to breakeven, nearly 8 years for modest returns.

Scenario 2: Buying at the top

- **Start December 2007:** The market is euphoric. Everyone is keen for more gains. You jump in at the top with $100,000.
- **February 2009:** Disaster. Your investment falls 47% to **$53,246.**
- **January 2013:** After years of holding on, you're finally at +4% to **$104,491**.
- **Time to recovery:** 5 years of anxiety to break even and then have a slight return.

---

43 Scenarios are based on the Dow Jones Industrial Average (DJIA). This analysis uses inflation-adjusted month-end DJIA price data sourced from publicly available sources, including the Wall Street Journal, which publishes data derived from S&P Dow Jones Indices. Calculations and scenario modelling are the author's own work.

44 Fear Of Missng Out.

Scenario 3: Perfect timing – if you had a crystal ball[45]

- **Start December 2007:** You think trouble is coming since the market has been rallying for a few years now. You park your money in an offset account and wait.
- **February 2009:** Market bottoms. You invest your $100,000.
- **January 2013:** Your portfolio grows to **$196,244**, up 96%.
- **Result:** Nearly doubled your money in less than 4 years by being patient and prepared (and in this case lucky to find the exact bottom).

Scenario 4: Buying during the crash

- **Start October 2008:** You've been watching the markets go down by 30%. You decide to invest $100,000 during the panic.
- **February 2009:** Your position dips to **$75,742** (down 24%).
- **January 2013:** You ride the recovery to **$148,639**, a 49% gain.
- **Result:** A decent return in about 4.5 years.

These four crash-test scenarios suggest one clear principle: investing big at market highs can backfire. Instead, strategic patience – waiting for value, or easing in with DCA – may lead to better outcomes. Even though you can't predict the exact bottom, investing after the crash has arrived can pay off, even if your position keeps going down after you jump in. You don't need a crystal ball, but you do need discipline, patience, acceptance of uncertainty, and a smart plan.

---

45 This scenario is for educational purposes only and does not imply that timing the exact bottom of the market is possible. It is a case study designed to illustrate potential outcomes. Data is based on historical Dow Jones Industrial Average (DJIA) month-end closing values, inflation-adjusted using headline CPI. Data is sourced from publicly available financial platforms, including the *Wall Street Journal* (derived from S&P Dow Jones Indices). Calculations and scenario modelling are the author's own work.

Four investor journeys

Entry scenario	Start value	Lowest point	Jan. 2013 value	Return	Years held
1. FOMO in 2005	$100,000	$69,295	$135,988	+36%	~8 years
2. Peak of 2007	$100,000	$53,246	$104,491	+4%	~5 years
3. Finding the bottom by luck (2009)	$100,000	N/A	$196,244	+96%	~4 years
4. During the crash (2008)	$100,000	$75,742	$148,639	+49%	~4.5 years

The chart overleaf shows the general progression of market prices for the 2008 GFC and the market recovery, including how long it took the market to double from the 2009 low point:[46]

46 This chart uses total return data for the Dow Jones Industrial Average (DJIA), including dividends. As a result, there may be slight variations in returns and recovery timing compared to charts based on price-only data. Data is sourced from publicly available financial platforms, including the Wall Street Journal (derived from S&P Dow Jones Indices). Calculations and adjustments are the author's own. Minor variations may exist between data providers due to methodology and rounding differences. Key dates and levels are based on historical DJIA data and may vary slightly depending on the data source and whether intraday or closing values are used. The Dow Jones doubled from its GFC low in approximately 3 years. It took closer to 4 years before the recovery felt firmly established.

GFC market recovery vs. growth

(Nominal price movements of Dow Jones Industrial Average Index)

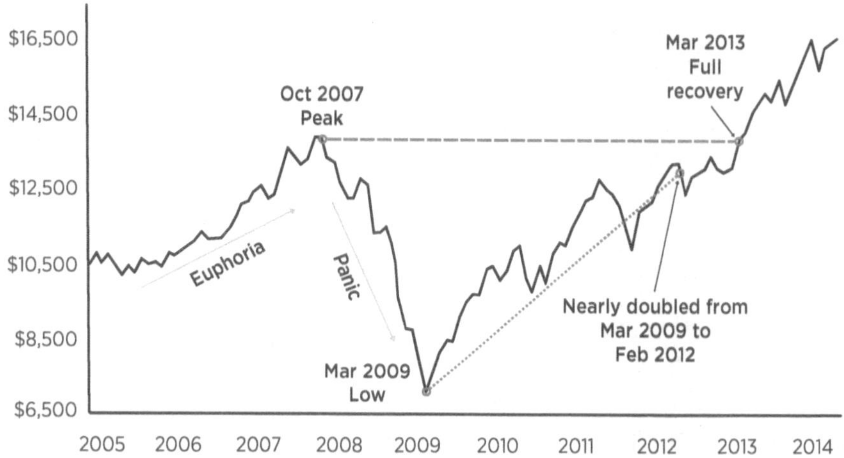

WHY CRASH INVESTING WORKS

- **You're buying value at a discount:** Great quality companies don't vanish in a crash, but their prices do.
- **Dividends become more attractive:** A share yielding 5% at $30 now yields 7.5% at $20.
- **Downturns don't last forever:** History shows markets bounce back. Crashes are often temporary. Rebounds are powerful.
- **Some investments won't recover:** You should also know that not all individual investments recover in the same way, and some may never return to previous levels.

History is a guide[47]

Let's look at a few crash examples.

47 Data reflects historical S&P 500 price index daily closing levels, excluding dividends and not adjusted for inflation. Figures are for broad market illustration only; individual securities may perform very differently and carry different risks. Source: publicly available S&P 500 index data. Time-to-double estimates in this section are based on the S&P 500, while the previous GFC chart references the Dow Jones Industrial Average (DJIA), which may result in slight variations.

Market recovery time after the fall:

- 1987 Black Monday: ~2 years
- 2000 Dot-com crash: ~7 years
- 2008 GFC: ~5.5 years
- 2020 COVID crash: ~6 months

How fast the market doubled from the bottom:

- 1987 Black Monday: ~5 years
- 2000 Dot-com crash: ~5 years
- 2008 GFC: ~2 years[48]
- 2020 COVID crash: ~1.5 years

How fast the market tripled from the bottom:

- 1987 Black Monday: ~8.5 years
- 2000 Dot-com crash: ~14.5 years
- 2008 GFC: ~5.5 years
- 2020 COVID crash: ~5.5 years

Market recovery vs. growth after crashes (S&P 500)

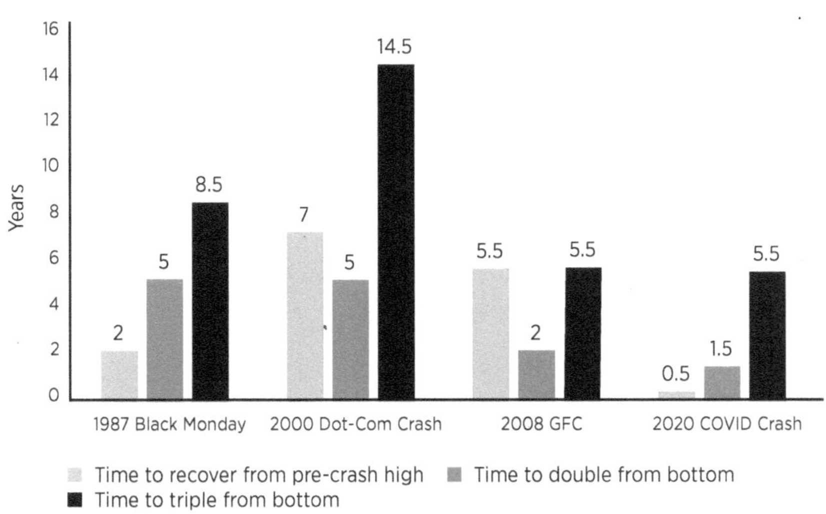

48 The 2008 GFC stands out as the slowest recovery to its prior peak relative to its doubling time: the S&P 500 doubled from its March 2009 bottom in roughly 2.1 years, but did not reclaim its October 2007 pre-crash peak until March 2013. Not all recoveries are rapid: even after strong gains from the bottom, fully recouping prior losses can take significantly longer

The takeaway? Markets fall. But they also recover. And when you invest while fear is high, the rewards can be worth it.

Now, while I have used actual market data to produce these charts, I'd like to point out the results can vary depending on the data used, the time period selected, and the method applied. Some recoveries have taken longer than expected, and there's no guarantee future markets will follow the same path.

But, I don't want to get bogged down with the nitty-gritty – that's not the point here. The point is to convey the general principle that *markets crash, but they also recover.*

SPOTTING A CRASH: WHAT TO LOOK FOR

So how do you know when a crash has arrived? Well, you'll never know the full extent of it. But here's a general guide:

- The market is down significantly (for example 10% or more).
- Media headlines are screaming panic.
- People around you are freaking out.

HOW TO INVEST DURING A CRASH, SMARTLY

First, I'd also like to point out that this is only a general framework to help you think about market conditions, not a precise formula or a rule-based strategy or recommendation. Make sure you always exercise your best judgment.

But I want to give you an example of a simple way to think about it:

You can look at whether the market has fallen meaningfully from recent highs (for example, around 10% or more).

How? Google 'ASX 200 index chart' for Aussie shares (or 'S&P 500 chart' as an indication for global markets). Google shows the performance numbers. You can filter the Google charts for 1 year, 5 years, and so on. Compare today's number to the recent high.

Decide on your approach and how much you want to invest. Here's an example of what this may look like:

- Smaller amounts: Consider investing all at once.
- Larger amounts: Consider splitting in two chunks.
- Very large amounts: Consider splitting into numerous parts.

What constitutes a small, larger, or very large amount depends entirely on your circumstances – $10,000 may be a small sum to some and a huge amount to others. So ultimately, you have to decide what you're comfortable with.

Normally investors start with the first portion. If the market keeps dropping, then the next portion can be invested. These chunks can be spaced out every few weeks depending on how events unfold. Use your best judgement without becoming distracted by noise.

If the market bounces back quickly, consider pausing. Don't worry. You haven't missed out, you've preserved your capital.

The key is to review your entries. Stick to the plan. Don't let fear or FOMO push you off track. Make sure you log your decisions in your Decision Log (more on this later).

And if you want to invest during a rising market? That's okay too, just use DCA. Invest gradually over time. It helps smooth out your entry points and avoids buying at a peak.[49]

And remember, markets can fall further, recover faster, or behave differently to any past example.

When this may not be suitable:

- If you cannot tolerate short-term losses.
- If you need access to the funds in the near term.
- If your financial position is already stretched.
- If you're reacting emotionally rather than strategically.

What could go wrong:

- Markets may continue falling after you invest.
- Some investments may never recover.
- Poor timing can delay recovery for years.
- Overconfidence can lead to overexposure.

49 Disclaimer: The strategies and examples in this section are for educational purposes only and do not constitute personal financial advice. Past performance is not a reliable indicator of future results. Always consider your own objectives, financial situation, and needs, and seek advice from a licensed financial adviser before acting.

RICH Rating

Risk ★★★☆☆: Reducing entry price lowers the risk of long-term losses.

Income ★★☆☆☆: Potential dividends. But not designed for income – this is a growth play.

Capital ★★★★★: You can deploy capital quickly when opportunities appear.

Hassle ★★★★☆: It feels uncomfortable. You need discipline, but it's not a daily grind.

TACTIC 10: Harvesting shares for steady dividend income

***Level:** Foundation to Advanced (all levels).*
***Best for:** Those who are focused on cashflow and consistency.*

When it comes to investing, sometimes cash in hand beats promises on paper. That's why some investors prioritise dividend yield over growth.

Why? Because income is real. It's in your account. You can spend it, reinvest it, or use it to pay the bills. But capital gains? They're just numbers on a screen until the day you sell, and markets love to play games with those numbers.

WHAT HAPPENS IF THE MARKET DROPS?

If you own shares in a company paying solid dividends and the market dips, you may still be able to collect income, although dividends are not guaranteed.[50] And here's the kicker: that dip becomes an opportunity.

You buy more shares at a lower price, which:

- lowers your average purchase cost
- boosts your potential capital gain when prices rebound
- increases your dividend yield, since you bought in at a cheaper price.

50 This is a general assumption for education purposes only. In fact, companies may reduce or pause dividend payments if they are in financial trouble during market downturns.

DIVIDENDS VS INFLATION

Another reason some investors prefer dividend-focused strategies? Dividend growth. Quality dividend-paying companies often raise their payouts over time. That's a natural hedge against inflation; your income keeps up with rising costs.

BUT WATCH FOR THE TRAP ...

Not all dividends are created equal. Some companies offer big payouts just to prop up their share price, even if they can't afford it. That's a red flag.

What you want is stability. Look for businesses with a long history of consistent, sustainable dividends. These are the ones that keep delivering, come rain or sunshine. Go back 10 years and see how the share has been paying dividends. Was it stable?

Also, it is worth remembering that companies don't have to pay dividends. So, this can fall away at any point randomly.

BOTTOM LINE

Dividends provide reliable income, peace of mind during downturns, and a powerful compounding effect when reinvested. In short, boring, dependable dividend shares might just be the most exciting part of your portfolio.

When this may not be suitable:

- If your focus is long-term growth over income.
- If you rely heavily on stable income from investments.
- If you're chasing high yields without understanding risk.

What could go wrong:

- Dividends can be reduced or removed.
- High yields may signal underlying issues with the investment.
- Share prices can still fall significantly.
- Overconcentration in income assets reduces diversification.

RICH Rating

Risk ★★★★☆: Established dividend stocks tend to be more resilient, though permanent loss is still possible.

Income ★★★★★: Designed to generate steady, real cashflow.

Capital ★★★★☆: Easy to access and sell, with generally steadier growth.

Hassle ★★★★☆: Largely hands-off once set up, with the occasional check-in.

TACTIC 11: Ride the storm, catch the sun – your all-weather investing plan

MUST READ

Level: *Foundation to Advanced (all levels).*
Best for: *Investors who want clarity, confidence, and a timeless strategy.*

If you're on **Track 1**, Tactics 8 to 10 should be treated as *Must Reads*. They break down each move step-by-step and give you the depth that makes this strategy really stick, so it's worth taking the time to read them properly.

If you're on **Track 2**, I highly recommend coming back to Tactics 8 to 10 when time allows. They explore what this tactic brings together in much more interesting depth.

If you're on **Track 3**, this tactic stands on its own for now and is enough to help you understand the concepts, but I do recommend you circle back to Tactics 8 to 10 before you start investing in shares.

We've now covered the big three tactics: *Dollar Cost Averaging*, *Crash Investing*, and *Dividend Harvesting*. You've got the tools. Now it's time to bring them together into one simple overarching but smart approach to navigate *any* market season, come rain, hail, or shine.

A SMART, ADAPTABLE APPROACH

Think of this as your *all-weather* investing plan. No matter what the market's doing, climbing, crashing, or coasting, you've got a smart, adaptable approach that keeps you moving forward.

Step 1: Take the market's temperature

Start by doing a quick market check. Just Google:

- **ASX 200 chart** for Australian shares
- **S&P 500 chart** as an indication for international shares.

Filter the view to show the past three or five years. You're simply reading the trend:

- **Market's been going up?** This is when DCA is your best friend. Invest smaller amounts regularly (weekly, fortnightly, monthly) to smooth out the bumps and avoid buying at a peak.
- **Market falling or crashing?** Now it's Crash Investing time. This is your moment to invest in quality companies while they're trading at a discount. Go in with lump sums in portions, just like we discussed earlier. Cool, calm, and cashed-up.

Step 2: Already in? Harvest while you wait

If you're already in the market and it starts heading south, don't panic.

Don't sell in fear. Keep collecting dividends.

That's where Dividend Harvesting shines. You're getting paid while you wait for recovery. And if you've got spare capital, it might even be a smart time to average down your cost, meaning you buy more shares at the lower prices and reduce your overall cost per share.

LET THE PLAN DO THE HEAVY LIFTING

To recap, here's your all-weather investment plan.

Market condition	What to do	Why it works
Market rising	Use **Dollar Cost Averaging** E.g., invest $200/month	Smooths entry, avoids peak pricing
Market declining	Use **Crash Investing**	Buy quality at a discount by investing big chunks

Market condition	What to do	Why it works
Market uncertain	**Harvest Dividends** and **Average Down**	Wait while earning income and improve long-term gains

You don't need to guess the future. You've now got a plan that *works with* the market instead of fighting it. This approach gives you:

- a consistent plan across any market condition
- a defence against emotional decision-making
- a proactive path to long-term wealth.

Easy to understand. Easy to execute. And extremely effective when done consistently.

Okay, now that you've figured out investing in shares, let's shift gears.

Next stop? Business plays. Where things get bold, personal, and potentially life-changing.

Let's keep rolling.

When this may not be suitable:

- If you prefer a simple, passive 'set and forget' approach.
- If you're not confident interpreting market conditions.
- If you struggle to stick to a structured plan.

What could go wrong:

- Misreading market conditions.
- Emotional decisions overriding strategy.
- Acting too frequently or not at all.
- Overconfidence leading to poor timing.

RICH Rating

Risk ★★★★☆: Structured to reduce permanent mistakes across market cycles.

Income ★★★★☆: Balanced between income and growth.

Capital ★★★★★: Flexible and liquid.

Hassle ★★★★☆: Requires structure, but not constant tinkering.

CHAPTER 23
BUSINESS TACTICS: WEALTH WITHOUT THE 9–5 GRIND

Let's be real, starting or buying a business is no small feat. It's a massive undertaking, full of moving parts, variables, and risk. So, while this book isn't a full-blown business manual, I've carved out this section to give you the essential insights and game-ready tactics to get started the smart way.

Covering business requires a separate book on its own. That's why I'm writing a second book, called *The Chameleon*, which is solely dedicated to business moves. Stay tuned!

For now, cast your mind back to the *RICH* metrics: Risk, Income, Capital, Hassle. Real estate and shares are easier to measure across these filters. But private business? That's the wildcard. Depending on the business and how it's managed, it can be a dream … or a total disaster.

Especially when it comes to hassle.

Bad systems.

Unreliable staff.

No time off and never-ending fires to put out.

If that's the trade-off, even a wildly profitable business can leave you burnt out, bitter, and wondering why you ever started. I've seen it too many times: brilliant business owners chained to their companies, working 70, 80, even 90 hours a week, rich in dollars, broke in freedom, and dreaming of a holiday.

That's not what we're after.

THE REAL GOAL: FREEDOM, NOT JUST PROFITS

In the *RICH Trifecta*, your private business arm must serve your life, not consume it. That means designing (or reshaping) your business with a clear aim: to reduce your involvement over time, not increase it.

If you're in the trenches right now, running a business that demands your blood, sweat, and sanity, this section is for you.

We'll explore:

- how to start a business with low hassle from day one
- how to grow a new business with a future exit plan from day one
- how to buy a freedom business instead of starting one.

Now let's be real. Chances are, you would still need to grind in the beginning, and that's okay. But the grind should be a means to an end. Because owning a business isn't real wealth if it steals your life.

This section is your launchpad for a freedom business, one that puts income in your bank account without putting stress on your soul. Let's build smart, build lean, and build free.

TACTIC 12: Start a smart, flexible side hustle

MUST READ

Level: *Foundation to Intermediate.*
Best for: *Those who want an additional income stream without burnout.*

Before we dive in, let's clear something up: when I say 'business', I'm not talking about legal structures like sole trader vs company. What I *am* talking about is this: simple income-generating ideas that run alongside your day job and quietly stack your wealth on the side.

A well-placed side hustle can be one of the most powerful tools in your financial arsenal. Why? Because it adds a brand-new stream of income, without needing a second job or second life. And when that extra cash is funnelled back into the *RICH Trifecta* – real estate, shares, or even another hustle – you've just put your wealth-building on rocket fuel.

The key is this: low effort. High return. Minimal stress.

The perfect side hustle isn't something that takes over your nights, weekends, and sanity. It's something that flows with your life, not crashes into it.

I've seen too many people chase 'passion projects' that turn into full-time headaches. Your side hustle should be like a Spotify playlist on repeat: smooth, low-maintenance, and making you money while you dance through life.

Renee and I have had one for many years, one that takes almost no effort and actually provides a great deal of enjoyment while producing an income stream. I'll tell you about it in the *GEAR UP* part, along with other hand-picked examples to get your wheels turning.

For specific examples and ideas, head over to the *GEAR UP* part.

When this may not be suitable:

- If your main job is already stretching you thin.
- If your personal life or health is under pressure.
- If you're chasing quick money instead of something sustainable.
- If you don't have the discipline to follow through consistently.

What could go wrong:

- It turns into a second job instead of a flexible income stream.
- Income is inconsistent, especially early on.
- You burn out trying to do too much at once.
- You invest time or money into an idea that doesn't gain traction.
- It distracts you from your main income source, which is still your foundation.

RICH Rating

Risk ★★★★☆: Because startup costs are usually low, any losses tend to be manageable.

Income ★★★☆☆: It can be strong, but it won't always be consistent.

Capital ★★★★☆: Low entry cost and easy to scale if it starts working.

Hassle ★★★☆☆: It takes effort, but it shouldn't run your life.

TACTIC 13: Build a hassle-free business (from day one)

Level: *Intermediate to Advanced.*
Best for: *Experienced professionals ready to scale income without scaling stress.*

Let's get one thing straight: when it comes to business, you don't want just any hustle, you want a *freedom business*. That means something you understand, can control, and eventually step away from. Your time is too precious to be trapped in a job you created for yourself.

So, here's the golden rule of starting a business:

Only build a business in a field you know like the back of your hand.

Yes, some people launch startups in industries they've never worked in. And yes, a few even succeed. But betting your financial future on being the exception? That's not a strategy, that's wishful thinking. And *Freedom Gameplan* is not built on wishful thinking. It's built on replicable, reliable, real-world tactics.

KNOW YOUR SWEET SPOT

Warren Buffett, the GOAT of investing, credits much of his success to the 'Circle of Competence' concept. He borrowed the idea from baseball legend Ted Williams, who famously only swung at pitches inside his sweet spot, where he knew he could hit hard and often.

Buffett applied this to investing. You'd do well to apply it to business:

- If you're a sparkie, don't start a Pilates studio.
- If you make great coffee, don't dive into trading stock options.

Stay in your lane, and dominate it.

- **Electrician?** Start an electrical services business.
- **Mechanic?** Set up your own repair shop.
- **Teacher?** Launch a tutoring business or online education platform.
- **Barista?** Open that café.
- **Personal trainer?** Go digital with coaching and programs.

Ignore the noise and the 'next big thing' pitches in industries you don't understand. They're a distraction, sometimes an expensive one.

Like Carnegie said: 'Put all your eggs in one basket, and then watch that basket closely.'

START WITH THE EXIT IN MIND

Let's be honest: starting a business takes sweat. You'll grind, hustle, and wear a lot of hats. But the goal isn't to keep doing that forever. The real trick is building the business to run *without* you.

Here's how.

1. **Set a revenue target.** Know how much you need to make before hiring your first team member to take over some of your workload.
2. **Hire smart, not cheap.** Bring on people who are capable, trustworthy, and motivated. Delegate the tasks that eat up your time.
3. **Build a rockstar team.** Invest in training. Give them real ownership and decision-making power. You don't want to be the only brain in the business.
4. **Step back without falling apart.** Gradually remove yourself from daily operations. Eventually, you should be able to check in weekly, not clock in daily.

FINAL THOUGHT

This isn't overnight. It might take a year. It might take five. But if you build it right, you'll wake up one day and realise your business is making money while you're on a beach, or sleeping in.

The end goal is freedom. Not just financial freedom, but freedom of time, headspace, and energy. The right business, done the right way, gives you all three. So don't just chase profit, build a machine that makes it without needing your constant attention.

If your business can't survive without you … then you don't own a business. You own a job.

And we're here to clock off the wage cage, not build a shinier one.

When this may not be suitable:

- If you don't have experience in the field you're entering.
- If you're not ready to commit time upfront to build systems.
- If you need immediate, stable income with low uncertainty.
- If you struggle with delegation or trusting others.

What could go wrong:

- You accidentally build yourself a job instead of a business.
- Poor hiring decisions create more stress, not less.
- Cashflow becomes inconsistent, especially in early stages.
- Lack of systems pulls you back into day-to-day operations.
- Growth stalls because everything depends on you.
- Burnout from trying to do everything yourself.

RICH Rating

Risk ★★★☆☆: The stakes are higher than a side hustle, but sticking to what you know keeps things recoverable.

Income ★★★★☆: Plenty of room to scale, even if the early days feel a bit uneven.

Capital ★★★☆☆: You'll need to commit capital and reinvest to help it grow.

Hassle ★★☆☆☆: Even with solid systems, you're still the one steering the ship.

TACTIC 14: Buy an established business – skip the startup pain

Level: *Advanced.*
Best for: *Experienced professionals ready to fast-track their freedom.*

Sometimes, buying an existing business is a smarter move than starting one from scratch.

Why? Because someone else has already done the hard yards, set up systems, built a customer base, generated revenue, and ironed out the early-stage headaches. You're stepping into a running car instead of building the vehicle yourself.

But, and believe me, this is a big BUT, how you approach this tactic will make or break you. Buy right, and you could fast-track your journey to financial freedom. Buy wrong, and you'll be drowning in stress, debt, and regret.

DO YOUR HOMEWORK (OR PREPARE TO PAY FOR IT)

Buying a business is like getting married. Do it right, and you've got a partner for life. Do it wrong, and you're heading for the world's most expensive breakup.

Here's how to keep the honeymoon phase from turning into a horror movie.

Stay in your circle of competence

If you wouldn't – or couldn't – work in the business, don't buy the business. Stick to what you understand. If you're a builder, don't buy a bakery. If you're a physio, don't buy a printing shop. This isn't the time to 'wing it'.

Dig into the financials

Profit & loss, balance sheet, cashflow. Know them by heart, or pay someone who does. Look for stable profits, manageable or no debt, and strong, predictable cashflow. Beware of erratic income or unexplained expenses. Numbers rarely lie, but sellers sometimes do.

Talk to the troops

Employees know what's really going on. Chat with the team. Are they happy? Do they respect the leadership? High staff turnover or bitterness behind the scenes could be a big red flag.

Check industry benchmarks

Don't just compare the business to your expectations; compare it to the industry. Is it outperforming its competitors or limping along? Context is everything.

See it in action

Spend time on the ground. Watch how things run. Talk to customers. Test the systems. If something feels off, it probably is.

Look past the sales pitch

Remember: the seller wants out. It's your job to uncover *why*. Ask tough questions. Be sceptical. If it sounds too good to be true, it usually is.

YOUR ENDGAME: BUILD A BUSINESS THAT RUNS WITHOUT YOU

When you buy a business, it's tempting to roll up your sleeves and dive in. That's fine, for a while. But don't forget the goal: *financial freedom with minimal hassle.*

The day you sign the papers, start planning your exit from day-to-day operations.

Here's how.

Hire a manager ASAP

Find a capable, trustworthy operator. Pay them well, train them well, and empower them to run the show. If your business depends on you, *it* owns *you*, not the other way around.

Systemise everything

Document every process. From onboarding new staff to managing inventory. The clearer your systems, the less you need to be there.

Set a timeline for your exit

Maybe you're fully hands-off in 12 months. Maybe you just review the numbers once a month. Define your North Star and stick to it.

FINAL THOUGHT

Buying a business isn't just a shortcut to cashflow, it can be a leap forward in your wealth-building journey. But only if you do it right.

Stick to what you know.

Dig deep before you sign.

Build systems.

Plan your exit.

You're not buying another job. You want to buy *freedom*, so treat it that way.

And when you've done it right? You'll wake up one day, sip your morning coffee, and realise the business is making money while you're deciding which beach to visit next.

When this may not be suitable:

- If you don't fully understand the industry or business model.
- If you're not comfortable reviewing financials or relying on expert advice.
- If you don't have access to sufficient capital or buffers.
- If you're not prepared to be hands-on initially.
- If you're risk-averse and uncomfortable with uncertainty.

What could go wrong:

- You overpay for a business that underperforms.
- Financials don't reflect reality (poor records, inflated earnings).
- Key staff leave after the sale, impacting operations.
- Revenue drops once ownership changes.
- Hidden issues (debts, legal risks, operational problems) surface later.
- It becomes more hands-on than expected, pulling you back into daily work.
- Debt used to acquire the business creates financial pressure and additional risk.

RICH Rating

Risk ★★☆☆☆: There's real money on the line here, so getting it wrong can hurt.

Income ★★★★★: You're stepping into an existing revenue stream, so cashflow can start from day one.

Capital ★★☆☆☆: It usually takes serious upfront capital, and you can't just cash out overnight.

Hassle ★★☆☆☆: Even with good systems, you're still responsible for what happens behind the scenes.

CHAPTER 24
CLEVER MOVES FOR MAXIMUM IMPACT

TACTIC 15: Get a helping hand

MUST READ

Level: *Foundation to advanced (all levels).*
Best for: *Everyday Australians who don't want to leave their future to chance.*

If you feel like you could use some help, that's usually a good sign you should reach out for it.

One of the biggest misconceptions I hear is that financial planners are 'only for the rich'. Nothing could be further from the truth. In reality, smart planning is often how everyday Aussies *become* wealthy in the first place.

Breaking this myth is one of my personal missions. Because I've seen firsthand how the right advice, at the right time, can change the direction of someone's life.

I've met people who genuinely believed they were out of options, until one good conversation helped them see a path forward. Let me show you what I mean with a story that could have ended very differently.

JOHN AND MARY'S CROSSROADS

No matter where you are in life, early career, mid-career, or staring retirement in the face, this story has something for you. Because in most cases, the real problems don't start at retirement. They start years earlier, with small decisions that quietly compound.

John and Mary (not their real names) were a hardworking, down-to-earth couple doing their best to prepare for retirement. They'd raised a family, paid the bills, and steadily added to their super over many years. Nothing flashy. Just consistent effort.

But as retirement crept closer, John started feeling that familiar knot in his stomach.

You know the one.

Will this be enough?

What if we run out?

What if we've left it too late?

Those questions play on repeat for a lot of Australians. And if you don't have a clear plan, anxiety has a habit of filling in the gaps.

That anxiety pushed John towards a decision he believed would fix everything. Eager to 'catch up', John was drawn into an online investment opportunity promising fast, impressive returns. It was mentioned by a colleague and sounded like a smart, sophisticated move. He was encouraged to leverage the family home and move a large portion of their retirement savings into a single investment, outside the usual channels.

It sounded confident. It sounded clever. It sounded like the solution he'd been waiting for.

But within months of investing the money, it was gone. Every dollar.

Decades of hard work disappeared so much faster than it had taken to build.

John was forced back into full-time work instead of the casual transition he'd planned. Retirement was no longer about *when*, but about *if*. When they first came to see me, they were exhausted, overwhelmed, and quietly terrified they'd run out of options.

John's natural instinct was to sell the home and possibly move in with family, just to free up cash to live. And honestly, I understood his thinking. Selling the house sounded like the obvious move.

But I knew that 'obvious' move would have caused another serious problem.

What almost went wrong

Under Centrelink rules, your principal home is exempt from the Age Pension assets test. But once you sell it, the cash from the sale can suddenly count as an assessable asset.

Had John and Mary sold their home, they would have gone from being eligible for government support to receiving little or nothing at all.

Imagine selling your home, thinking you've secured your future, only to discover you've accidentally cut yourself off from vital support.

The power of good advice

Instead of reactively selling in panic, we helped John and Mary downsize *strategically*:

- They kept a comfortable home.
- They freed up cash to rebuild their super.
- They retained Centrelink pension eligibility.
- And most importantly, John was finally able to retire for good.

The difference between financial devastation and a secure retirement came down to one thing: getting appropriate advice *before* making a life-altering decision.

Whether you're 25, 45, or 65, the lesson is the same. What feels like the 'logical' answer in the moment isn't always the best one when you zoom out. Every day, people make costly mistakes by following tips from well-meaning friends, overconfident workmates, or the latest guru on social media. But here's the truth: financial planning is often most valuable for people who *don't* feel wealthy enough to seek it.

Before you worry about maximising returns, you need to protect yourself from the kind of mistakes that can knock your entire game-plan off course. Avoiding disaster is always step one.

Before making any major financial decision, consider speaking with a professional. Start by asking friends or family for a referral to a financial planner they trust. Across Australia, there are many skilled planners who genuinely care about helping people get back on track.

The real cost of not seeking advice is that small mistakes can snowball into major setbacks.

When this may not be suitable:

- If you're not ready to act on advice.
- If you're unwilling to invest time or money into planning.
- If expectations of advice are unrealistic.

What could go wrong:

- Poor advice can lead to poor outcomes.
- Costs may outweigh perceived value.
- Miscommunication can lead to misunderstandings.
- Lack of implementation reduces benefits.

TACTIC 16: A smarter way to balance super and your mortgage

Level: *Intermediate to Advanced.*
Best for: *Homeowners in their late 40s and 50s with a mortgage and a decent income.*

> Before we go any further, I want to clarify that strategies involving superannuation, tax structuring, and debt reduction can have complex and long-term consequences. The following example is just general information. So please do not rely upon this without first considering your personal circumstances.

If you're in your late 40s or 50s and still chipping away at your mortgage, you've probably had this thought: *I should throw every spare dollar at the home loan and get it off my back.*

It *feels* responsible. It *sounds* smart. But what if I told you there may be an alternative approach, one that could cut your mortgage years earlier and hand less of your money to the tax office along the way?

Let me introduce you to an underrated tactic in the wealth-building playbook: using super instead of your mortgage for extra contributions.

THE BIG IDEA: USE THE TAX SYSTEM TO YOUR ADVANTAGE

Most people treat their mortgage like a moral mission, 'must pay it down no matter what'. But we're not here for moral victories. We're here for *financial wins.*[51]

Here's how this approach could work in certain scenarios.

Your income is taxed at your marginal tax rate, often 32% or higher.

Super contributions (up to your concessional cap) are taxed at just 15%.

Compared to taking the income as salary and directing it to the home loan, this can create a tax difference of around 17%, depending on your situation.

The tax break plus compounding means you could be *thousands ahead.*

Still with me? Good. Let's see an example.

James and Rose's alternative strategy

James and Rose are both 50. They bought their family home five years ago with a 30-year loan. That leaves them with 25 years to go, and an $800,000 mortgage.

Life's a little more comfortable now. Thanks to James's promotion, they have $2500 a month ($30,000 a year) in additional wages.

The question is simple: *what's the smartest way to use it?*

Option 1: Smash the mortgage

Put the full $30,000 additional wage each year straight into their home loan. This will be $20,400 once they've paid tax on it.

---

51 Disclaimer: Strategies involving superannuation should only be undertaken after speaking with a licensed adviser. Access to super is subject to specific eligibility and legislative requirements. This is general information for education purposes only and is not intended as personal financial advice.

After 15 years, the mortgage will be fully paid out as a result of consistent extra repayments.

Mortgage-free in their mid-60s – great outcome. Solid and logical, but perhaps not the most optimal solution.

Option 2: Supercharge the super[52]

Instead of paying extra to the bank, they salary sacrifice $15,000 each into their respective super funds ($30,000 total).

Because super is taxed at 15% instead of their marginal rates (32%), they save about $5100 in net tax every year, combined.

Now two things are happening at once:

- **Super grows:** Their contributions (after tax inside super) add around $25,500 each year. With 4% growth, that compounds to ~**$511,000** over 15 years.
- **Mortgage continues to shrink:** Even with only the minimum repayments each year, the loan falls to ~**$441,000.**

At age 65, under current rules, they could withdraw a lump sum from super to pay out the mortgage. So effectively:

$511,000 extra super less $441,000 loan = ~$70,000 advantage.

Now, this is a simplified projection and does not account for market volatility, legislative changes or individual circumstances. But I'm using this example to explain how this all works because the benefit doesn't come from extra cashflow today, but from keeping more of their income inside a tax-advantaged environment over time.

52 Figures assume marginal tax rate of 32% for both James and Rose. Super contributions taxed at 15%, and assumes they have available concessional contributions caps. Employer contributions count toward the concessional contributions cap. If your income is high, Div 293 may add another 15% tax to some concessional contributions. Super growth assumed at 4% p.a., compounded annually. May be higher or lower; using 4% is for illustration only. The loan interest rate remains at 5%. Actual outcomes depend on tax law, super rules, and investment performance. Super carries market risk, though conservative options can reduce this. Access to super is subject to current rules and future legislation (generally tax-free at retirement from age 60). Assumes current super legislation. The strategies and examples in this section are for educational purposes only and do not constitute personal financial advice. Always consider your own objectives, financial situation, and needs, and seek advice from a licensed financial adviser before acting.

THE BOTTOM LINE

- **Mortgage focus:** Mortgage free. No extra super.
- **Super focus:** Mortgage free, extra $70,000 in super.
- **Result:** More super available for their retirement.

Now, I know what you're thinking: 'But wait, what about the risk in super?'

Yes, good job, you are right. Super does carry investment risk. If markets wobble right before retirement, balances can take a hit. But for this portion, James and Rose could choose a conservative option to smooth out market ups and downs. The above scenario assumed fairly conservative super return of 4%.

SO WHY DOESN'T EVERYONE DO THIS?

Because super feels like a black box, and mortgages feel tangible. But just because something feels logical doesn't mean it's optimal.

This strategy works best when:

- you're over 50, or in your late 40s (so super isn't locked away too long)
- you're earning a decent income that puts you at least in the 32% marginal tax bracket (so the tax benefit is meaningful)
- you don't need access to that money until at least after age 60 (extra repayments into the mortgage may be accessible, where in super this will be locked away).

FINAL THOUGHT

Most people aim to be debt-free. But the real prize is financial freedom, and that comes from structuring things smartly, not just slogging harder.

You can consider letting your super do the heavy lifting. Stack up the tax savings. Let compounding go to work. Then wipe out your loan when you can access super.[53] But you should still know that in some scenarios, prioritising mortgage reduction may be more appropriate, particularly where flexibility, risk tolerance, or access to funds is a concern. Because this tactic sits at the intersection of super, tax, and your mortgage, consider getting a licensed financial planner and a registered tax agent in your corner before making any changes.

When this may not be suitable:

- If you need access to funds before retirement.
- If you are uncomfortable with market volatility.
- If tax advantages are minimal for your income level.
- If flexibility is a priority.

What could go wrong:

- Investment returns may underperform.
- Super rules or tax settings may change.
- Funds are locked away and inaccessible.
- Market downturns near retirement can impact outcomes.

RICH Rating

Risk ★★★★☆: Risk depends on how you invest inside super; conservative options lower the chance of permanent loss.

Income ★★★☆☆: Helps long-term wealth, but doesn't increase your cashflow today.

Capital ★★☆☆☆: Money is locked away until preservation age, so flexibility is limited.

Hassle ★★★★☆: Needs some planning around caps, but salary sacrificing can help to run it quietly in the background.

Now, let me show you how a small shift can change the entire finish line. Meet Dan.

---

53 Want to see how others are applying this? Jump into the FG Community and see real stories, ask real questions, and learn from what's working at: www.rodnia.com.au or scan the QR code:

REAL PEOPLE, REAL SUCCESS STORIES

DAN

'Hard work matters. But where you aim it matters just as much.'

Dan is an impressive fellow Aussie who has always done the right thing. He worked hard, raised a family, and served his community. Now 63, retirement is on the horizon. He can see it, feel it, almost reach out and touch it. But one thing keeps tugging at the back of his mind:

'I don't want to carry this mortgage into retirement.'

It isn't a massive debt, but for Dan, it's a reminder that he isn't quite ready to retire yet.

At first, he did what most people do: made extra repayments, chipping away at the loan bit by bit. It helped … but not fast enough.

Then he discovered a smarter way to use super to reduce his mortgage. A small shift on the surface, but one that changed the pace entirely.

Suddenly, everything moved faster. The weight started lifting. Momentum took over, and he felt confident that he could finally clear the mortgage and retire.

Today, Dan stands just a breath away from full retirement – mortgage-free, confident, and proud. Not because he worked harder, but because he worked smarter. He found a better way.

And now, that finish line is no longer in the distance. It's almost beneath his feet.

Well played, Dan.

TACTIC 17: The Decision Log – your secret weapon for better choices

Level: *Foundation to Advanced (all levels).*
Best for: *Those who want to build bulletproof decision-making muscles.*

Your life's path will mirror the quality of your decisions.

We've already talked about how your decisions shape your outcomes, financial and otherwise.

That's why I keep a tool I call the *Decision Log.*

And let me tell you, this isn't just something I 'like'. I love it. I've been jotting down the reasoning behind every big decision, especially the financial ones, for years. Not just *what* I did, but *why* I did it.

Why? Because your brain can be a sneaky little liar. Hindsight makes our memory foggy. We remember wins bigger than they were, downplay our losses, and convince ourselves we knew what we were doing all along. A Decision Log cuts through that nonsense. It keeps you honest.

And here's the kicker: it saves you from two big traps.

Trap 1: Thinking you're a genius when you just got lucky.

Trap 2: Throwing away a perfectly good strategy just because the outcome didn't pan out.

You see, sometimes a smart decision loses. And sometimes a dumb decision wins. That's why judging by results alone is a risky business.

It's like this: if you give someone great advice and they ignore it, then stumble into a win by accident, was your advice bad? Of course not!

Or picture this: you fling a basketball backwards from half-court and it happens to swish in. Does that make you Michael Jordan? Obviously not. It makes you lucky. Once. But good luck pulling that trick twice.

The real truth is simple: good decisions win most of the time, even if they occasionally lose.

Bad decisions might pay off once, but eventually, the consequences come knocking.

That's why I think people who get lucky with bad investment decisions are worse off than those who make solid calls and lose. The 'lucky' ones start thinking they've cracked the code and double down until the whole thing blows up. But the others learn, adjust, and come back smarter.

Think of it like roulette. The wheel has 37 slots: 18 red, 18 black, 1 green zero. Bet on red and you've got a 48.65% chance of winning, close to 50/50, but not quite. That lone zero is the house edge. You might win a few spins, but play long enough and the house wins.

That's how bad decisions work. They might pay off once, but over time they'll sink you. But good decisions, even when they lose now and then, put you in the winner's circle over the long haul.

Someone who gets lucky with a bad decision is in more danger than someone who loses with a good one.

And that's why tracking your reasoning matters more than tracking your results. With a *Decision Log*, you're not just guessing six months later; you're reviewing. You can see your thought process clearly, and you learn from it. Every entry sharpens your thinking, improves your judgement, and compounds your decision-making skill, just like how interest compounds money.

The longer you use it, the stronger your 'decision muscle' gets. And when tough calls come up, and they always do, you'll be ready.

When this may not be suitable:

- If you are biased towards a specific outcome when logging your decisions.

What could go wrong:

- Over-analysis can delay action.
- Misinterpreting past decisions can reinforce poor habits.

DECISION LOG HYPOTHETICAL

1. Decision summary

What are you deciding?[54] *Whether to invest a lump sum into a diversified portfolio of shares now, or phase it into the market over time.*

Date: *13 March 2022.*

2. Strategic goal

Grow long-term wealth with discipline, while managing the emotional and timing risks of entering the market.

3. The options

Option A: *Invest the full lump sum immediately.*

Upside: *Maximises time in the market and potential for long-term compounding; captures early gains if markets recover quickly.*

Downside: *Risk of investing just before a market decline. Potential for short-term losses. No more capital available for averaging down, if the prices continue to decline.*

Option B: *Phase the investment over time (for example, monthly contributions).*

Upside: *Reduces timing risk and smooths entry into the market.*

Downside: *May miss out on gains if markets rise quickly; slower exposure to compounding.*

4. Core reasoning

Markets are unpredictable in the short term, but tend to grow over time. Investing sooner increases time in the market, which supports long-term compounding. While short-term volatility is possible, the decision is based on a long-term investment horizon rather than attempting to time market movements. A disciplined approach reduces the risk of emotional decision-making.

---

54 Disclaimer: This is a hypothetical example for education only, not personal financial advice. Borrowing to invest increases both potential gains and losses. Always consider your own circumstances and seek advice before acting.

5. RICH Rating

Risk ★★★☆☆
Income ★★★☆☆
Capital ★★★★☆
Hassle ★★★★☆

6. Review date

Review in 6 to 12 months.

NOW IT'S YOUR TURN

Use the following worksheet to log your next decision. Don't worry about getting it perfect. The goal is to think clearly, not to predict the future.[55]

Once you've completed your 30-day Freedom Kickstart or made a few logged decisions, keep the momentum going by starting the Freedom Ritual: act, reflect, share. It's how you'll learn faster, stay accountable, and help others rise with you.

55 You can download your Decision Log template at www.rodnia.com.au or scan the QR code below and start your first entry today.

DECISION LOG WORKSHEET

Before you judge your success, judge your process.

Use this worksheet to log your reasoning behind any major decision. The goal is to improve the quality of your thinking over time.

1. Decision summary

What are you deciding? e.g., whether to buy an investment property using the equity release tactic, or wait another 2 years to save a 20% deposit.

____

____

____

Date: ______________

2. Strategic goal

What are you ultimately trying to achieve with this decision? e.g., get into the property market early to avoid being priced out.

3. The options

What are your main options?

Briefly note the key trade-offs for each.

Option A: ______________________________

Upside: ______________________________

Downside: ______________________________

Option B: ______________________________

Upside: ______________________________

Downside: ______________________________

4. Core reasoning

Why are you making this choice based on what you know today? What facts or strategic logic are guiding you?

____

____

____

____

____

____

5. RICH Rating (at the time of decision)

Risk ☆☆☆☆☆
Income ☆☆☆☆☆
Capital ☆☆☆☆☆
Hassle ☆☆☆☆☆

This rating reflects how the decision was expected to behave when made, not how it turned out.

Rate each category based on how predictable, income-generating, capital-efficient, and hassle-free you expect it to be. Don't overthink this, just score it based on what you know now.

6. Review date

Review this decision in 6 to 12 months and ask: was the thinking sound, even if the result didn't go as planned? If the results were positive, was it because of luck, or sound reasoning?

Date: ____________________

Remember: A good decision is one made with clarity, not certainty. You can't control the outcome, but you can always control your thinking.

CHAPTER 25
BEYOND THE HYPE

TACTIC 18: Your Freedom Ritual

MUST READ

Level: *Foundation to Advanced (all levels).*
Best for: *Anyone wanting to clock off the wage cage.*

Tactics give you power. Rituals give you momentum.

Now that you've got a full playbook of strategy and tactics, it's time to make them stick.

This is where the Freedom Ritual comes in, your weekly five-minute ritual that locks in learning, builds habits, and fuels real, lasting change.

On the next few pages, you'll find a 10-Week Freedom Ritual Tracker. Use it to:

- recalculate your Freedom Score
- log one financial decision per week
- share wins, lessons, or insights in the FG Community.

This is your rhythm for progress. Your anchor in motion.

> Science shows that when you pair a habit with a consistent cue, like playing the same music, lighting a candle, or sitting in the same spot, you strengthen the neural pathways that make that habit automatic. That's why I recommend creating a Freedom Ritual: pour a drink, light something up, hit play on the same playlist. Over time, your brain learns: ah, it's ritual time.

This is how you earn your freedom, one ritual at a time.[56]

Track your weekly progress below.

When this may not be suitable:

- If you're unwilling to commit to regular reflection.

What could go wrong:

- Inconsistency reduces impact.
- Early slow progress may reduce motivation.

Week	Date	Freedom Score	Key decision logged	Insight or win shared in FG Community? (Yes/No)	Progress notes
1					
2					
3					
4					
5					
6					
7					
8					
9					
10					

Use the tags #FreedomRitual1, #FreedomRitual2, etc. when posting in the FG Community to track your journey.

56 Want a downloadable version? Visit www.rodnia.com.au.

TACTIC 19: Day trading – why even the smartest monkey can lose

Level: *Foundation to Advanced (all levels).*
Best for: *Those who can spot Jesus in toast but not risk in charts!*

This one is more about what *not* to do, an *anti-tactic*, if you will.

Alright, now it's time for me to have a bit of a vent!

This one is personal. Because every time I see someone on YouTube with a chart, some jargon, and a '100% win rate strategy', I want to throw my coffee at the screen.

Technical trading, reading charts, patterns, and trends to make short-term trades, sounds smart. It's filled with confidence, data, and clever names like 'Golden Cross' and 'Relative Strength Index'. It makes traders feel like they have cracked some market code.

And hey, on paper, it all looks great. They've back-tested their system. The numbers look tidy. They've noticed trends: *when the S&P 500 goes up, gold often goes down; every September for the past three years, the market has dropped during reporting season, around 10% each time*. They've even nailed a decent 'strike rate'.

It feels predictive. It feels clever.

But here's the catch: *our brains love patterns, even when they're not real.*

JESUS IN TOAST

Here's one you will enjoy! In the '70s, a woman in Florida saw the face of Jesus ... in a burnt piece of toast.

The toast then went viral (in pre-Internet terms), and years later, it sold for $28,000! Imagine that!

This is a true story, just Google 'Jesus in toast' and you can find it for yourself.

Funny? Absolutely. But it tells us something powerful: the human brain is a pattern-seeking machine. It finds shapes in clouds, voices in white noise, and signals in market noise.

Traders do the same thing with share charts. They spot patterns that 'must mean something', when in reality, they're just randomness in a bunch of charts.

MEET THE SMARTEST MONKEY ON WALL STREET

I love this piece that I read in the book the *Art of Thinking Clearly*. Let's see if you agree.

I want you to picture 10,000 monkeys sitting at share trading terminals. Each one has two buttons in front of them, and they press the 'buy' or 'sell' button completely at random, which would place the corresponding trade. After every round, those monkeys who lost money are eliminated. Eventually, only one monkey is left.

That monkey made all the right moves, survived the gauntlet, and is hailed as a genius!

He now gets a book deal, a podcast, and a YouTube channel.

But did he win because he's smart? Of course not. He just happened to be the random one that got lucky.

This is survivorship bias in action, where we celebrate the winner and ignore the thousands of failures behind them. In trading, luck can *look* like skill, until it doesn't.

A REALITY CHECK FROM THE FRONTLINES

As a financial planner, I regularly sit down with professional analysts and fund managers, people whose *job* is to beat the market. They're paid very well to find trading opportunities before anyone else does.

They're glued to quad-screen terminals 24/7, have access to massive institutional research, and teams of economists and quants behind them. We're talking tens of millions in research budgets and entire departments dedicated to making this stuff work.

But here's the kicker: even they struggle to consistently make it work.

So, do you really think a bloke in his kitchen in his trackies, staring at candlestick charts on his MacBook, is going to beat these guys at their own game? Remember, this is a zero-sum game; for him to win, someone has to lose. He's not just trading against 'the market', he's going against the pros.

JARGON DOES NOT EQUAL GENIUS

Now allow me to drive my point (rant!) home.

Here's the thing: the more complex something sounds, the more legit it feels. In fact, that's exactly how scammers reel people in.

'Resistance levels', 'momentum oscillators', 'technical divergence' – they sound scientific and imply expertise. But most of the time, they're just fancy ways of saying, 'I think the line might go up'.

Still sceptical?

Try this: 'Our back-tested CQI model leverages Trans-Dynamic Theta Synchronisation and Theta-to-Omega Conversion Rates to predict market shifts with an 82% strike rate.'

Sounds impressive, right?

Yet, it's total nonsense. I've made up almost every word. Wrap gibberish in jargon, and suddenly people think: *geez, this guy must be onto something.*

THE HIDDEN COSTS OF DAY TRADING

I'm not even done yet! Let's say you *do* manage to make a profit. Don't celebrate just yet:

- Brokerage fees eat into your returns.
- Capital gains tax slices another chunk.
- You miss out on franking credits due to the 45-day rule.
- You lose compound growth by constantly moving in and out.

And as you know by now, if your share price drops 50%, you don't just need a 50% bounce to recover. You need a 100% gain just to break even. That's harder than most traders realise.[57]

THE WORST THING THAT CAN HAPPEN IS EARLY SUCCESS IN TRADING

Here's the cruel twist: if you fail at trading early, you're lucky. You learn. You quit. You live to invest another day.

---

57 Disclaimer: This example is intended to highlight behavioural risks and should not be taken as a recommendation for or against any investment style.

But if you *succeed* early? That's dangerous. Because now you think you're brilliant. You double down. You start taking bigger swings. And eventually, you blow up.

Success in the wrong game teaches all the wrong lessons.

CHOOSE THE PATH THAT WORKS

This isn't just about day trading. It's about being honest with yourself.

- Are you making decisions based on real principles?
- Or are you hoping your dart lands near the bullseye?

You can follow the flash, or follow the framework.

One dazzles.

One delivers.

When this may not be suitable:

- If you are a professional-level technical analyst with sufficient resources, time or expertise.

What could go wrong:

- Rapid and permanent capital loss.
- High costs and taxes eroding returns.
- Emotional decision-making leading to poor outcomes.
- Overconfidence after early wins leading to bigger losses.

RICH Rating

Risk ★☆☆☆☆: For most people, this is one of the fastest ways to permanently damage capital.

Income ★☆☆☆☆: There's no steady income here, just wins, losses, and a lot of uncertainty.

Capital: ★★☆☆☆: Your money is liquid, but frequent trading and costs quietly eat away at it.

Hassle: ★☆☆☆☆: It demands constant attention, emotional energy, and screen time.

DO One-Step Action

Log one decision.

Open your Decision Log, choose one meaningful decision from your week, and record your reasoning. This one habit can transform how you grow.

PART III RECAP

TURN SMART MOVES INTO REAL PROGRESS

If you've reached this point and feel like your head is full, that's a good sign. It means you've learned enough to start. You don't need more information; you need motion.

Tactics only matter if they move your *Freedom Score* forward. Choose the ones that increase income, reduce expenses, or accelerate the gap between them.

KEY TAKEAWAYS

- **Property tactics:** Learn how to buy your first home with little or no deposit, sidestep auction traps, borrow against equity smartly, and turn negatively geared properties into cashflow winners. Real estate becomes a tool for leverage, not just ownership.
- **Share market tactics:** Master DCA, investing during crashes, and Dividend Harvesting. Understand when to stay consistent and when to strike. You now know how to ride market waves instead of drowning in them.
- **Business tactics:** Explore hassle-free side hustles, launch lean startups, or buy established businesses to skip the painful early grind. Business ownership isn't just about making money, it's about taking control.
- **Clever moves for maximum impact:** Use your super strategically to pay off your mortgage, keep a Decision Log to sharpen your thinking, and create a Freedom Ritual. Clarity is your most powerful tool.

UP NEXT: GEAR UP

You've now explored the real-world tactics that separate action-takers from armchair experts. But tools matter too, and in the next part, we're opening the toolbox.

From here, your tactics come alive, revealing the options, platforms, and structures that amplify results, safeguard progress, and keep your financial life running smoother than ever.

All of the tactics we just covered will now come to life.

If the *DO* part is your workout movements, then *GEAR UP* is your gym bag, packed with the right gear for each exercise.

Real progress begins when you gear up.

PART IV
GEAR UP

Your Wealth Toolkit

> **A note from the legal department**
>
> This part contains general information and educational concepts only. It does not take into account your personal objectives, financial situation, or needs. Before making any financial decisions or investing in any products mentioned in this book, consider seeking personal financial advice from an Australian Financial Services (AFS) licensee or authorised representative. Any reference to third-party research tools, platforms, ratings, data providers, or analyst reports is for educational illustration only. These references are not endorsements, recommendations, or financial product advice. Third-party research contains opinions that may change and may be wrong. Any tax outcomes depend on current law, product rules and your personal circumstances.

WHAT TO SET UP SO IT BECOMES AUTOMATIC

Welcome to the toolkit section of the Freedom Framework, where plans become action through the use of real-world tools. Everything in this part directly supports the same three engines you saw in the Freedom Map and explored in the DO section:

- Property
- Shares
- Business

If you've printed your Freedom Map™, keep it nearby.

As you move through GEAR UP, you'll start to see exactly where each tool plugs into your journey.

Similar to the DO part, this section is not about mastering every tool. It's about knowing what exists, when to use it, and where to go deeper when the time is right.

Think of this section as optional upgrades.

Helpful, not mandatory.

Useful, not urgent.

This is where the gears of the *RICH Trifecta* start to turn. The right tools don't just support your assets individually, they enable

Synergification, helping your property, shares, and business tactics fire in unison.

And if you're not sure where to start, don't worry, the 30-Day Kickstart at the end of the book will later walk you through this step by step and help you choose your moves.

KICK-OFF: WHAT YOU'RE ABOUT TO DISCOVER

This part is your boots-on-the-ground guide to the tools, platforms, and products that help turn financial strategy into real-world action.

Here's what you'll walk away with:

- **How to evaluate property quality**, houses vs townhouses vs units, and why land is valuable.
- **How to avoid traps** like flood zones, crime pockets, and overpriced 'shiny new' homes.
- **How to use valuation tools** like PropertyValue.com.au
- **The manual for active and passive share investing** and how to combine both.
- **How to use investment and research platforms**, without needing a finance degree.
- **Side hustles and business ideas** that actually work.
- **Insurance, super switches, investment bonds, and more** to protect your wealth from life's curveballs.
- **The RICH Rating:** a simple way to *score and compare* any opportunity, so you can instantly tell what deserves your time, energy, and capital.

These are the tools you can start using in your quest to freedom.

Time to *GEAR UP*.

WHAT YOU'RE REALLY INVESTING IN

Back in the 1830s, a Belgian mathematician named Adolphe Quetelet dropped a big idea: individual behaviour is unpredictable, but when you look at large groups, clear patterns start to emerge. That principle still runs the world today.

Think about Facebook, Google, Amazon. They don't market to *you*. They market to the group you belong to: new parents, gym fanatics, and makeup enthusiasts. You're not being targeted as *you*. You're being targeted as one of *them*.

And here's the kicker: it works. Because while individuals are unpredictable, the masses are surprisingly consistent.

Now, let's bring it back to investing. Industries are the crowd. Companies are the individuals.

DON'T CONFUSE THE TWO

This is where most people slip up. They assume: 'If the industry is hot, every company in it must be a winner.' Nope. That's like assuming every singer in the '80s could become Michael Jackson.

Take electric vehicles as an example. The future is electric, no doubt. But does that mean Tesla wins forever? Not necessarily. Twenty years ago, Tesla wasn't even a thing. Twenty years from now? It might not be *the* thing.

A booming industry doesn't mean booming returns for every business in it.

History proves it over and over:

- Nokia owned mobile phones … until Apple showed up.
- Blockbuster owned Friday nights … until Netflix mailed a DVD.
- Kodak literally invented digital cameras … and then got destroyed by them.

Trends lift industries. But execution makes or breaks companies.

SAME RULE FOR PROPERTY

The same applies to property. Just because the national market is hot doesn't mean every suburb, or even every street, will boom. Micro factors like school zones, flood maps, or oversupply can make or break performance.

As we step into the toolkit zone, here's the mindset I want you to lock in: you're not investing in ideas. Not even industries. You're investing in *execution*.

Do the research. Ignore the hype. Don't assume yesterday's winner will also be tomorrow's winner.

That's your lens now: hype last, homework first.

By the end of this part, you'll know which tools to use before you spend a dollar, and which ones protect you after you do.

Let's get to work.

CHAPTER 26
PROPERTY POWER TOOLS: SPOT WINNERS, DODGE DUDS

The point of these tools is not to make you a property nerd. It's to help you choose assets that are more likely to improve your Freedom Score.

Okay, now that we've made it this far, let's get one thing straight about property. I haven't covered commercial property in this book at all. However, commercial property can work well if you know what you are doing. For our purposes though, we will focus on residential directly held property.

And remember, these tools aren't just for navigating real estate. When paired with your share and business strategies, they unlock true *Synergification*.

PROPERTY VALUE LADDER: WHAT YOU'RE REALLY BUYING

One of the first questions people ask when stepping into the property market is: 'What type of property should I buy – house, townhouse, or unit?'

It's a great question. And while most people instinctively lean towards the kind of dwelling they've lived in themselves (which makes sense from a lifestyle perspective), we need to step back and remember something critical: this isn't a lifestyle decision, it's one of the biggest investment decisions of your life.

Whether it's your first home or an investment property, you need to know the hierarchy of residential property types from an investment point of view. Here's how it stacks up.

1. Freehold house (detached dwelling)

Many long-term investors consider this the gold standard. A free-standing house on its own block of land (not part of a strata or body corporate) gives you the potential for greater long-term value for one simple reason: **historically, land appreciates. Buildings depreciate.**

When you buy a house, you want a good chunk of it to be the land value relative to the total purchase price. Land is a *limited resource*, and as the population grows and urban areas expand, the value of land tends to rise, significantly over time.

So, even if a house is in a less 'prestigious' or central location, it often has stronger long-term growth characteristics than a shiny new apartment in the inner city.

An entry-level house in a prime suburb may be a wiser choice than a 'nicer' house at the top end of a second-rate suburb.

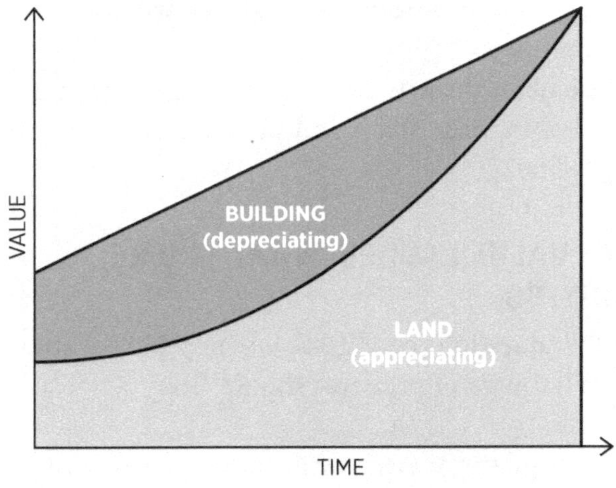

2. Townhouse

Townhouses are the next best option. They usually come with some land, like a courtyard or small yard, but it's shared under a common title (often strata), so you don't get full control or benefit.

The big catch? Body corporate fees.

These ongoing costs can eat into rental yield or increase your cost of living, often cancelling out the perceived advantages. Add in the rules, restrictions, and potential disputes with other owners, and townhouses come with extra hassle that freehold homes don't.

Still, if you're priced out of standalone houses, a well-located townhouse can be a solid investment.

3. Unit or apartment

You own little to no land, but you do get the privilege of paying hefty body corporate fees (sometimes $700-plus a month), just for the right to share walls and ask permission before hanging a picture.

Units, especially in high-rise blocks, sit at the bottom of the property hierarchy for a few reasons:

- minimal land ownership
- shared facilities and infrastructure
- steep ongoing fees, particularly with lifts, pools, or gyms.

That said, units aren't 'bad'. If it's all you can afford, and it's in a high-demand area, a unit can still be a useful stepping stone. It's just handy to know where it sits in the investment food chain.

BOTTOM LINE

A house means full control of the land.

A townhouse means shared land and shared decisions.

A unit means only a fraction of the land – with higher costs and limited upside.

Buildings age, break, and need repairs. Land doesn't. That's why property success is less about shiny finishes and more about how much earth you actually own. Of course, every market cycle and location is different, and there are exceptions to every rule. So, as always make sure you do your research first.

SUPPLY & DEMAND 101: WHY SOME PROPERTIES SKYROCKET AND OTHERS DON'T

In recent years, even units and apartments have experienced strong price growth across Australia. This surge has largely been driven by a national housing shortage, more people want to buy homes than there are properties available. And when demand outstrips supply, prices inevitably rise. It's basic economics. This has led many people to believe that units are great investments for capital appreciation.

But here's the thing: markets move in cycles. At some point, this dynamic will shift. Prices don't rise forever. And just because you haven't personally experienced the downward cycle in your lifetime yet, doesn't mean it doesn't exist. History tells us it does, and will again.

Now, here's where the type of property you invest in becomes critically important. Let's ask a simple question:

Which type of dwelling can be built the fastest, in the largest numbers, and in the smallest space?

You guessed it, units.

So, when governments and developers respond to housing shortages, their solution is often to build more units, not houses. And when the market gets flooded with supply? Prices drop. This is why units are much more vulnerable to oversupply and price corrections.

Contrast that with freestanding homes. These properties require land, more materials, and more labour. There's only so much usable land, and the process of building detached homes is slower and more expensive. That's why the supply of these homes is naturally restricted, even as demand continues to grow.

This supply constraint makes freehold properties more resilient during market downturns. In fact, it's entirely possible that when unit prices start to fall from oversupply, freestanding home values may continue to rise, as investors and homeowners shift their attention to the more stable, scarce asset.

Between 1992 and 2022, across the combined capital cities, house values went up 453%, compared to 307% for units.[58]

So, while units may currently be riding the wave of rising property prices, history suggests that freehold homes may be better positioned for long-term performance and defensiveness. But of course these outcomes based on general observations can vary significantly depending on location, timing, supply conditions and individual circumstances.

---

58 Sourced from CoreLogic Australia: Property Pulse: The long game – 30 years of housing values (Aug. 2022).

> Understanding how supply and demand shape property cycles helps explain why freestanding homes often sit at the top of the residential property hierarchy. Historically, they've tended to show greater resilience than other dwelling types, something to keep in mind when weighing options, depending on your goals and circumstances.

VALUATION TOOLS: KNOW BEFORE YOU GO

Before you go to a house inspection, there's one critical move that separates savvy investors from emotional buyers: getting the numbers.

The moment you walk into a property, your brain becomes vulnerable to all sorts of mental shortcuts. Remember all sneaky mental shortcut we covered in the THINK part? This is where your judgment gets swayed by the asking price, the agent's pitch, or the smell of fresh cookies at the open home.

Why it matters

Real estate agents are professionals. Their job is to sell, and they're trained to shape your perception of value. If you show up unprepared, you're using their narrative as your baseline, not independent data. That's how people end up overpaying ... or buying the wrong property altogether.

One way some buyers approach this is to use platforms such as PropertyValue.com.au (powered by Cotality), or other reputable data providers.[59]

> **Bonus:** If you're purchasing an investment property, some research costs like the subscription could be considered a tax-deductible expense (depending on the circumstances). Always confirm deductibility with your accountant or tax adviser.

---

59 Disclaimer: The information in this section is general in nature and does not take into account your personal objectives, financial situation, or needs. It is educational only and not a recommendation to buy, sell, or hold any property or financial product. Always do your own research and seek professional advice before making financial decisions.

What you can do

Before the inspection:

- Check the estimated property value and confidence level.
- Review recent comparable sales in the area.
- Look up rental yield estimates and past rental history.
- See the ownership and sales history for the property.

Research the suburb:

- Median prices, capital growth rates, and time on market.
- Rental yields for houses vs units.
- Resident income levels and demographics.
- Owner-occupier vs investor breakdown.
- School catchments and more.

Step-by-step: how to use valuation tools

- **Search the address** – Pull up the full property profile.
- **Review estimated value** – Check the valuation range and how confident PropertyValue is in that estimate.
- **Dig into the sales history** – See how often the property has changed hands and when.
- **Check suburb performance** – View growth, yield, and vendor discounting trends.
- **Compare suburbs** – Stack your shortlisted suburbs side-by-side.
- **Print the report** – Take it to the inspection. It's your data-driven defence against sales tactics.

Quick word of warning

These are automated valuations. They're algorithm-based, not eyeball-based. Treat them as guidance, not gospel. If the home is heavily renovated, unique, or distressed, factor that in.

This isn't about becoming a data nerd, it's about walking into the game with a playbook. You're not just buying a property. You're buying *well.*

> "You make your money when you buy property, not when you sell.

How to spot overpricing

Say PropertyValue.com.au estimates a home at $640,000 … but the agent says the seller wants $750,000. Ask *why*.

If they explain it's due to renovations or high demand, verify that with real comparisons in the area. If they can't justify it, it's likely fluff. Investigate further, reconsider the opportunity, or just walk away.

Same goes for rental yields. The platform may use the estimated value in its yield calculation, which can skew results. Instead, run this yourself:

Rental yield (%) = (Weekly rent × 52) ÷ Purchase price × 100

Even if you're buying a home to live in, it could become an investment one day. A strong yield means it'll work for you, not against you.

Cross-check with realestate.com.au

Want another layer of truth? Jump on RealEstate.com.au or its app:

- Filter for *sold* properties in the same suburb.
- Match filters to the property you're evaluating (beds, baths, land size).
- Compare actual sale prices to the one you're looking at.

Final word

Smart investing starts with objective thinking, and that begins *before* the open home. Use tools like PropertyValue.com.au and RealEstate.com.au to walk in with clarity, not emotion. Because once you're in love with a place, it's harder to walk away.

Data keeps your decisions rational. And rational decisions build wealth.

And remember, the art of negotiating a good deal, is in the willingness to walk away.

BUYING TO LIVE IN? HERE'S WHAT MATTERS

Even if you're purchasing your primary residence, these principles still apply. Ideally, you want your home to grow in value too, even if it's not purely an investment.

If a house is out of reach in the area you want to live in, consider moving a little further out where you can afford a freestanding property. You'll likely get better long-term growth, more privacy, and less hassle.

BUYING TO INVEST? HERE'S WHAT CHANGES

The principles we've covered matter even more if you're buying an investment property. Because you're not living in the property, you can make decisions purely based on the numbers, not emotion. That means:

- buying in suburbs with growth potential
- prioritising land over building
- minimising overheads like body corporate fees
- looking for good yields and future development potential.

In many cases, a modest house in an up-and-coming suburb will outperform a flashy apartment in a saturated market.

FLOOD ZONES: THE EXPENSIVE SURPRISE YOU CAN AVOID

Buying in a flood zone without checking the maps is like sunbaking without sunscreen – feels fine at first, but the pain shows up later, and it stings! Always check the flood maps before you buy. Seriously, there are two big reasons why this step is non-negotiable.

- **The obvious issue – damage:** A flood can cause catastrophic damage to your property. Even if it doesn't reach the floorboards, water damage to the foundations, walls, electrical systems, and finishes can cost tens (if not hundreds) of thousands to repair. Worse still, some damage may not be covered by standard insurance policies if you're in a flood-prone zone.
- **The hidden issue – insurance costs:** Even if your property never floods, if it's *classified* as high-risk, insurers will price your premiums accordingly. You may not discover this until after signing the contract, when you go to arrange building insurance and are quoted an annual premium that's through the roof,

or worse, told that it's uninsurable. Some buyers only realise after the fact that they're paying three to four times the normal premium for a flood risk area.

How to check flood risk

Flood maps are published by local councils and state governments, and most are freely available online. You can usually search by suburb or even by specific address.

For example: if you're buying in **Cleveland, QLD**, you can check the Redland City Council's Flood Information Portal. This interactive map allows you to:

- search by address
- view the predicted flood extents for different storm scenarios (such as 1-in-100-year events)
- check overlays for creek, overland flow, and tidal surge zones.

> **Expert tip:** Before signing the contract, get an insurance quote for the property. An inflated premium, say $6,000 on a $1M house, can be a red flag that may warrant further investigation. Premiums are the insurer's way of pricing risk, and if they're high, there's usually a reason you won't spot on a walk-through, like flood risk.

CRIME RATES, COMMUTES, AND THE CASE FOR CHECKING EVERYTHING

Safety comes first, for you and your investment.

When it comes to choosing the right investment property, location is everything. But beyond proximity to schools, transport, and shops, one of the most overlooked (yet crucial) factors is the crime rate in the area. Don't just fall in love with the house, get to know the neighbours. If the local crime map lights up like a Christmas tree, you might want to keep shopping.

A high-crime neighbourhood doesn't just make tenants feel unsafe, it can directly impact your rental returns, property value, and your own peace of mind. Tenants in these areas are more likely to move frequently, vacancy rates are higher, insurance premiums can spike, and resale down the track may become more difficult.

How to check crime stats in your state or territory

Safety matters, for you, your tenants, and your long-term returns. Fortunately, most Australian states and territories provide free, publicly available crime maps or statistics online. These tools help you move beyond 'gut feel' and base your decisions on hard data.

Here's where you can find them:

- **Queensland** – Queensland Police Crime Map: search by suburb, filter crime types, and view interactive heat maps and trends.
- **New South Wales** – NSW Bureau of Crime Statistics and Research (BOCSAR): detailed crime trends, suburb breakdowns, and customisable graphs.
- **Victoria** – Crime Statistics Agency: access reports by suburb, explore trend dashboards, and download data.
- **South Australia** – SA Police Crime Mapper: search by suburb and crime type with clear visual mapping.
- **Western Australia** – WA Police Crime Statistics: view data by local government area or category, with downloadable reports.
- **Tasmania** – Tasmania Police (Our Performance – Crime Stats): monthly and annual offence reports by category.
- **Australian Capital Territory** – ACT Policing Crime Statistics: suburb-level crime data, updated regularly.
- **Northern Territory** – NT Police Crime Statistics: offence summaries by district and year.

What you might find:

- moderate levels of break-and-enter offences around rental-heavy pockets.
- low rates of violent crime in residential zones.
- more activity around public transport hubs and commercial areas.

This helps you compare similar suburbs and make better-informed decisions based on actual data, not just assumptions.

Why it matters

- **Safety drives demand:** Renters (especially families and professionals) prefer safe neighbourhoods.
- **Resale value:** Safer areas historically perform better in capital growth.
- **Insurance premiums:** Some insurers charge more in high-crime suburbs.
- **Tenant turnover:** Higher in unsafe areas, leading to increased management costs.

> **Expert tip:** Visit the area at different times of day, what feels peaceful at 10 am can look very different after dark. Spend time at the local shopping centre to get a feel for the demographics, then pair your impressions with crime stats. Compare those stats to a suburb you know well to put them in context.

DEVELOPMENT FORECASTS: WHAT'S COMING TO THE NEIGHBOURHOOD?

What's coming next for your area can make or break your investment. When choosing an investment property, you're not just buying the land and structure, you're buying into the future of the surrounding area. That future is often written in development applications (DAs) and infrastructure projects, and ignoring them could cost you.

Why it matters

A new train station or shopping centre nearby could boost values and rental demand. A 20-storey apartment complex next door could block views and flood the market with supply. A proposed motorway extension might increase accessibility, or bring unwanted noise.

Understanding the development pipeline gives you a huge edge in making informed investment decisions. It's like reading tomorrow's news today.

How to find out what's coming

1. **Use local council websites.** Every local council in Australia publishes DAs online. You can search by suburb, street, or even specific lots.

   Example: Brisbane City Council

   - Go to developmenti.brisbane.qld.gov.au.
   - Search by suburb or address.
   - View applications for dwellings, high-rise proposals, rezoning, commercial builds, and more.

   Expert tip: Look at approved, pending, and recently completed applications to get a full picture.

2. **State Government infrastructure plans:** Major infrastructure like hospitals, highways, or rail links are often part of long-term state or federal plans.

   Example: Queensland Government

   - Visit www.qld.gov.au and search for 'Infrastructure Projects' or go to your local State Development, Infrastructure, Local Government and Planning portal.
   - Review major initiatives in housing, transport, and utilities.

3. **Talk to real estate agents and property managers:** Local agents often have the inside scoop on what's happening in the area, especially unlisted or soon-to-be-announced developments. Just make sure to verify their claims independently.

   What to watch for: positive developments

   - New schools, hospitals, or universities.
   - Shopping centres or lifestyle precincts.
   - Major transport hubs or upgrades.
   - Rezoning for low or medium density housing (good for growth).

   What to watch for: red flags

   - High-density unit developments next door.
   - Infrastructure that causes noise or congestion (such as motorways, industrial parks).
   - Overdevelopment that leads to oversupply.

Bottom line

The value of your property isn't just about what exists today, it's about what's coming. A little research can mean the difference between buying into a dead-end street or the next hotspot.

THE GOLDEN RULE: LOCATION STILL REIGNS SUPREME

When it comes to real estate, one golden rule has stood the test of time: *location, location, location*. You've probably heard this a thousand times, and for good reason. The location of a property has more impact on its performance than just about any other factor. A great location can turn an average property into a high-performing asset, while a poor location can make even the most beautiful home a dud investment.

So how do you assess a *great* location?

Let's break it down.

Shops and amenities

People want convenience. Think about it, when you're choosing where to live, how nice is it to be close to a good café, a shopping centre, or even a decent takeaway joint? Properties located within walking distance or a short drive to grocery stores, gyms, pharmacies, and lifestyle centres tend to attract higher demand from both renters and buyers.

From an investment point of view, this translates into two big wins:

- lower vacancy rates for rentals
- stronger resale value in the future.

Schools

Even if you don't have kids, buying in a good school catchment is an incredibly smart move. Properties located within highly regarded public school zones are often more expensive and more in demand. Parents will go to great lengths, including paying a premium or even renting in an area, just so their children can attend a better school.

> **Expert tip:** Look up the school catchment maps for the area you're interested in. In many cases, you'll find that the value of two similar properties on the same street can be vastly different if they fall on opposite sides of a school boundary line.

Public transport

Properties with easy access to public transport, especially train stations and major bus routes, are more desirable. People want to cut down on commute times, fuel costs, and general traffic headaches. The closer your property is to convenient transport options, the broader your tenant pool and the more resilient your investment becomes.

Hospitals and medical facilities

Locations near hospitals, health clinics, and aged care facilities are ideal for long-term demand. They're particularly attractive to health-care workers, retirees, and families with older relatives. While these may not be as trendy as cafés and restaurants, they offer something even more valuable: stability.

How to assess a location

When evaluating a property for investment, here's a quick checklist:

- Is it within one to two kilometres of shops or supermarkets?
- Does it fall within a desirable school catchment zone?
- Is there a train station or bus stop nearby?
- Are there medical centres or hospitals in reasonable proximity?
- Is the area known for parks, green spaces, or recreational amenities?
- Does the suburb have a low crime rate and good community facilities?

Invest where people want to live, and where they'll want to keep living. That's how you build wealth that stands the test of time.

> **Expert tip:** Once you sign the contract, you're legally responsible for the property, even before settlement. If fire, storm damage, or accidents occur in that period, the cost

could fall on you. Protect your investment: take out building insurance the moment the contract is signed, not on settlement day.

DON'T BE BLINDED BY BLING: HOW TO ASSESS A BUILDING'S TRUE CONDITION

As you know by now, the longer you own the property, the more valuable the land becomes, but the building on top slowly loses value over time. This is why, from an investment perspective, a less-than-perfect house on a bigger block is often a far better buy than a stunning, brand-new build on a tiny parcel of land. Similarly, if you're choosing between a prime location with an average house or a pristine home in an inferior location, try to favour location. As the old saying goes, *you can fix the house, but you can't move the land.*

The sweet spot: 10 to 15 years old

When it comes to the actual structure, I think the ideal age of a building to purchase is often around 10 to 15 years old. Why? Because the previous owner has already worn the brunt of the depreciation, especially the accelerated depreciation that occurs in the early years, but the building is still in excellent condition, assuming regular maintenance.

Think of it like buying a car. The moment you drive a new car off the lot, it drops in value, by as much as 30% in the first three years. Most savvy car buyers aim for a vehicle that's two to four years old because the depreciation curve flattens after that. The same logic applies to real estate.

Buying a relatively new but not brand-new property gives you:

- a modern build with good materials and design
- reduced risk of major repairs in the near term
- a lower purchase price due to reduced depreciation
- potentially better tax deductions if it's an investment (due to remaining building depreciation available under ATO rules).

Avoid the 'shiny new' trap

Brand-new properties might look and feel appealing, especially when marketed with glossy brochures and fancy appliances. But from an investment standpoint, they often come at a premium. And that premium disappears as soon as the property is no longer 'new'. Not to mention that many new developments, especially high-rise apartments or house-and-land packages in fringe areas, may come with hidden issues like oversupply, inflated developer margins, and subpar construction.

> **Expert tip:** If you're buying an older home (20-plus years), always factor in the potential renovation or maintenance costs. These can be significant, and if not accounted for, may erode your expected return.

WAYS TO ADD VALUE WITHOUT OVERSPENDING

One of the smartest ways to increase your return on investment is by adding value to a property you already own. Whether you're preparing to sell, boost rental income, or simply grow your equity position, strategic improvements can pay off in a big way.

These improvements work well whether it's your own house or an investment property.

But not all renovations are created equal. Some upgrades are time-consuming, expensive, and offer minimal return. Others are simple, cost-effective, and deliver strong results, both in terms of increased valuation and rental yield.

Here are three of the easiest and most profitable value-adding improvements.

1. Add a garage or covered carport

In most Australian suburbs, off-street parking is a big win. Whether it's a garage, carport, or even a simple driveway expansion, providing a safe and secure place to park instantly makes the property more functional and appealing to buyers and renters.

Expert tip: Where council allows, consider converting an underused area or shed into a lockable garage, it may end up being cheaper than you think.

Benefits:

- Increases rental appeal, especially for families or professionals with multiple cars.
- Adds perceived security and convenience.
- Can increase overall property value by tens of thousands depending on location.

2. Add a second bathroom

Expert tip: If space is tight, look for opportunities to convert a laundry area or under-stair space into a small second bathroom (with council approval).

One bathroom in a three or four-bedroom house? That's a pain point for most renters and buyers. A second bathroom (even a compact ensuite or powder room) can be a game-changer in usability and liveability.

Benefits:

- Allows for higher rent and quicker leasing.
- Makes the property more appealing to families and house-sharers.
- Boosts valuation due to improved functionality.

3. Add an extra bedroom

More bedrooms mean more people, and more people mean higher rental yield. In many cases, a second living area or large dining space can be enclosed to create an extra bedroom without major structural work.

Benefits:

- Direct impact on valuation, property agents often price homes by number of bedrooms.

- Opens up new rental market segments (for example, larger families or roommates).
- Can significantly increase rental income.

Expert tip: Always check that the new bedroom meets minimum size and legal requirements to be considered a bedroom under the local council's rules.

The smart approach

When completing renovations, always ask:

'Will this change attract more buyers or renters?'

'Is the cost of the upgrade likely to be outweighed by the increase in value or income?'

The best value-adding improvements are ones that balance cost, effort, and return, and the three listed above strike that balance perfectly. Start with these low-hanging fruits before taking on larger renovation projects, and you'll be surprised how much more your property can earn you without a complete overhaul.

And always make sure you first get approval from your council for any changes.

Now, let me show you what smart value-adding looks like when it's done right.

Meet Lani and Bryce.

REAL PEOPLE, REAL SUCCESS STORIES

LANI & BRYCE

'Tomorrow is built on the actions you take today.'

At just 18 years old, Lani made a bold decision that some people twice her age wouldn't dare to make – she wanted to buy her first property.

Armed with vision and determination, she teamed up with her brother Bryce and their mother to purchase a rundown house from the estate of a family friend who had recently passed away. Calling it a 'fixer-upper' would have been

generous. This place was practically a horror film set: waist-high weeds blanketed the yard, rooms were piled with junk, plaster walls hung loose at the corners, paint peeled from moisture damage, and cobwebs draped over everything like curtains. It was the kind of property that made you want to walk away as fast as you could.

But Lani and Bryce didn't flinch. Given the poor state of the property, they secured a great deal. Instead of being overwhelmed, they rolled up their sleeves – literally. Over the following months, the family became a renovation crew. They hacked back the overgrown jungle, cleared out years of neglect, and taught themselves how to rebuild a home through YouTube tutorials, a few scraped knuckles, and more trips to Bunnings than they could count.

Before

After

What happened next was nothing short of remarkable. In just six months, that rundown house was transformed. Lush gardens replaced weeds. Clean white walls replaced grime. A sleek, modern interior replaced rot and ruin – the kind of place that turns heads and sparks bidding wars. The before-and-after photos barely do it justice. You had to see it. I was astonished when I walked into the property after the renovation. The transformation was jaw-dropping.

And the payoff? Their hard work likely added an estimated $500,000 in value – not through luck or waiting, but through determination, grit, and a willingness to learn, adapt, and act. Lani and Bryce didn't just buy their first property – they created wealth at 18 and 20. They built equity, confidence, and momentum for their future. They showed that, with the right mindset and a bit of elbow grease, you can turn a ruin into a real estate triumph.

If that's not a winner's story, it's hard to know what is.

STRUCTURING YOUR PURCHASE: GET THIS WRONG AND IT COULD COST YOU THOUSANDS

Before you sign on the dotted line for your home or investment property loan, it's crucial to get the structure right. Because what looks like a small decision today could cost you tens of thousands down the track.

Here are just a few traps to watch out for:

- **Ownership matters:** Putting the property in the higher income earner's name might save you a bit of tax in the short term, but can seriously backfire with land tax, capital gains tax, and estate planning complications later.
- **Loan features matter too:** Fixed vs variable rates, redraw vs offset, and Loan to Valuation Ratio (LVR) rules can all impact your flexibility, tax outcomes, and future borrowing capacity.
- **Your future might look different:** What if your income changes? What if the property becomes positively geared? What if something unexpected happens?
- **Bottom line:** Don't just chase short-term tax benefits. Play the long game, and structure things right from the start.

For the full breakdown, including real examples, key numbers, and clever structuring tips, head to the *Bonus Material* section at the end of this book.

CHAPTER 27
YOUR SHARES TOOLS: PLAY THE MARKET WITH CLARITY

If the idea of picking shares gives you cold sweats, or you'd rather watch grass grow than follow quarterly earnings reports, don't worry. There's a way to grow your wealth that doesn't require a second degree in finance or a crystal ball.

PASSIVE SHARE INVESTING: LET THE MARKET DO THE HEAVY LIFTING

For many readers, this will be one of the simplest long-term ways to keep nudging their Freedom Score higher.

Passive investing is like having the market do the heavy lifting while you sit back, sip your coffee, and let time and discipline do their thing.

Now, I'm not here to talk about a product or tell you what platform to use. There are many platforms out there. You should choose one that suits your needs. If you're not sure where to start, try searching terms like 'investment platform Australia automated investing'.

Look for something simple, low-cost, with regular investing and clean tax reporting.

Here are some common features you might find on platforms like this:

- Automated investing options like DCA on autopilot.
- Clean, simple tax reporting – because nobody wants a spreadsheet-induced headache when it's tax time.

- Optional adviser access, if you want to tag in a professional down the line.

Think of this like a Toyota Corolla for your portfolio: no flash, low maintenance, and gets you to your destination without leaving you stranded.

If you are curious about setting up your platform of choice, it might roughly look like:

1. Open a platform account that matches your needs.
2. Think about your investment choices in terms of your goals.
3. Set up a regular investment plan.
4. Review now and then, don't obsess, get advice if things start to get complex.

Track it to stack it: your spending reality check

Before you start putting your money to work for tomorrow, make sure you know exactly where it's going today. If you don't, it's like trying to build a house without first checking whether the ground is level. If your perception of your spending doesn't match what's really happening, you'll end up building plans on shaky ground. That's where a little tech magic comes in.

I'm a big fan of using smart tools to make life easier. And when it comes to tracking your spending, there are some useful options out there.

Apps like WeMoney and Frollo link to your accounts and automatically categorise your spending. Also, many banks have built-in options that work brilliantly too (like CommBank's Money Plan, NAB's Spending Tracker, and Westpac's Budget Planner). These are just examples; there are plenty of other tools out there. The key is picking one that works for you. The tool doesn't matter as much as the habit. The key is to pick one tool, use it consistently, and let it keep you honest.

Here's an example of what this might look like in action.

Groceries	-$912.33	20.03%
Coffee/take out	-$587.92	12.91%
Fuel	-$501.12	11.00%
Restaurants	-$450.21	9.88%
Services	-$678.97	14.91%
Internet/phone	-$120.00	2.63%
Entertainment	-$70.00	1.54%
Clothing	-$250.76	5.50%
Other	-$983.90	21.60%
Total	**-$4555.21**	**100%**

Notice how spending is broken down into clear categories with easy-to-read summaries. This is how you get the real picture of where your money's going. Once you see it, you can plan accordingly.

Bottom line? The more accurate your numbers, the more powerful your plan.

ACTIVE SHARE INVESTING: OUTSMARTING THE MARKET WITH RESEARCH

If you're someone who enjoys rolling up your sleeves and getting involved with your investments, welcome to the research lane.

Now before we get too far, let's be clear: this section isn't about what you should buy, or when. It's simply a peek into how smart investors use research tools to make more informed choices, and avoid chasing 'hot tips' from the cousin's mate who 'knows a guy'.

Why research matters (and glossy brochures don't)

Would you buy a house without going in for an inspection, checking the suburb, the council rates, or whether it has plumbing?

Of course not.

Yet people do this with shares every day, buying based on a headline, a hunch, or because someone shouted 'AI is the future!' on YouTube.

Here's the smarter approach: treat investing like buying a business. And before you buy any business, you want to know two things:

- What is the fair value?
- What is it actually doing?

That's where third-party research tools can come in. One example some investors use is tools such as Morningstar, alongside broker research, ASX announcements, annual reports, and other independent sources. This is just one of the many tools out there, but I am using it to illustrate my point.

What third-party research tools offer

Some of the useful features to investors include:

- **Fair value estimates:** Gives you an idea of what analysts think a company is worth.
- **Ratings (often 1 to 5):** Quick snapshot of valuation.
- **Research reports:** Structured analysis combining data and analyst opinion.

These tools can help everyday investors cut through the hype. You still need to do your homework. But at least now you've got a better ruler to measure with.

And no, you don't need to be a Wall Street analyst to use it. That's the beauty. The researchers have crunched the numbers, so you can focus on understanding the logic, not reinventing calculus.

But wait … what do the stars mean?

Some investors look at the rating system like this:

- **★** or **★★:** Possibly overpriced (might be time to watch, not act)
- **★★★:** Fairly valued (sit tight or do more digging)
- **★★★★** or **★★★★★:** Potentially undervalued (worth closer attention as a prompt for further research, not as a reason on its own to buy).

Important reminder: these are opinions, not prophecies. Even five-star shares can fall. That's investing. The ratings reflect analyst opinion at a point in time and can change. Different platforms present this information in different ways, and no single tool should be relied on in isolation.

A caution, with love

Look, tools like this are fantastic *if* you're the kind of person who'll actually use them. But just having a subscription doesn't make you Warren Buffett. If it did, we'd all be billionaires.

And even the best analysts get it wrong. Markets move. CEOs change. Once in a century events like the Covid-19 pandemic show up. So, use research tools to inform you, not to lull you into thinking risk has left the building.

> “A share report can guide you, but it can't predict the future.

Take a moment to think about how you may be able to use the share tools to work with the other components of your *RICH Trifecta* in a way that would create true *Synergification.*

FRANKING CREDITS

Franking credits are tax credits attached to dividends from Aussie companies that have already paid tax (usually 30%). When you receive a dividend, you also get a tax credit, reducing your tax bill or sometimes even giving you a refund, depending on your circumstances and eligibility.

For example:

Receive a $700 dividend + $300 franking credit
= $1000 taxable income.

If you're in the tax-free threshold, that $300 could come back to you in a cash refund. It's one of the best-kept secrets of the Aussie tax system, and a big reason shares are so powerful.

To qualify, you must hold the shares at least 45 days (excluding buy/sell days). Sell too soon and you lose the credit.

CHAPTER 28

BUSINESS TOOLS FOR WEALTH BUILDERS: SHORTCUTS THAT SAVE YEARS

Remember the side hustle I mentioned Renee and I have back in the DO part? We have been dog sitting for years and absolutely love it. It's given us the joy of furry company, without the long-term commitment, and a bit of side income too.

SIDE HUSTLE IDEAS

Here are some side hustle ideas that can complement your path to financial freedom: easy to start, relatively low-cost, and scalable if done right. Of course, your results will depend on your own effort, market demand, and how you manage the details. The earnings examples below are simplified for illustrative purposes. These should not be treated as expected, typical or likely earnings.

My aim here is to spark your imagination so you can explore which ideas might help you step closer to escaping the wage cage. The goal is to generate additional income that can be directed to your *RICH Trifecta* machine and create *Synergification*.

Each side hustle below is rated by a **RICHness ★**, which measures how effectively it can feed your *RICH Trifecta* machine based on four factors:

- **Risk:** how stable or volatile it is.
- **Income:** how much income potential it has.
- **Capital:** how much starting capital is needed.
- **Hassle:** how much time and effort it takes to maintain.

The higher the RICH Rating, the better it aligns with your wealth-building strategy:

- ★★★★★: Low risk, strong income, minimal hassle and capital.
- ★★★: A balanced, moderate opportunity.
- ★: High hassle, capital-intensive, or low return, better for a hobby.

Alright, let's look at some real-world examples.

1. Pet sitting at your own home

Potential earnings: $50–$80 per night per pet
RICH Rating: ★★★★☆

Platforms like MadPaws and Pawshake let you offer pet sitting from your own home. If you love animals, it's a great way to turn that into income without much disruption to your routine.[60]

Benefits:

- No upfront investment.
- Low overhead.
- Recurring clients build up over time through word of mouth.

Example: Two dogs a week at $50 each per night for 2 nights could bring in up to around $10,400 per year.

2. Vending machines

Potential earnings: $400–$1200+ per month
RICH Rating: ★★★☆☆

A vending machine placed in a good location can become a source of semi-passive income. The upfront cost is the machine and stocking it, but after that, it's mostly maintenance.

---

60 These examples are not income guarantees. They are starting points to spark your ideas. Always do your research. Every opportunity has variables like demand, competition, and upfront investment. And if you're unsure whether a side hustle affects your tax position or legal obligations, chat to an accountant or adviser first.

Good for those with access to gyms, schools, or busy offices. Think if it would make sense to put one at your work. Ask for approval for this from your employer.

Some vending machine operators make their best deals by approaching businesses directly and offering them a revenue share or free machine placement in exchange for space.

Benefits:

- Can scale with more machines.
- Relatively hands-off after setup and re-stocking.

Example: A machine earning $15/day could bring in about $5000 a year. Two or three such machines might push your income higher, depending on expenses and site conditions.

3. Renting out unused space (garage, driveway, storage)

Potential earnings: $100–$500+ per month per space
RICH rating: ★★★☆☆

If you've got an empty garage, driveway, or storage space, platforms like Spacer, Parkhound, or Share With Oscar can help you connect with people who need parking or storage. With minimal ongoing effort beyond setup and occasional maintenance, it's a way to generate extra income.

Example: Renting a garage for $250/month could earn you around $3000/year, before expenses and factoring in occasional vacancies.

4. Automated online store (print-on-demand, dropshipping)

Potential earnings: Varies, some earn hundreds, others thousands
RICH Rating: ★★★☆☆

Platforms like Shopify, Etsy, and Redbubble let you sell products with your custom designs, without holding any inventory. Orders are fulfilled automatically. If you have a craft hobby, something you enjoy anyway, you could earn a little side money from it, without it taking over your life.

Benefits:

- No stock needed.
- Entirely online.
- Potential to scale with marketing.

Example: Selling 20 novelty print shirts a day at $5 profit could bring in up to $3000/month. But this depends heavily on consistent demand, low production & shipping costs, minimal returns, and successful promotion.

5. Airbnb arbitrage (renting out properties without owning them)

Potential earnings: $1000–$1500+ per month
RICH Rating: ★★☆☆☆

Airbnb arbitrage involves renting a property long-term and re-renting it short-term through Airbnb. It sounds simple, but make sure you:

- have landlord permission
- understand the local regulations
- furnish the property well
- check Airbnb's terms of service.

Example: If you rent for $2000/month and earn $3000/month from guests, your gross profit could be $1000, before expenses and tax.

6. Digital course or ebook

Potential earnings: $500–$1500+ per month (long-term potential)
RICH Rating: ★★★☆☆

If you have knowledge or skills others want to learn, you can package it into an online course or ebook. Platforms like Teachable, Udemy, and Amazon Kindle make publishing accessible.

Benefits:

- One-time effort can lead to long-term passive income.
- Zero inventory or shipping.
- Fully scalable.

Example: Selling a $20 e-book to 50 customers in a month brings in about $1000 in gross sales. After platform fees (~30%), that's around $700. Subtract a modest marketing budget of $150, and your net profit could be roughly $550/month. Of course, results depend on your pricing, audience, and promotion.

7. Office plant watering

Potential earnings: $200–$400+ per month
RICH Rating: ★★★★★

Many offices have indoor plants but no one to care for them properly. Offer a weekly or fortnightly watering service, you may be able to drop in after hours on your way home, or even on weekends.

Benefits:

- Easy to start with basic tools.
- Flexible timing.
- Quiet, peaceful side income.

Example: Watering plants at two offices for $30/week per office could earn $260/month.

Final word

Don't just rely on my RICH Ratings. Run every opportunity, no matter the asset class, through the RICH filter yourself. The real power of the model is in how *you* apply it to your own life and goals.[61]

These side hustle ideas aren't just about extra cash, they're freedom accelerators. Remember to check in with your Freedom Score after any new income stream. Watch the needle move!

---

61 I've kept this list short and sweet to keep the book lean and laser-focused, but you'll find a growing library of extra Aussie-friendly ideas that I keep updating at www.rodnia.com.au or scan the QR code below to explore them.

RICH RATING: YOUR DECISION COMPASS

The beauty of the *RICH Trifecta* is its flexibility. The RICH Rating™ isn't a formula to follow. It's a lens for clear thinking. Think of it like a compass, not a GPS. It won't tell you exactly what to do, but it'll make sure you're heading in the right direction. Its real purpose is simple: to help you choose options that are more likely to improve your Freedom Score, not just impress you on paper.

Every investment or side hustle can be viewed through four simple lenses. Score each from 1 to 5. Don't overthink it.

Dimension	★ (Poor)	★★★ (Moderate)	★★★★★ (Excellent)
Risk	High chance of permanent loss, low control	Uncertain but manageable downside	Predictable, low chance of permanent loss, high control
Income	Low or unpredictable returns	Decent yield or growth	Strong, stable income stream
Capital	High initial capital needed, illiquid (hard to cash out)	Moderate capital required, moderately liquid	Low capital or leverage-friendly, highly liquid
Hassle	Very hands-on, time consuming	Manageable involvement	Minimal hassle or fully passive

Quick and easy RICH Rating

1. Give each filter a score from 1–5. Just use your best judgement.
2. Add up your scores and divide by 4 to get a quick average.
3. Match the number to the stars:

Average score	Star rating	Meaning
1.0–1.9	★	Poor fit / hobby income
2.0–2.9	★★	Speculative / niche play
3.0–3.9	★★★	Solid fit
4.0–4.5	★★★★	Strong strategic fit
4.6–5.0	★★★★★	Freedom accelerator

Don't stop at the number – reflect

Here's a critical rule: don't average away red flags. A high overall score can be misleading if one category is dangerously weak. For example, an opportunity might score like this:

- **Risk ★**
- **Income ★★★★**
- **Capital ★★★★**
- **Hassle ★★★★**

That averages to 3.25 star rating (solid fit).

But let me be very clear: a one-star risk rating is a serious warning sign you should not ignore. If there's a high chance of permanent loss, it doesn't matter how good the income or capital efficiency looks. One weak link, especially in Risk, can break the entire chain.

Don't let a strong average convince you to ignore a serious flaw.

In many cases, a single low score should be enough to pause, dig deeper, or walk away.

The real power isn't in the star rating.

It's in why you gave those scores.

After scoring, ask yourself:

- What assumptions am I making about each factor?
- How does this align with my stage of life and goals?
- What would need to change for this opportunity to score higher?

This reflection separates blind optimism from strategic clarity.

On the other hand, if something scores low, don't immediately throw it away. Ask how it could be improved, can you reduce the hassle, lower the risk, or boost the income?

Personalising the score: weighing what matters most

Not everyone values each factor equally:

- A time-poor professional might give Hassle extra weight.
- A retiree might weigh Risk more heavily.
- A young investor might prioritise Income or Capital efficiency.

If you enjoy numbers, you can add a personal weighting to each factor to make the RICH Rating truly reflect *your* priorities.

If maths isn't your thing, don't worry. The simple star rating above already works great. Think of this step as 'optional seasoning', not a required recipe.

Let's say you decide how important each factor is to *you*, for example:

- Risk is worth 30% of your decision
- Income 30%
- Capital 20%
- Hassle 20%

Just make sure the total of the four factors adds up to 100%. Then you simply multiply the importance by the star rating you gave each factor:

- **Risk:** 30% × 3 stars = **0.9**
- **Income:** 30% × 5 stars = **1.5**
- **Capital:** 20% × 4 stars = **0.8**
- **Hassle:** 20% × 3 stars = **0.6**

Total: 0.9 + 1.5 + 0.8 + 0.6 = 3.8 → 3.5 to 4-star rating.

This turns your RICH Rating into a personal decision compass, not a generic checklist.

The same opportunity that might be a 2-star for one person could be a 5-star for another, depending on their stage of life, circumstances, and goals.

Example: pet sitting vs Airbnb arbitrage

Opportunity	R	I	C	H	Average	RICH Rating
Pet sitting	4	4	5	4	4.25	★★★★☆
Airbnb arbitrage	2	4	3	1	2.5	★★☆☆☆

Neither is 'right' or 'wrong'. But one might align more closely with your life right now. You'll encounter countless opportunities for what to do with your money over time. The power of the RICH Rating is that it lets you compare them on level ground, so you can make smarter, more confident decisions.

Every investment, whether it's a property, a business, shares, or a side hustle, would be run through your personal RICH filter. And over time, you'll find that your clarity compounds just like your wealth.

And as always remember, the RICH Rating is a personal thinking tool only. It is not a substitute for due diligence, professional advice, or product suitability assessment.

THE CASE FOR BUYING A FRANCHISE

If you're new to business ownership or want a lower-risk option, buying into an established franchise could be worth considering in some situations. With a franchise, you inherit a recognised brand, a proven business model, and built-in support systems, which reduces risk and hassle compared to starting or buying an independent business.

Why franchises work well

- **Training and support** – Most franchises offer comprehensive training, marketing assistance, and operational support, helping you avoid beginner mistakes.
- **Brand recognition** – A well-known franchise comes with built-in customer trust and demand, reducing the challenge of establishing credibility.
- **Easier access to financing** – Lenders are often more willing to finance a franchise purchase compared to an independent startup, because the risk is lower.
- **Proven systems** – Unlike a typical business where you have to figure everything out from scratch, a franchise provides step-by-step operational procedures, making it easier to get up and running.

The downsides of franchises

- **Higher initial costs** – Buying into a reputable franchise can be expensive. Expect franchise fees, royalty payments, and marketing levies.
- **Less flexibility** – As a franchise owner, you must follow the rules and systems set by the franchisor. This means you can't innovate or make drastic changes to the business model.
- **Ongoing fees** – Most franchises charge monthly royalties or marketing fees, which can cut into your profits.

How to choose the right franchise

Just like anything else in life, not all franchises are created equal. Here's how to find one that fits well for you within the *RICH Trifecta* Framework:

- **Stick to your circle of competence:** As always, stick to what you know, choose a franchise in an industry you understand. If you've worked in hospitality, a food franchise could be a good fit. If you have experience in fitness, a gym franchise might be ideal.

- **Check profitability:** Some franchises generate strong returns, while others are notorious for low margins. Speak to existing franchisees to get a real-world picture of potential earnings.
- **Understand the commitment:** Some franchises require significant personal involvement (for example, fast food chains), while others can be semi-passive (for example, laundromats or vending machine businesses). Choose one that fits your time commitment goals.
- **Assess the franchisor's support:** Research how much support you will receive. A good franchisor offers ongoing training, marketing assistance, and operational guidance.

CHAPTER 29
THE UNSEXY TOOLS THAT SAVE FORTUNES

This chapter covers the essential tools that protect your wealth from life's unexpected curveballs, because even the best wealth plan can unravel without proper protection.

PERSONAL INSURANCE: YOUR FINANCIAL AIRBAG

Before we start sprinting towards financial freedom, let's make sure we've packed the right safety gear.

You can build wealth brilliantly, but without the right insurance, one accident, illness, or crisis could undo it all. Life insurance isn't just a 'nice to have', it can play a critical role as a safety net that ensures you and your family stay afloat, no matter what life throws your way.

The generic covers you can buy online may not always be tailored to your situation. Proper insurance should be tailored to your situation and best structured with the help of a qualified financial planner. That way, you avoid the lesser-known disadvantages that could leave you stranded when you need help the most.

> **Expert tip:** Most people already have some insurance inside their super without even realising it. But these default policies can be inadequate or poorly structured. If you're serious about safeguarding your wealth and income, it may be worth reviewing these to ensure they meet your needs.

Here are the four common types many people consider.

1. Life insurance (death cover)

What it does: Pays a lump sum to your beneficiaries if you pass away.

Why it matters: It can help protect your loved ones, cover debts, funeral costs, and ongoing living expenses. Without it, your family could be left financially vulnerable.

2. Total & permanent disability (TPD) insurance

What it does: Pays a lump sum if you become permanently disabled and can't return to work.

Why it matters: A serious injury or illness can end your career overnight. TPD cover gives you a financial lifeline, so you're not forced to drain your savings or face financial hardship.

3. Income protection insurance

What it does: Replaces a portion of your income (often up to around 70%, depending on policy terms), plus your employer superannuation contributions, if you can't work due to illness or injury.

Why it matters: For many people, their ability to earn is their most important asset. If it stops, so does your financial progress. Income protection can help make sure the bills still get paid.

4. Trauma insurance (critical illness cover)

What it does: Pays a lump sum if you're diagnosed with a major illness like cancer, stroke, or heart attack.

Why it matters: A health crisis affects more than your body, it hits your bank account too. This cover helps you pay for treatment, take time off, or make lifestyle changes with less financial pressure.

Protect before you invest

You've got the roadmap. You know the strategy. But none of it matters if a single event can blow up your plan.

Most people don't think about insurance until it's too late. And it's a mistake most only recognise later.

Review your existing cover, especially inside your super.

Consider whether it's structured to match your needs.

Before making any changes, pause and check what you may be giving up. Reducing or cancelling cover can leave a gap at exactly the wrong time, especially if replacement cover has not yet been accepted.

A qualified financial planner can help you structure this appropriately.

Because the right policy can be a life saver.

And remember, the type and level of cover required varies significantly depending on your personal circumstances, and these covers may not be necessary for everyone.

> **Expert tip:** If you're unsure how this applies to you, talk to a reputable financial planner to help you with your insurance. This is a complex area, and expert advice can make all the difference.

SUPERANNUATION SWITCHES: DON'T LET A SIMPLE CHOICE COST YOU THOUSANDS

It's easy to be tempted by media headlines shouting things like 'Best Super Funds of the Year!' or 'Lowest Fees Ranked!'. You glance at your statement, see a higher fee or a lower return than you'd like, and suddenly you're clicking around comparing super funds.

The media loves to pit super funds against each other like it's the Melbourne Cup. It's true that fund performance, fees, insurance terms, investment options, and service can all matter. But switching without understanding the consequences can have serious financial implications.

What you could lose

Before you hit 'transfer', take a deep breath and consider the two big risks people often overlook:

You might lose your insurances

Most people don't realise life, TPD, or income protection cover could be bundled inside their super. If you switch funds and close the old one without checking first, your insurance is gone. And worse, you might not be able to replace it if your health has changed.

There have been cases where people discovered, only when they needed cover most, that their insurance had been cancelled when they switched funds. This can leave families exposed to financial hardship, or individuals without income protection during illness or injury.

You could forfeit a tax deduction

If you made personal contributions to super and intend to claim a tax deduction, you need to submit a 'Notice of Intent to Claim a deduction' to your super fund before you roll over or close that fund. If the fund is closed before lodging the notice, you may lose the ability to claim the deduction.

Before you switch

- **Check for insurance** inside your current fund.
- **Check whether cover can be kept**, or whether replacement cover might be needed first.
- **Submit your Notice of Intent to Claim** for any personal contributions you want to claim as a tax deduction. Wait until it's been acknowledged before transferring funds.
- **Ask: Am I switching for the right reasons?** Fees and performance matter, but they're not the only factors.

> **Expert tip:** Switching super funds is like changing lanes on the highway; do it without checking your blind spots, and you might crash. Ask questions. Consider seeking advice from a licensed financial planner.

AN OVERLOOKED TAX-ADVANTAGED WEALTH TOOL (HIDDEN IN PLAIN SIGHT)

Remember the lesser-known investment account I teased back in previous parts that could help manage or reduce tax on some investments? Well, enter investment bonds. These often fly under the radar, but for the right people in certain situations, they can be a useful tool in the wealth building arsenal. This can be especially relevant when thinking about early retirement or investing tax-effectively outside of super.

What's an investment bond?

An investment bond is really like a tax-paid investment portfolio. You invest your money, choose from a range of investment options (just like in super), and let it grow inside the bond structure.

Here's the kicker: if all the rules are met and the bond is held for 10 years or more, proceeds can be tax-free in your hands. That can mean no capital gains tax, no annual income distributions adding to your tax return, and no extra admin for you. The tax is paid within the bond structure (currently up to 30%), which may be lower than some individual marginal tax rates (e.g. 32%, 39%, 47% brackets incl. Medicare), depending on personal circumstances. But of course, this is subject to current legislation and compliance with contribution rules.

Who are investment bonds for?

In general, some investors consider investment bonds in situations like:

- Higher-income earners looking to invest without increasing taxable income from distributions.
- Those planning to retire before super is accessible and need another tax-effective investment bucket.
- Parents saving for kids' education, a future nest egg, or simply long-term wealth.

The 125% rule

This is a very important point about investment bonds. To keep the 10-year tax-free status intact, you need to stick to the 125% rule. This means that each year, you can contribute up to a maximum of 125% of what you contributed in the previous year.

If you exceed that, the 10-year clock resets. So, if you're five years in and over-contribute, you start again from year 1.

What's inside the bond?

Think of an investment bond like a wrapper. Inside it, you can build a diversified investment portfolio: Aussie or International shares, listed property, fixed income, all depending on the provider you choose. Most providers offer plenty of choice.

It's simple, automated, and can be set up to invest regularly. It can suit long-term, hands-off approaches like the DCA tactic we covered in the DO part.

Investment bonds aren't for everyone, but they can be worth exploring as part of a broader plan, depending on your circumstances. Just be sure to structure it right and stick to the rules. Whether an investment bond is appropriate depends on your tax position, time-frame, contribution pattern, and broader strategy. The returns are dependent on the underlying investments and are not guaranteed. Fees, tax treatment, and product rules vary between providers.

Speak to a financial planner

Investment bonds can be a powerful tool, but only when used in the right context. A financial planner can help you:

- pick the right provider and investment mix
- plan your contributions without breaking the 125% rule
- ensure it fits your broader strategy alongside super, shares, and other assets.

Quick Tip: Financial planners are like any other service provider, some are excellent, some are average, and not all will be the right fit for *you*. You're not just hiring expertise … you're building a relationship. You'll talk about money secrets, fears, health, mistakes, the whole lot. So, look for someone licensed, trustworthy, and human. Someone who can say, 'No worries, let's walk through it together', when you say, 'I've got no bloody idea where to start'.

CHAPTER 30
CRYPTO: THE PINK HEELS OF MODERN FINANCE

If you've made it this far my friend, first of all, well done! But I can almost hear you wondering: 'Wait on Amir, what about crypto? Are you not even going to mention it?'

Now, here's the fun part. Let me tell you a little story that sums up my take on cryptocurrency. By now, I reckon you expect a story or two from me, don't you?

Okay, what if I told you that there was a time when high heels and pink clothing (almost like dresses) weren't just acceptable for men but were actually symbols of power and prestige?

Not long ago, I visited the Palace of Versailles in France, the grand court of Louis XIV, one of the most powerful monarchs in European history. If you ever get the chance, I highly recommend visiting. It's a stunning reminder of how fleeting trends can be.

As I walked through the lavish halls, I noticed a painting of King Louis XIV in an almost theatrical pose. Then something caught my eye. *Was the mighty king wearing high heels and stockings?* At first, I thought I was imagining things. It had been a long day, and maybe my mind was playing tricks on me. But the more I looked, the more obvious it became: Louis XIV, the mighty Sun King, was rocking a pair of red heels! Here's the painting I'm talking about (overleaf).

So, I looked it up.

It turns out that in the 17th and 18th centuries, it was common for aristocratic men to wear high-heeled shoes, stockings, and extravagant pink garments. These weren't just fashion choices; they were symbols of power, status, and wealth. Red heels, in particular, were reserved exclusively for nobility, and Louis XIV even passed an edict declaring that only members of the aristocracy could wear them. If you had red heels, you were somebody.

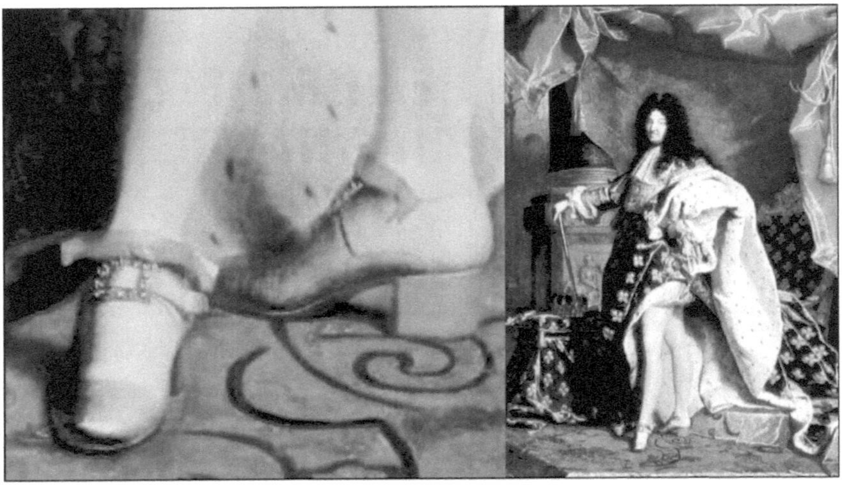

Similarly, Madame de Pompadour, the influential mistress of Louis XV, helped popularise the colour pink for both men and women in French high society. At the time, it was considered elegant, sophisticated, and even masculine.

Now imagine walking into a modern boardroom where the executives are rocking red heels, stockings, and pink dresses. These days, you probably wouldn't assume you were in the presence of royalty. More likely, you'd think that you'd wandered into a themed costume party.

That's the power of trends: yesterday's status symbol is today's curiosity.

So, what does all this have to do with cryptocurrency?

I respect that some people see opportunity in crypto. But my philosophy isn't chasing trends, it's building freedom on solid ground.

Now, if you want to dabble a little, that's okay. Just remember: it *is* speculation. So treat it like play money, and don't bet the farm on it.

THE BITCOIN PROBLEM

For some reason, those red high heels and pink coats reminded me of a conversation I had with someone I met briefly a few years ago. He was a smart man, a well-educated and thoughtful schoolteacher. But no matter how hard I tried, I couldn't convince him that maybe, just maybe, crypto might not be as sure a thing as he thought. He was utterly convinced that Bitcoin was the future, that it would replace gold, and that it was an unstoppable force of wealth creation.

But here's my problem with that way of thinking.

Crypto isn't really backed by anything.

There are no tangible assets behind it.

There is no company or central authority responsible for it.

It doesn't produce any income.

Now here's a perspective-shifter for you: the United States, the world's largest economy, holds around $630 billion worth of gold in reserves. That's the wealth of Fort Knox, the gold bars in the Fed, the whole lot.

And yet, Bitcoin, a digital code created in 2009 with no physical backing, is now worth nearly twice that, as of this writing.

Pause and think about that. A digital token that lives on the internet now commands more value than the entire US government's gold holdings.

That's why I'm sceptical of crypto as a store hold of wealth; instead I see it more as a hype cycle on steroids, a fleeting fashion trend just like the red heels and stockings of Louis XIV.

Gold has been a store of wealth for thousands of years, used by ancient civilisations, great empires, and modern economies alike. It is rare, difficult to mine, and universally accepted.

And yet somehow, a digital currency created in 2009 with no physical presence or intrinsic backing is expected to stand the test of time like gold, a substance that civilisations have bled for.

No, I don't think Bitcoin is a safe haven asset like gold; it's speculation wrapped in hype. And history is filled with examples of 'sure things' that were supposed to make everyone rich … until they didn't.

Let's rewind the tape …

Lessons from history: the dangers of mania

Tulip Mania (1600s)

Believe it or not, in the 17th century the Dutch went absolutely wild for tulip bulbs. Yes, you read that right, tulips. Prices soared to unimaginable levels, and people traded everything they had to get in on the action. It was the hottest investment of its time. And then, boom! The market collapsed, and fortunes were wiped out overnight.

The South Sea Bubble (1700s)

In the early 1700s, Britain was buzzing with a new investment opportunity: the South Sea Company, a trading enterprise promising unimaginable riches from commerce with South America. Backed by a royal charter and clever marketing, the company's shares skyrocketed, fuelled more by hype and speculation than actual profits.

People from all walks of life rushed to buy in. The price of South Sea shares surged over 1000% in a matter of months, creating one of the world's first major financial bubbles.

Even Sir Isaac Newton, one of the most brilliant scientists in history, got caught up in the mania. He initially made a small, tidy profit and sold. But as he watched friends grow vastly wealthier, he couldn't resist. He re-entered the market near its peak … and lost what would be the equivalent of millions in today's dollars. He later summed up his painful experience: 'I can calculate the motion of heavenly bodies, but not the madness of men.'

The South Sea Company crashed spectacularly, wiping out fortunes and ruining reputations. Newton's quote endures as a timeless reminder: no one is immune to the psychological forces of greed, fear, and crowd behaviour. Even a genius couldn't outthink human emotion.

Bernie Madoff's Ponzi scheme (1990s-2000s)

One of the most successful financial frauds in history lasted for 40 years before it collapsed. Federal investigators found nothing suspicious for decades. Everything *looked* legitimate. Investors who thought they were making incredible returns discovered too late that they had lost everything.

The dot-com bubble (1990s-2000s)

Companies with no real revenue, no business model, and no tangible product saw their share prices skyrocket simply because they had '.com' in their name. Then the crash came, and billions were lost.

A disaster waiting to happen?

My personal view is that cryptocurrency will eventually suffer the same fate as these past manias. Perhaps it will be the biggest financial disaster since the Great Depression.

Now, I could be wrong. I am not arrogant enough to claim otherwise. But if history is any guide, the signs are flashing red.

Here's the real question: Why take the risk?

You don't need to gamble on speculative assets to build wealth. We've already covered proven, time-tested strategies and tactics in this book. You don't need crypto. You don't need Dogecoin. You don't need the latest hyped-up digital token promising to be the next big thing.

Instead, build your wealth on a solid foundation. Invest in real assets, businesses, real estate, productive investments that generate value over time. Stick to what works.

Crypto's story is still unfolding. Unlike proven asset classes with centuries of history behind them, crypto remains an experiment in progress. Maybe it becomes the future of money. Maybe it goes to zero. The problem is: nobody really knows.

And when nobody knows, I'd rather watch the ride from the sidelines than be strapped into the roller coaster when the bottom falls out.

The RICH Rating score of crypto

Let's strip away the hype for a second and run crypto through the same clear-eyed lens we've applied throughout this book, the RICH Rating.

Here's how it stacks up:

- **Risk score: 1** – This isn't just market movement. It's the very real possibility of total loss, from hacks, regulatory changes, or holding platforms disappearing overnight.

- **Income score: 1** – Or zero if we could give it. Crypto doesn't produce any cash flow, rent, or dividends.
- **Capital score: 1** – To make any meaningful crypto return, you need to invest a large lump sum in one speculative asset.
- **Hassle score: 3** – While technically 'passive', most holders live with constant background stress, price swings, hacks, FOMO, and exit timing anxiety.

  Average RICH Rating: 1.5 stars: speculative territory, not wealth-building.

This isn't about whether crypto will go up or down. It's about whether it fits the RICHness of sustainable wealth. And right now, it doesn't.

But of course, this is simply how I view crypto through the lens of long-term wealth building. It is not a recommendation to buy, sell, or hold cryptocurrency or any other digital asset.

AVOID THE HOT TIPS

To me, crypto is just another version of a hot tip. Why? Because the only way you make money is if someone else is even more excited, and more willing to pay for it, than you are. It's not investing. It's musical chairs.

Over the years, I've seen too many people crash and burn chasing hot tips. One person, during the COVID-19 market crash in 2020, was told to move all her super into cash. So, she did. Then she watched, helplessly, as the market soared in one of the strongest rebounds in history. Panicked by FOMO, she jumped back in, right at the peak. That's the double whammy: sell low, buy high.

Thankfully, with some solid planning, she eventually recovered. But her story shows just how damaging a 'hot tip' can be.

The only time I ever followed a hot tip was when a guy walked up to me while I was out shopping and said, 'Mate, if you've got shares in [Company X], sell them now, it's about to tank.'

Amused and intrigued, I looked into the share he mentioned. Sure enough, the price was plummeting. But when I checked the fundamentals, the business looked really good. It looked like a classic case of panic selling. So, I bought in, and made a tidy profit.

Moral of the story? Most hot tips are just hype. But if you know what you're doing, sometimes a red flag is actually a green light in disguise.

OUTSMART THE DIGITAL PICKPOCKETS

We've talked about shiny objects in investing, now let's talk about something even shinier, and far more dangerous: scams. I've heard too many horror stories not to touch on this. The truth is, scammers aren't just after the careless anymore, they're after everyone. They've evolved. They sound like your bank, look like your adviser, and write emails that would fool a professional copywriter.

That's why protecting your wealth isn't just about growing it, it's about guarding it.

Here's how to make yourself a hard target:

- **Limit the damage.** Keep your main savings, offset, and investment accounts completely separate from your everyday spending. Use a low-limit debit account or a credit card for daily purchases, and only transfer in what you need from your Hub Account. Think of it as putting a firewall between your freedom and their fraud.
- **Slow them down.** Set low daily transfer limits on your banking app. It sounds simple, but it's one of the most powerful forms of self-defence. It can mean the difference between losing a few dollars or a few thousand. If you ever need to change your daily limit for a bigger transaction, make sure that you remember to change it back.
- **Add extra locks.** Turn on two-factor authentication (2FA) for every financial and email account. Use strong, unique passwords for each login. It's not paranoia, it's protection.
- **Verify before you trust.** If you get a text, email, or call claiming to be from your bank or super fund, never click the link or call the number they give you. Instead, look up the official contact details yourself. Real organisations will never rush you, threaten you, or ask for remote access to your device. Same thing for your partner or family members suddenly asking for money.

Call them directly rather than acting on a text message or email from them. Scammers try to pose as a family member in trouble who needs immediate cash.

- **Stay alert.** Scammers are masters of emotion. They'll trigger urgency, fear, greed, or curiosity to get you to act fast. When something feels off, pause. Talk to your bank's fraud team, your adviser, or even a trusted friend before you act.

For up-to-date scam alerts and safety tips, visit Scamwatch.gov.au. It's the official Australian Government resource for staying one step ahead of scammers.

> Growing wealth is one skill. Protecting it is another.

Here's the hard truth: it can take years to earn money, but only seconds to lose it.

So stay vigilant, stay sceptical, and don't assume it could never happen to you, because that's exactly what every scammer is counting on.

GEAR UP One-Step Action

Pick one thing from the below options:

- an asset you already own
- something you're thinking of buying
- a side hustle idea you've considered.

Now give it a quick RICH Rating.

Don't overthink it. Gut feel is perfectly fine for what you want here.

And if you'd like to go deeper, you can use the weighted version explained earlier in the 'Personalising the Score' section, but that's optional.

PART IV RECAP

ARM YOURSELF WITH THE RIGHT TOOLS TO WIN

The right tools don't just build wealth. They move your Freedom Score forward and protect it from setbacks. The tools themselves don't create freedom, the decisions you make with them do. Every decision either moves your Freedom Score forward … or it doesn't.

KEY TAKEAWAYS

- **Property:** Land is where the long-term value lives. A freestanding house may work better than townhouses and units due to limited supply and greater appreciation. Use valuation tools (like PropertyValue.com.au), flood maps, and crime data before buying. Location is still king, but data is your crown.
- **Shares:** Combine passive (ETFs, index funds) and active (hand-picked shares) investing. Use a platform of your choice to automate your DCA strategy, and research data to evaluate value, risk, and potential before you buy.
- **Business:** There are many low-capital side hustles that can scale: pet sitting, vending machines, space rentals, or e-commerce. Or go bigger with franchise or business acquisitions, if it makes sense for your situation. Use the *RICH* metrics (Risk, Income, Capital, Hassle) to assess each investment.
- **The unsexy tools that save fortunes:** Protect your progress. Get the right insurance (life, TPD, trauma, income protection), don't lose cover when switching super, and consider investment bonds depending on your circumstances or if you want to invest outside super.
- **Avoid hype:** Crypto, 'hot tips', or trendy sectors may sound exciting, but the real magic lies in timeless, grounded execution. History rewards discipline, not speculation.

- **Stay scam-smart:** Scammers are getting smarter every day. Keep your savings and offset accounts separate from spending accounts, set low transfer limits, and enable two-factor authentication. Always verify who you're talking to before acting. Protecting your wealth is just as important as building it.

UP NEXT: WRAP UP

Deep down, true reflection is where meaning lives – when you reflect on what you've learned and consider how it can transform not only your own life, but also the lives of those around you.

In this final part, we zoom out one last time.

Now it's time to explore what financial freedom is really for, and how to use it to create a life of meaning, contribution, and impact.

Keep in mind that taking the time to reflect, reset, and rise is just as important as your gameplan.

Ultimately, it's all about connecting your wealth to your purpose, and helping others find theirs.

Make it count. Let's finish strong. Let's go full circle and wrap up.

PART V
WRAP UP

Beyond Wealth

CHAPTER 31
WHY WEALTH ALONE ISN'T ENOUGH

First of all, congratulations on making it this far. Most people never even pick up a book like this, let alone finish it. You are about to fulfil the promise you made yourself when you first started reading.

And if at any point you caught yourself thinking, *I wish I'd known all this earlier*, let me be clear: you're not late.

There is no universal timeline for getting money right. Wherever you are today is exactly where your next decision begins. Awareness is progress, and progress compounds.

People who learn this stuff notice the same thing: they start seeing money differently.

And once that happens, it doesn't go away.

You've now moved through all four stages of the *Freedom Framework*. In the updated diagram overleaf, you'll notice something new: the *Freedom Ritual* now sits alongside the Framework. That's because true mastery doesn't come from doing something once. It comes from doing the right things consistently, with intention.

The Framework *gets* you free. The Ritual *keeps* you free. The Freedom Framework is your full-spectrum transformation, from awareness to action. But the real shift happens when you finish the cycle and begin again.

As you know by now, that's the purpose of the Freedom Ritual, a simple but powerful three-part practice:

1. **Act** – Try one idea from this book. Big or small, just start.
2. **Reflect** – What worked? What didn't? What surprised you? Record it in your Decision Log. Glance at your *Freedom Map* to spark your imagination.
3. **Share** – Post your story in the FG Community. Help someone else. Spark a conversation.

Then repeat. Again. And again. That's how freedom is built, one small step at a time.

> “The first pass through the Freedom Framework builds freedom. The next few build mastery.

THE BIGGER WHY

So, in a while, your systems are humming. Your Freedom Score is rising. The stress is melting away.

And now, the real question surfaces: what is it all for? What kind of life will you build with the time, space, and choice you've earned?

Despite the title, this part isn't about wrapping things up. It's about levelling up. Financial freedom isn't a finish line, it's a *launchpad*. Once you reach the *GEAR UP* stage, you don't stop … you reflect, recalibrate, and re-enter the flow with sharper clarity and purpose.

Wealth is not the goal. It's the tool. It gives you the space to step back, ask deeper questions, and live on your own terms.

Yes, the idea of wealth is intoxicating. The mansion. The car. The jet. The dream holiday. But let's be honest, their novelty will eventually fade.

That dream home becomes just another place to sleep.

The car, just a way to get from A to B.

The trip, a blur of airport queues and time zone fatigue.

You've felt it before. Maybe when you got that thing you really wanted. It felt amazing … for a week. But then it's just another object.

That's the moment where *reflection* matters most. Because now, you're ready to stop chasing, and start choosing.

THE POWER OF PURPOSE OVER POSSESSIONS

So, if financial freedom isn't the endgame, what is?

Purpose. Contribution. Fulfilment.

True fulfilment comes from doing something meaningful with the time, energy, and the options money buys you. Raising a family, starting a movement, making art, mentoring others, or solving problems that matter – these are the real treasures.

Wealth gives you options. What you choose to do with those options defines your *life*.

Helping others is where the real joy begins.

You don't need to donate a million dollars or save the world.

A single act of kindness can change a life.

What if someone is struggling so deeply that they're on the brink, and a few sincere words from you gives them enough hope to keep going?

You may never know the impact you had ... but it's real.

And this is why financial freedom matters.

It gives you the space, clarity, and tools to show up for others, not just survive your own stress. Because once you're free ... you can help others get free too.

WHY 1 + 1 = 100: THE SCIENCE OF COLLECTIVE INTELLIGENCE

Collective intelligence isn't just philosophy; science backs it up.

Harvard research shows that group intelligence isn't about who's smartest. It's about who listens, collaborates, and brings diverse perspectives to the table. Neuroscience shows that when people think together, their brains sync. Biology teaches us that ants, bees, and termites achieve remarkable feats, not alone, but as superorganisms.

Humans are no different. Our best breakthroughs, scientific, financial, social, are born from collaboration.

> “You are powerful. But you are unstoppable with the right tribe.

WHY I BUILT THE FREEDOM GAMEPLAN COMMUNITY

People often ask me why my cooking always seems to hit the spot. The truth is that it's not technique or ingredients, it's love. Any time I cook, I put my heart into it. And that's also exactly how I approached this book.

I poured everything into these pages. I don't even know how many countless hours, but at its core, it was made with love. And like my cooking, it's meant to be shared.

But here's the thing: I'm just one guy. As much as I would love to, I can't answer everyone's questions or be there for every single person on this journey. That's why I created the **Freedom Gameplan Community**, a dedicated, free space where readers can support each other. Some will share stories, some will ask questions, and others will step up to guide, but together we create something much bigger than one voice.

Of course, I'm in there too. I'm part of the conversation. But think of me as a support act, not the lead. The real magic happens when people help each other.

Here's what you can do when you first arrive:

- **Share** your lightbulb moments.
- **Partner** up with others for your Freedom Ritual.
- **Join** or start a Gameplan Crew.
- **Ask** questions and spark conversations.

This isn't just another Community. It's a movement. A place where ideas turn into action, and where your story can inspire the next person's quest to freedom.

Let's learn from each other's mistakes. And wins.

Let's build the Freedom Gameplan together.

You're welcome to join at: www.rodnia.com.au.

KICK OFF YOUR 30-DAY FREEDOM KICKSTART

You're about to finish the book. But your freedom journey has only just begun. It's time to start the 30-Day Freedom Kickstart in the following pages. It's a simple, structured plan that helps you turn the ideas from this book into action.

THE FINAL THOUGHT: ACTIVITY, ACTIVITY, SPEED!

This book is filled with quotes, but I want to leave you with one of my all-time favourites. It's from Napoleon Bonaparte, who is arguably history's greatest general. It goes:

> 'Activité, Activité, Vitesse!'
> *(Activity, Activity, Speed!)*

I can't think of a better phrase to close this book.

Success with money doesn't come from waiting.

It comes from moving.

From acting.

From staying engaged, making decisions, taking steps, building momentum, all before the moment passes you by. That's why I wanted to write a book that blends knowledge and action. One that empowers you to activate the knowledge through action.

Those who hesitate, stay stuck.

Those who act, grow.

Those who keep moving, win.

We've walked this journey together, page by page. Now it's your turn to carry it forward, into action, into life, into freedom.

Most people will be stuck in the wage cage.

But you? You know the way out.

So, I'll leave you with the same question I asked you at the beginning of your *Freedom Gameplan* journey.

Will you be money's master … or its slave?

Remember: you've got to make the dash before you get the cash. Fair dinkum action, my friend.

Choice is the real fruit of freedom.

Actions, not intentions, shape your financial destiny.

Stay true to the path you've designed.

Here's to your freedom. See you on the other side.

Amir Rodnia

LOVED THE FREEDOM GAMEPLAN?

If *Freedom Gameplan* inspired or helped you, I'd be very grateful if you leave a review. Your feedback helps others discover the book, and means the world to me as an author. Just scan the QR code or visit: www.rodnia.com.au.

Upward and onward, towards freedom.

Amir Rodnia

PART VI
YOUR NEXT MOVE

Put Your Freedom Gameplan to Work

THE 30-DAY FREEDOM GAMEPLAN KICKSTART

Clarity. Momentum. Freedom.

'You don't need to be a millionaire. You just need to be free.'

This is your activation ritual.

In just 30 days, you'll gain visibility, set up your systems, start applying what you've learned, and track your progress towards real financial independence.

You don't need to do everything.

You just need to begin.

If this book is the map, the next 30 days are the journey.

If you miss a week or take longer than 30 days, that's totally okay. Progress doesn't expire.

Week 1: See where you stand

Theme: *Awareness*
Mission: *Get a clear picture of your financial position and Freedom Score.*

Clarity is power. Progress starts with knowing your numbers.

Checklist

- Complete a full Money Snapshot: list all income, expenses, debts, assets, and investments in one place.
- Work out your annual living expenses: How much would you need each year to live freely, without relying on active (employment) income?
- Calculate your Freedom Score: Passive income (current) ÷ Expenses × 100 = Your percentage progress towards freedom.

- Your Freedom Score doesn't just track isolated wins; it measures the compounding effect of *Synergification*, when your shares, property, and business work in sync rather than in silos.
- Use the goals worksheet to define one outcome you want to achieve by improving your Freedom Score, keeping the number tied to meaning, not just maths.
- Build the habit. Update your Freedom Score weekly as part of your Freedom Ritual (from week 4 onwards), and continue tracking your spending using your preferred budgeting app. Numbers don't lie, but memory does.
- Use your tools: Refer to The Freedom Gameplan Glossary at the end of the book whenever you need a quick refresher on key concepts.
- Think about suitable people who could become your *Gameplan Crew*. Set a time to discuss this idea with them and find out if they are interested.
- Take action: Earn your first Freedom Score badge in the community:
  - 0–25%: Wage cage
  - 26–50%: Breakaway
  - 51–75%: Power shift
  - 76–100%: Freedom edge
  - 100%+: Clocked off

Week 2: Set the flow

Theme: *Focus*
Mission: *Centralise your cashflow and create financial clarity.*

Buckets help you manage. A Hub Account helps you master.

Checklist

- Open or designate your Hub Account.
- Use your offset account, or the highest-interest fee-free account you have for this. If you feel more comfortable having multiple accounts, set them up as offset accounts, if possible.

- Redirect all income to this account. Salary, side hustles, dividends, everything flows *in.*
- Automate your fixed costs. Bills, rent, insurance, mortgage, get them flowing *out* of the Hub Account automatically.
- Consolidate or close scattered accounts.
- Visibility is the new discipline. Keep it clean and simple.

Week 3: Spark the *RICH Trifecta*™

Theme: *Wealth building*
Mission: *Take one small but meaningful step in one of the Trifecta assets.*

You don't need to sprint. You just need to start.

Options

Real Estate:

- Check borrowing power or equity.
- Explore offset savings potential.
- Review First Home Guarantee or valuation tools.

Shares:

- Open a brokerage or platform investing account of your choice.
- Invest your first $500 in an ETF (passive) or individual shares (active).
- Set up an auto-investing plan (monthly, fortnightly).

Private business:

- Pick one side hustle or business idea.
- Think of people for potential collaboration.

Bonus tool: Map your next move

As you work through this Kickstart, keep your **Freedom Map** you printed in the PLAN part nearby.

This is your personal compass, the roadmap that helps you think about your next move.

You don't have to figure it all out at once. Just begin at '*Start Here*' and follow the path that fits your situation.

One step at a time, that's how freedom is built.

Get the printable colour version of the map (I suggest A3 size) and put it on your wall. You can get it at: www.rodnia.com.au.

Week 4: Enter the Freedom Ritual

Theme: *Mastery through motion*
Mission: *Cement your progress with a weekly ritual that builds lasting freedom.*

Freedom isn't a finish line. It's a ritual. A rhythm. A weekly return to the one question that matters: am I moving closer to freedom, or drifting away?

Checklist

- Schedule your first Freedom Ritual: Choose a consistent weekly time (for example, Sunday evening) to reflect, refocus, and reset. It can take as little as five minutes.
- Review your Freedom Score: Track your progress and, where possible, involve your partner or someone on the journey with you (Gameplan Crew).
- Log a decision: Record one financial decision – big or small – in your Decision Log.
- Engage with the community: share a win, question, or insight in the FG Community using tags such as #FreedomRitual1, #FreedomRitual2, and so on to keep track of your progress.
- As part of your regular ritual, spend one minute with your **Freedom Map**. Ask yourself: *Am I moving forward on my path?*
- Use it to spot your next action, realign your goals, stay in momentum, and remind yourself how far you've come.
- Build your RICH buffer: Set a minimum reserve in your Flow Account (for example, three months of expenses). This acts as both your safety net and your springboard.
- Set your next badge goal: Review your Freedom Score and identify your next milestone. What could increase your score by 5% to 10% over the next 6 to 12 months?

- Recalculate your Freedom Score (after Day 30): You've completed the Kickstart, but the journey is just beginning. Look for small improvements – reducing unnecessary expenses, adding income streams, or starting a side hustle – as every step moves your score forward.

What happens next?

You've taken real action. You've built clarity, momentum, and habits.

Now it's time to practice it, every week.

That's how mastery is formed. That's how freedom compounds.

Keep up the good work.

Bonus power move: Anchor a ritual

Want to make this habit stick even faster? Anchor your Freedom Ritual sessions to a small, repeated ritual. Light a candle, sit in the same chair, or play the same song each day before starting. This simple trick tells your brain: 'This is my moment'. Over time, this creates a mental shortcut that helps you snap into focus and build momentum with less effort.

THE FREEDOM GAMEPLAN GLOSSARY

This isn't just a book. It's a new way of thinking. And with any new way of thinking comes a new language – short, sharp, powerful terms that help you see money differently and act with confidence. Use these as your personal toolkit: in your planner, on your fridge, or even around the dinner table.

30-day Freedom Kickstart Kit: A practical 30-day action plan, available at the back of the book or online at www.rodnia.com.au, designed to help you assess your current position, set up your Hub Account, activate your *RICH Trifecta*, and build early momentum.

Decision Log: A tool for sharper financial decisions. Record your major financial decisions, including your reasoning and expectations. Over time, this helps you identify patterns, avoid repeat mistakes, and think more strategically. Available at www.rodnia.com.au.

Freedom Framework™: A structured pathway to financial freedom built on four stages – THINK, PLAN, DO, GEAR UP – guiding you from clarity to action and long-term results. While designed for financial transformation, it can be applied to other areas of life, providing a practical system for building, executing, and refining your strategy over time.

Freedom Gameplan Community (FG Community): A peer support network offering real stories, insights, accountability, and encouragement. Join at www.rodnia.com.au.

Freedom Ritual: A weekly review process where you set aside 5 to 10 minutes, update your Decision Log, review your *RICH Trifecta*, and refocus. Think of it as your personal board meeting. A tracker is available at www.rodnia.com.au.

Freedom Score™: The percentage of your annual living costs covered by passive income. It is the core metric of this book and the clearest measure of how close you are to financial freedom.

Hub Account: Your central financial account where all income is received, expenses are paid, and financial momentum builds. Ideally, this is your mortgage offset account; otherwise, use your highest-interest savings account. Centralised control beats fragmentation.

RICH Metrics: A four-part decision framework used to assess any financial move: Risk – what could go wrong; Income – does it generate cashflow; Capital – how much do you need to get in, and how easily can you get it out; Hassle – how much time, energy, or complexity is involved. Use it as a practical tool for clearer, more structured decisions.

RICH Rating™: A five-star scoring system for evaluating investments, strategies, or opportunities across four dimensions: Risk, Income, Capital, and Hassle. It replaces gut feel with structured clarity, helping you choose options aligned with your goals, stage of life, and Freedom Gameplan.

RICH Reset: A cashflow optimisation strategy for property investors typically 1–3 years into a principal and interest mortgage. By resetting the loan term to 30 years, repayments may be reduced while rental income continues to grow, potentially shifting a property from negatively geared to cashflow positive. This is about timing, not trickery. See Tactic 7 in the DO section.

***RICH Trifecta*™:** A core wealth-building framework based on three key asset classes – real estate, shares, and private business – providing control, growth, and leverage. The goal is to build them in balance over time, not all at once.

Synergification™: The alignment of asset classes for compounded growth. More than diversification, it describes the amplification that occurs when property, shares, and business work together, accelerating growth through compounding momentum rather than simply spreading risk.

BONUS MATERIAL
FOR THE CURIOUS, THE TACTICAL, AND THE OBSESSIVE

If you've made it this far, bravo. Most people never finish the books they start. But you? You've just completed a full-blown money transformation roadmap. You now understand the *why*, the *what*, and the *how* behind financial freedom.

So, what's next?

For some of you, this is the perfect place to close the book and start taking action. But for others, the curious, the tactical, the detail-driven, you might be thinking, *wait, is there more?*

Oh yes. There's more.

What's in the bonus section?

On the website, you'll unlock an entire vault of advanced strategies, deep dives, and juicy extras that didn't quite fit in the main parts. We're talking about:

- **Professional hacks** like how doctors, lawyers, and accountants can buy property with lower deposits, and pay *zero* Lender's Mortgage Insurance (LMI).
- **SMSF traps and tricks** to help you avoid barbecue horror stories and stay compliant.
- **Business transformation moves** to turn your grind into a scalable, sellable, lifestyle-friendly asset.
- **Land tax bombs, CGT curveballs, and estate planning blind spots** that cost people tens of thousands if ignored.

Where to access it

You can read all of it, completely free, at www.rodnia.com.au.

Or scan the below QR code:

This is the stuff we couldn't squeeze into the print version without turning the book into a doorstop. But it's waiting for you online, ready when you are.

Why it's separate

The core content of *Freedom Gameplan* is designed to be practical, inspiring, and *easy to finish*. But I know some of you want to go deeper, geek out, and optimise every edge. That's where the Bonus Section comes in.

Think of it as the **afterparty for your *Freedom Gameplan* journey**, more advanced, a little nerdier, and ridiculously useful.

ABOUT THE AUTHOR

Amir Rodnia is a financial planner, author, and entrepreneur on a mission to help Australians break free from the wage cage and reclaim their time, purpose, and peace of mind.

Before advising clients or writing books, Amir was just like many of the people he now helps, scraping together coins for fuel, hustling through 80-hour weeks, and feeling the panic of an overdrawn account. Those lived experiences drive his belief that anyone can turn their financial life around with the right blueprint.

Amir holds a Master of Financial Planning (MFinPlan) and specialist credentials including SMSF Specialist Adviser (SSA®), Accredited Behavioural Finance Professional (ABFP®), and Chartered Retirement Planning Counsellor (CRPC®). But he'll be the first to say: wisdom doesn't just come from textbooks, it comes from failure, resilience, and fierce determination.

Blending technical expertise with a passion for psychology, history, and strategy, Amir created the Freedom Gameplan philosophy: a practical, human, and independent roadmap to financial freedom. He is also the founder of Rodnia Wealth Partners (RWP) and is completing a PhD on financial literacy and business survival.

When he's not writing or advising, Amir enjoys history, travel, slow-cooked meals, and good conversation, but his favourite moments are seeing the spark of confidence when someone takes their first step toward freedom.

If you've enjoyed reading **FREEDOM GAMEPLAN** and you'd like to know how you can work with **AMIR RODNIA**, the next few pages are for you.

Rodnia Wealth Partners provides financial advice in accordance with its licensing obligations. Any advice provided will take into account your personal circumstances, goals and needs. The workshops and educational programs are general in nature and do not constitute personal financial advice.

WOULD YOU LIKE TO TAKE A PROACTIVE APPROACH TO YOUR WEALTH KNOWLEDGE?

This book gives you the framework. The next step is learning how to apply it in real life.

If you're looking for structured guidance, education, and practical tools, there are a range of workshops, masterclasses, and programs designed to help you go further.

These experiences are built around the Freedom Gameplan, giving you a clearer way to think, plan, and act when it comes to money.

You'll learn how to:

- Think strategically about money
- Make more confident financial decisions
- Build a system that works in the real world
- Stay consistent as your life evolves

If you want general guidance and education, these programs are designed to help you go deeper with the ideas from this book.

EXPLORE WORKSHOPS AND MASTERCLASSES

Visit www.rodnia.com.au or scan the QR code to explore workshops, masterclasses, and upcoming programs.

NEED A SPEAKER FOR YOUR EVENT?

Amir brings a fresh perspective on money, freedom, and modern wealth building.

If you need a speaker to challenge the status quo around money and wealth, Amir Rodnia is the man for the job. Author of Freedom Gameplan, Founder of Rodnia Wealth Partners, and doctoral researcher, he is rejuvenating the conversation around money.

Topics Amir covers include:

- Why most people work 40 years...
  and never realise they were never free
- The "wage cage": why modern life feels comfortable, but quietly traps you
- Why earning more money often makes people feel more stuck, not less
- Why most financial advice sounds good...
  but fails in real life
- The real cost of money: how people are unknowingly trading their life away
- The Freedom Score: the simple metric that shows if your life is actually moving forward

INVITE AMIR TO SPEAK

To enquire about getting Amir to speak at your event, visit www.rodnia.com.au or scan the QR code to connect.

WOULD YOU LIKE TO INTERVIEW AMIR RODNIA?

Amir is all about shifting the conversation around money, and he does that with the perfect balance of passion and deep knowledge.

As the Author of Freedom Gameplan, Founder of Rodnia Wealth Partners, and doctoral researcher, Amir is perfectly positioned for media interviews across all platforms.

Available for:

- Podcast interviews
- Guest articles and opinion pieces
- TV and radio segments
- Regular columns

REQUEST AN INTERVIEW OR MEDIA COMMENT

To enquire about interviews or media opportunities:
visit www.rodnia.com.au or scan the QR code to connect.

www.ingramcontent.com/pod-product-compliance
Lightning Source LLC
LaVergne TN
LVHW102100210926
848480LV00013B/828
9781923630369